CURIOSITIES
AND
SPLENDOUR

EDITED BY MARK MACKENZIE

CONTENTS

Introduction – *Mark MacKenzie*   4

Station Life in New Zealand – *Mary Anne Barker*   6

A Lady's Life in the Rocky Mountains – *Isabella Bird*   15

The Road to Oxiana – *Robert Byron*   26

The Worst Journey in the World – *Apsley Cherry-Garrard*   38

Voyages – *James Cook*   50

The Voyage of the Beagle – *Charles Darwin*   59

American Notes – *Charles Dickens*   71

The Journal of a Voyage to Lisbon – *Henry Fielding*   86

Summer on the Lakes – *Margaret Fuller*   95

The Histories – *Herodotus, trans. by George Rawlinson*   104

Tales of the Alhambra – *Washington Irving*   113

English Hours – *Henry James*   125

A Journey to the Western Islands of Scotland – *Samuel Johnson*   138

Sea and Sardinia – *DH Lawrence*   145

Missionary Travels and Researches in South Africa –
David Livingstone   157

The Cruise of the Snark – *Jack London*   165

Letters – *Lady Mary Wortley Montagu*   178

My First Summer in the Sierra – *John Muir*   186

Farthest North – *Fridtjof Nansen*   197

Travels in the Interior of Africa – *Mungo Park*   209

Discovery of a North-West Passage – *William Edward Parry*   218

The Travels of Marco Polo – *Marco Polo*   227

With the Tibetans in Tent and Temple – *Susanna Carson Rijnhart*   236

Through the Brazilian Wilderness – *Theodore Roosevelt*   245

South – *Ernest Shackleton*   256

Travels with a Donkey in the Cévennes – *Robert Louis Stevenson*   267

Life on the Mississippi – *Mark Twain*   277

In Morocco – *Edith Wharton*   287

Letters Written during a Short Residence in Norway,
Sweden and Denmark – *Mary Wollstonecraft*   295

Index   308

INTRODUCTION
BY MARK MACKENZIE

The best travel writing evokes not just a sense of place, or of wonder, but relates its story with a distinctive voice. Unsurprisingly, the authors collected here are nothing if not observant. Classics of the genre are more than the sum of their parts, revealing not simply the where and when, but the extent to which the author was changed by a particular destination, or vice versa. The soaring prose of Robert Byron, for example, whose descriptions of the architectural splendours of Isfahan show a young man in the throes of revelation. Or the coruscating wit of DH Lawrence, complaining his way around Sardinia and by so doing confirming the bitterness of exile. Washington Irving, in contrast, waxed so lyrical about the Alhambra, in Granada, that his account did much to save it from absolute ruin.

The books selected have inspired countless travellers and writers, in some cases explicitly. Mary Wollstonecraft's portrayal of the brooding Norwegian scenery directly informed the landscape of *Frankenstein*, the Gothic novel penned by her daughter, Mary Shelley. Later, the richly poetic nature writing of John Muir helped give rise to the American conservation movement.

Social attitudes have, of course, changed. Dominions no longer need civilising; 'natives' have gods of their own. Some of the travellers featured here, judged by modern standards, seem driven by little more than vanity; witness Theodore Roosevelt crashing through the Brazilian wilds, self-appointed saviour of Amazonian tribes. Or Jack London, sailing not quite around the globe in a boat sufficiently small enough to endorse his own ideas about machismo. It might be argued that any form of travel is some form of indulgence, yet what redeems them is both the quality of their writing and the extent to which each became a force for good; Roosevelt's expedition shone an early light on the fragility of the rainforests, while London's visit to a Hawaiian leper colony helped change attitudes to the disease. And those works that tell of landscapes lost, such as Mark Twain's *Life on the Mississippi,* or Margaret Fuller's *Summer on the Lakes,* serve as salutary reminders of the consequences of progress.

Then there are the pure explorers. Held alongside great stylists, such as Lawrence or Twain, accounts of Fridtjof Nansen's bid to be first to the north pole, or Ernest Shackleton's similar ambition for Antarctica, might seem destined to pale by comparison. Yet the strength of will to record even perfunctory details while under extreme physical duress – and the subsequent effort to shape them into a compelling narrative – has its own virtues.

Part of the explorer's motivation, of course, is to be seen as a pioneer, and it is worthwhile to pause and reflect whose voices made it onto the record of the early history of travel writing. Again and again it is the adventuring Western imperialist whose reaction to new lands is recorded, whether they are surveying places newly subjugated, as Samuel Johnson does in the Hebrides, or purposefully bringing outside religion to another culture, as David Livingstone does. Occasionally it is a woman, but inevitably she is of a wealthy class, able to indulge in leisure travel, albeit representing an independent spirit that set an example for later generations. In almost all cases, the intrusion is not an invited one. We can appreciate the glimpse into long-gone scenes and simultaneously question the underlying motives of the observer.

A collection such as this should also be notable for its contrasts. So, alongside travels of great historical importance, such as Herodotus wandering through the Greco-Persian wars, you will find adventures less epic. Edith Wharton, long before she became the great woman of American letters, toured Morocco with a discerning eye for architectural detail. Robert Louis Stevenson, meanwhile, keen to take his mind off relationship problems, trotted alongside a donkey through the mountains of France. Both write about their travels with such distinction that at no point do their undertakings feel trivial; in fact, quite the opposite. Perhaps all that needs to be said is that the very finest travel writing, such as Henry James' descriptions of the foggy bustle of London, elevates the everyday to the sublime.

5

MARY ANNE BARKER
INTRODUCTION

Mary Anne Barker's *Station Life in New Zealand*, published in 1870, recounts a three-year stay during which the author and her husband hoped to establish a sheep farm. The husband in question, her second, was Frederick Napier Broome, a British administrator who gave his name to Broome in Western Australia.

Lady Mary Anne Barker's pen name and title were a consequence of her first husband, Sir George Robert Barker. A British brigadier, Mr Barker had served with distinction at the Siege of Lucknow in India in 1857, for which he was knighted. Finding it commercially useful, Mary Anne retained the name, under which she published more than 22 books. *Station Life in New Zealand*, a collection of letters home to her sister, Jessie Stewart, was by some margin the most successful, reprinted in several editions and translated into a number of languages.

The Broomes travelled to New Zealand from England in 1865, following the purchase of a homestead, Steventon, on the Selwyn River. Mary Anne was a child of Empire (her father, Walter Stewart, had been Island Secretary of Jamaica), an advocate of both civilising Britain's dominions and seizing the opportunities they presented. *Station Life* was intended to convey the simple pleasures, and challenges, of homemaking, writ large across the colonial landscape. Prior to their arrival, the Broomes had commissioned new stonework and timbers to improve the house, and which were brought from Christchurch. 'It seems wonderful that so expensive and difficult an engineering work,' Barker wrote, 'could be undertaken by such an infant colony.'

Steventon already had literary connections. The vendors, brothers Arthur and Richard Knight, were great-nephews of Jane Austen. (The farm was named after the Hampshire village where Austen grew up.) The Broomes were to oversee renovations personally and in April 1866 moved in, with the house still under construction. 'We hurried here as soon as ever we could get into the house,' Barker noted, 'and whilst the carpenters were still in it.' Barker was heavily pregnant, and wished desperately for the baby to be born in the house. The occasion duly arrived but the child, a boy, died shortly after. 'No doubt there are bright and happy days in store for us yet,' Barker wrote, 'but these first ones here have been sadly darkened by this shadow of death.'

The popularity of the book lay in Barker's depiction of everyday life. The book's most well-known passage, featured in the extract here, concerns the weather. The Barkers had the misfortune to be lambing during the winter of 1867 when, in July, a freak storm hit.

The snow began on 29 July and lasted for a week. Completely cut off – even the dogs needed digging out from their kennels – the Barkers' only food was two chickens. These they shared between the entire household, including dogs and farmhands. When the snow eased, they went in search of the sheep. Fearing the worst, their shepherd urged Barker not to come. What they found makes for grim reading, thousands of animals either frozen to death or drowned when meltwater flooded the gullies in which they had taken shelter.

Barker's account of the storm became an important social document, in part because other witnesses, notably the local Māori whom Barker claims prophesied the storm, passed on the event as oral history. Whenever New Zealand experiences similarly extreme weather, for example in 1939 and 2010, Barker's account is invariably referenced.

Back in a still largely rural England, both landowners and tenant farmers related to Barker's plight. For city readers, it was pure drama. Indeed, her description of the loss of their stock – half the sheep and 90% of the lambs – still elicits sympathy. The Barkers abandoned their New Zealand dream that same year.

STATION LIFE IN NEW ZEALAND
BY MARY ANNE BARKER

LETTER XX: THE NEW ZEALAND SNOWSTORM OF 1867

Wednesday morning broke bright and clear for the first time since Sunday week; we actually saw the sun. Although the 'nor-wester' had done so much good for us, and a light wind still blew softly from that quarter, the snow was yet very deep; but I felt in such high spirits that I determined to venture out, and equipped myself in a huge pair of Frederick's riding boots made of kangaroo skin, well greased with weka oil to keep the wet out. These I put on over my own thick boots, but my precautions 'did nought avail', for the first step I took sank me deep in the snow over the tops of my enormous boots. They filled immediately, and then merely served to keep the snow securely packed round my ankles; however, I struggled bravely on, every now and then sinking up to my shoulders, and having to be hauled out by main force. The first thing done was to dig out the dogs, who assisted the process by vigorously scratching away inside and tunnelling towards us. Poor things! how thin they looked, but they were quite warm; and after indulging in a long drink at the nearest creek, they bounded about like mad creatures. The only casualties in the kennels were two little puppies, who were lying cuddled up as if they were asleep, but proved to be stiff and cold; and a very old but still valuable collie called 'Gipsy'. She was enduring such agonies from rheumatism that it was terrible to hear her howls; and after trying to relieve her by rubbing, taking her into the stable – and in fact doing all we could for her – it seemed better and kinder to shoot her two days afterwards.

We now agreed to venture into the paddock and see what had happened to the bathing place about three hundred yards from the house. I don't think I have told you that the creek had been here dammed up with a sod wall twelve feet high, and a fine deep and broad pond made, which was cleared of weeds and grass, and kept entirely for the gentlemen to have a plunge and swim at daylight of a summer's morning; there had been a wide trench cut about two feet from the top, so as to carry off the water, and hitherto this had answered perfectly. The first thing we had to do was to walk over the high five-barred gate leading into the paddock just the topmost bar was sticking up, but there was not a trace of the little garden gate or of the fence, which was quite a low one. We were, however, rejoiced to see that on the ridges of the sunny downs there were patches, or rather streaks, of tussocks visible, and they spread in size every moment, for the sun was quite warm, and the 'nor-wester' had done much towards softening the snow. It took us a long time to get down to where the bathing place had been, for the sod wall was quite carried away, and there was now only a heap of ruin, with a muddy torrent pouring through the large gap and washing it still more away. Close to this was a very sunny sheltered down, or rather hill; and as the snow was rapidly melting off its warm sloping sides, we agreed to climb it and see if any sheep could be discovered, for up to this time there had been none seen or heard, though we knew several thousands must be on this flat and the adjoining ones.

As soon as we got to the top the first glance showed us a small, dusky patch close to the edge of one of the deepest and widest creeks at the bottom of the paddock; experienced eyes saw they were sheep, but to me they had not the shape of animals at all, though they were quite near enough to be seen distinctly. I observed the gentlemen exchange looks of alarm, and they said to each other some low words, from which I gathered that they feared the worst. Before we went down to the flat we took a long, careful look round, and made out another patch, dark by comparison with the snow, some two hundred yards lower down the creek, but apparently in the water. On the other side of the little hill the snow seemed to have drifted even more deeply, for the long narrow valley which lay there presented, as far as we could see, one smooth, level snow field. On the dazzling white surface the least fleck shows, and I can never forget how beautiful some swamp hens, with their dark blue plumage, short, pert, white tails and long bright legs, looked as they searched slowly along the banks of the swollen creek for some traces of their former haunts; but every tuft of tohi-grass lay bent and buried deep beneath its heavy covering. The gentlemen wanted me to go home before they attempted to see the extent of the disaster, which we all felt must be very great; but I found it impossible to do anything but accompany them. I am half glad and half sorry now that I was obstinate; glad because I helped a little at a time when the least help was precious, and sorry because it was really such a horrible sight. Even the first glance showed us that, as soon as we got near the spot we had observed, we were walking on frozen sheep embedded in the snow one over the other; but at all events their misery had been over some time. It was more horrible to see the drowning, or just drowned, huddled-up 'mob' (as sheep en masse are technically called) which had made the dusky patch we had noticed from the hill.

No one can ever tell how many hundred ewes and lambs had taken refuge under the high terrace which forms the bank of the creek. The snow had soon covered them up, but they probably were quite warm and dry at first. The terrible mischief was caused by the creek rising so rapidly, and, filtering through the snow which it gradually dissolved, drowned them as they stood huddled together. Those nearest the edge of the water of course went first, but we were fortunately in time to save a good many, though the living seemed as nothing compared to the heaps of dead. We did not waste a moment in regrets or idleness; the most experienced of the gentlemen said briefly what was to be done, and took his coat off; the other coats and my little Astrachan jacket were lying by its side in an instant, and we all set to work, sometimes up to our knees in icy water, digging at the bank of snow above us – if you can call it digging when we had nothing but our hands to dig, or rather scratch, with. Oh, how hot we were in five minutes! the sun beating on us, and the reflection from the snow making its rays almost blinding. It was of no use my attempting to rescue the sheep, for I could not move them, even when I had scrattled the snow away from one. A sheep, especially with its fleece full of snow, is beyond my small powers: even the lambs I found a tremendous weight, and it must have been very absurd, if an idler had been by to see me with a little lamb in my arms, tumbling down at every second step, but still struggling manfully towards the dry oasis where we put each animal as it was dug out. The dear doggies helped us beautifully, working so eagerly and yet so wisely under their master's eye, as patient and gentle with the poor stiffened creatures as if they could feel for them. I was astonished at the vitality of some of the survivors; if they had been very far back and not chilled by the water, they were quite lively. The strongest sheep were put across the stream by the dogs, who were obedient to their master's finger, and not to be induced on any terms to allow the sheep to land a yard to one side of the place on the opposite bank, but just where they were to go. A good many were swept away, but after six hours' work we counted 1400 rescued ones slowly 'trailing' up

11

the low sunny hill I have mentioned, and nibbling at the tussocks as they went. The proportion of lambs was, of course, very small, but the only wonder to me is that there were any alive at all. If I had been able to stop my scratching but for a moment, I would have had what the servants call a 'good cry' over one little group I laid bare. Two fine young ewes were standing leaning against each other in a sloping position like a tent, frozen and immoveable: between them, quite dry, and as lively as a kitten, was a dear little lamb of about a month old belonging to one; the lamb of the other lay curled up at her feet, dead and cold; I really believe they had hit upon this way of keeping the other alive. A more pathetic sight I never beheld.

It is needless to say that we were all most dreadfully exhausted by the time the sun went down, and it began to freeze; nothing but the sheer impossibility of doing anything more in the hardening snow and approaching darkness made us leave off even then, though we had not tasted food all day. The gentlemen took an old ewe who could not stand, though it was not actually dead, up to the stable and killed it, to give the poor dogs a good meal, and then they had to get some more rails off the stockyard to cook our own supper of pork and maize.

The next morning was again bright with a warm wind; so, the effect of the night's frost soon disappeared, and we were hard at work directly after breakfast. Nothing would induce me to stay at home, but I armed myself with a coal-scoop to dig, and we made our way to the other 'mob'; but, alas! there was nothing to do in the way of saving life, for all the sheep were dead. There was a large island formed at a bend in the creek where the water had swept with such fury round a point as to wash the snow and sheep all away together, till at some little obstacle they began to accumulate in a heap. I counted ninety-two dead ewes in one spot, but I did not stay to count the lambs. We returned to the place where we had been digging the day before, and set the dogs to hunt in the drifts;

wherever they began to scratch we shovelled the snow away, and were sure to find sheep either dead or nearly so: however, we liberated a good many more. This sort of work continued till the following Saturday, when Frederick returned, having had a most dangerous journey, as the roads are still blocked up in places with snowdrifts; but he was anxious to get back, knowing I must have been going through 'hard times'. He was terribly shocked at the state of things among the sheep; in Christchurch, no definite news had reached them from any quarter: all the coaches were stopped and the telegraph wires broken down by the snow. He arrived about midday, and, directly after the meal we still called dinner, started off over the hills to my 'nest of Cockatoos', and brought back some of the men with him to help to search for the sheep, and to skin those that were dead as fast as possible. He worked himself all day at the skinning, a horrible job; but the fleeces were worth something, and soon all the fences, as they began to emerge from the snow, were tapestried with these ghastly skins, and walking became most disagreeable, on account of the evil odours arising every few yards.

We forgot all our personal sufferings in anxiety about the surviving sheep, and when the long-expected dray arrived, it seemed a small boon compared to the discovery of a nice little 'mob' feeding tranquilly on a sunny spur. It is impossible to estimate our loss until the grand muster at shearing, but we may set it down at half our flock, and all our lambs, or at least 90 percent of them. Our neighbours are all as busy as we are, so no accurate accounts of their sufferings or losses have reached us; but, to judge by appearances, the distant 'backcountry' ranges must have felt the storm more severely even than we have; and although the snow did not drift to such a depth on the plains as with us, or lie so long on the ground, they suffered just as much, for the sheep took shelter under the high riverbanks, and the tragedy of the creeks was enacted on a still larger scale; or they drifted along before the first day's gale till they came to a wire fence, and there they were soon covered up, and trampled each other to death. Not only were sheep, but cattle, found dead in hundreds along the fences on the plains. The newspapers give half a million as a rough estimate of the loss among the flocks in this province alone. We have no reliable news from other parts of the island, only vague rumours of the storm having been still more severe in the Province of Otago, which lies to the south, and would be right in its track; the only thing which all are agreed in saying is, that there never has been such a storm before, for the Māoris are strong in weather traditions, and though they prophesied this one, it is said they have no legend of anything like it ever having happened.

ISABELLA BIRD
INTRODUCTION

In 1892, Isabella Bird was the first woman to be elected a Fellow of the Royal Geographical Society. All the more extraordinary, perhaps, given that this pioneering Scottish writer, photographer and naturalist did not take up globetrotting until she was into her forties.

Her destinations included Australia, India, Tibet and the Middle East, but Bird reserved a particular fondness for North America. In 1873, she headed for the Rockies, and for Estes Park; now a town near Boulder, then a fledgling wilderness retreat founded by the prospector Joel Estes, and where Bird hoped the dry air would be beneficial for health. Bird related her experiences in a series of letters to her sister, Henrietta, and published, in 1878, as *A Lady's Life in the Rocky Mountains*. She began her Rockies odyssey in San Francisco, first by train, through Utah and Wyoming.

Cosmopolitan by Victorian standards, Bird was a woman of a class, possessed of withering opinions. The frontier town of Cheyenne, Wyoming, she observed, 'is...a God-forsaken, God-forgotten place. That it forgets God is written on its face. It owes its existence to the railroad [and is] mainly inhabited by rowdies and desperadoes, the scum of advancing civilization'.

On reaching Estes Park, Bird was in no mood to rest. She took part in high-octane cattle mustering, describing how 'I had not expected to work like a vachero'. And on land so wild that 'cows have to be regularly broken in for milking, being as wild as buffaloes'. She fulfilled too her ambition to summit Longs Peak. Her guide on the 14,000ft ascent was 'Mountain Jim' Nugent, a trapper and scout with a fearsome reputation. Bird developed a crush nonetheless, despite Nugent being a little wilderness worn. 'As he spoke I forgot both his reputation and appearance, for his manner was that of a chivalrous gentleman,' she wrote. 'He told me that the loss of his eye was owing to a recent encounter with a grizzly bear, which, after giving him a death hug, tearing him all over, breaking his arm and scratching out his eye, had left him for dead.' Nugent would be the John Brown to Bird's Queen Victoria, the rough outdoorsman rendered unobtainable by circumstance. (Nugent was shot dead nine months after they met.)

Bird's journey was, in truth, just beginning. An accomplished horsewoman, her intention from the outset had been to explore the mountains. From Estes Park, she ventured forth astride 'Birdie', a bay pony. 'A little beauty,' she wrote to Henrietta, 'with legs of iron, fast, enduring, gentle and wise; and with luggage for some weeks, including a black silk dress, behind my saddle, I am tolerably independent.'

They 'toured' for 800 miles, often alone, often at altitude. At times, Bird's bravura bordered on foolhardiness. 'The fierce heat caused soul and sense, brain and eye, to reel,' she recalls in the extract featured here. 'I was at a height of 12,000ft...the sun, he was white and unwinking like a lime-ball light [and] I suffered so from nausea, exhaustion and pains from head to foot, that I felt as if I must lie down.'

And so it went on, for weeks on end, Bird summoning the strength of will to record events daily. 'It is not easy to sit down and write after ten hours of hard riding,' she wrote to Henrietta, 'especially [when]...wholesome fatigue may make my letter flat when it ought to be enthusiastic.' On the occasions the mountains relented, they worked their magic. In Lower Canyon, Bird found 'a valley...of great sublimity. The sky and the earth combine to form a wonderland every evening – such rich, velvety colouring in crimson and violet; such an orange, green and vermilion sky; such scarlet and emerald clouds; such an extraordinary dryness and purity of atmosphere, and then the glorious afterglow which seems to blend earth and heaven.'

A LADY'S LIFE IN THE ROCKY MOUNTAINS

BY LADY ISABELLA BIRD

It was another cloudless morning, one of the many here on which one awakes early, refreshed and ready to enjoy the fatigues of another day. In our sunless, misty climate you do not know the influence which persistent fine weather exercises on the spirits. I have been ten months in almost perpetual sunshine, and now a single cloudy day makes me feel quite depressed. I did not leave till 9.30, because of the slipperiness, and shortly after starting turned off into the wilderness on a very dim trail. Soon seeing a man riding a mile ahead, I rode on and overtook him, and we rode eight miles together, which was convenient to me, as without him I should several times have lost the trail altogether. Then his fine American horse, on which he had only ridden two days, broke down, while my 'mad, bad bronco', on which I had been travelling for a fortnight, cantered lightly over the snow. He was the only traveller I saw in a day of nearly twelve hours. I thoroughly enjoyed every minute of that ride. I concentrated all my faculties of admiration and of locality, for truly the track was a difficult one. I sometimes thought it deserved the bad name given to it at Link's. For the most part it keeps in sight of Tarryall Creek, one of the large affluents of the Platte, and is walled in on both sides by mountains, which are sometimes so close together as to leave only the narrowest canyon between them, at others breaking wide apart, till, after winding and climbing up and down for twenty-five miles, it lands one on a barren rock-girdled park, watered by a rapid fordable stream as broad as the Ouse at Huntingdon, snow fed and ice fringed, the park bordered by fantastic rocky hills, snow covered and brightened only by a dwarf growth of the beautiful silver spruce. I have not seen anything hitherto so thoroughly wild and unlike the rest of these parts.

I rode up one great ascent where hills were tumbled about confusedly; and suddenly across the broad ravine, rising above the sunny grass and the deep green pines, rose in glowing and shaded red against the glittering blue heaven a magnificent and unearthly range of mountains, as shapely as could be seen, rising into colossal points, cleft by deep blue ravines, broken up into sharks' teeth, with gigantic knobs and pinnacles rising from their inaccessible sides, very fair to look upon – a glowing, heavenly, unforgettable sight, and only four miles off. Mountains they looked not of this earth, but such as one sees in dreams alone, the blessed ranges of 'the land which is very far off'. They were more brilliant than those incredible colours in which painters array the fiery hills of Moab and the Desert, and one could not believe them forever uninhabited, for on them rose, as in the East, the similitude of stately fortresses, not the grey castellated towers of feudal Europe, but gay, massive, Saracenic architecture, the outgrowth of the solid rock. They were vast ranges, apparently of enormous height, their colour indescribable, deepest and reddest near the pine-draped bases, then gradually softening into wonderful tenderness, till the highest summits rose all flushed, and with an illusion of transparency, so that one might believe that they were taking on the hue of sunset. Below them lay broken ravines of fantastic rocks, cleft and canyoned by the river, with a tender unearthly light over all, the apparent warmth of a glowing clime, while I on the north side was in the shadow among the pure unsullied snow.

The dimness of earth with me, the light of heaven with them. Here, again, worship seemed the only attitude for a human spirit, and the question was ever present, 'Lord, what is man, that Thou art mindful of him; or the son of man, that Thou visitest him?' I rode up and down hills laboriously in snowdrifts, getting off often to ease my faithful Birdie by walking down ice-clad slopes, stopping constantly to feast my eyes upon that changeless glory, always seeing some new ravine, with its depths of colour or miraculous brilliancy of red or phantasy of form. Then below, where the trail was locked into a deep canyon where there was scarcely room for it and the river, there was a beauty of another kind in solemn gloom. There the stream curved and twisted marvellously, widening into shallows, narrowing into deep boiling eddies, with pyramidal firs and the beautiful silver spruce fringing its banks, and often falling across it in artistic grace, the gloom chill and deep, with only now and then a light trickling through the pines upon the cold snow, when suddenly turning round I saw behind, as if in the glory of an eternal sunset, those flaming and fantastic peaks. The effect of the combination of winter and summer was singular. The trail ran on the north side the whole time, and the snow lay deep and pure white, while not a wreath of it lay on the south side, where abundant lawns basked in the warm sun.

The pitch pine, with its monotonous and somewhat rigid form, had disappeared; the white pine became scarce, both being displayed by the slim spires and silvery-green of the miniature silver spruce. Valley and canyon were passed, the flaming ranges were left behind, the upper altitudes became grim and mysterious. I crossed a lake on the ice, and then came on a park surrounded by barren contorted hills, overtopped by snowy mountains. There, in some brushwood, we crossed a deepish stream on the ice, which gave way, and the fearful cold of the water stiffened my limbs for the rest of the ride. All these streams become bigger as you draw nearer to their source, and shortly the trail disappeared in a broad rapid river, which we forded twice. The trail was very difficult to recover. It ascended ever in frost and snow, amidst scanty timber dwarfed by cold and twisted by storms, amidst solitudes such as one reads of in the High Alps; there were no sounds to be heard but the crackle of ice and snow, the pitiful howling of wolves and the hoot of owls. The sun to me had long set; the peaks which had blushed were pale and sad; the twilight deepened into green; but still 'Excelsior!' There were no happy homes with light of household fires; above, the spectral mountains lifted their cold summits. As darkness came on I began to fear that I had confused the cabin to which I had been directed with the rocks. To confess the truth, I was cold, for my boots and stockings had frozen on my feet, and I was hungry too, having eaten nothing but raisins for fourteen hours.

More than half of the day was far from enjoyable. The morning was magnificent, but the light too dazzling, the sun too fierce. As soon as I got out I felt as if I should drop off the horse. My large handkerchief kept the sun from my neck, but the fierce heat caused soul and sense, brain and eye, to reel. I never saw or felt the like of it. I was at a height of 12,000 feet, where, of course, the air was highly rarefied, and the snow was so pure and dazzling that I was obliged to keep my eyes shut as much as possible to avoid snow blindness. The sky was a different and terribly fierce colour; and when I caught a glimpse of the sun, he was white and unwinking like a lime-ball light, yet threw off wicked scintillations. I suffered so from nausea, exhaustion and pains from head to foot, that I felt as if I must lie down in the snow. It may have been partly the early stage of soroche, or mountain sickness. We plodded on for four hours, snow all round, and nothing else to be seen but an ocean of glistening peaks against that sky of infuriated blue. How I found my way I shall never know, for the only marks on the snow were occasional footprints of a man, and I had no means of knowing whether they led in the direction I ought to take. Earlier, before the snow became so deep, I passed the last great haunt of the magnificent mountain bison, but, unfortunately, saw nothing but horns and bones. Two months ago Mr Link succeeded in separating a calf from the herd, and has partially domesticated it. It is a very ugly thing at seven months old, with a thick beard, and a short, thick, dark mane on its heavy shoulders. It makes a loud grunt like a pig. It can outrun their fastest horse, and it sometimes leaps over the high fence of the corral, and takes all the milk of five cows.

The snow grew seriously deep. Birdie fell thirty times, I am sure. She seemed unable to keep up at all, so I was obliged to get off and stumble along in her footmarks. By that time my spirit for overcoming difficulties had somewhat returned, for I saw a lie of country which I knew must contain South Park, and we had got under cover of a hill which kept off the sun. The trail had ceased; it was only one of those hunter's tracks which continually mislead one. The getting through the snow was awful work. I think we accomplished a mile in something over two hours. The snow was two feet eight inches deep, and once we went down in a drift the surface of which was rippled like sea sand, Birdie up to her back, and I up to my shoulders!

At last we got through, and I beheld, with some sadness, the goal of my journey, 'The Great Divide', the Snowy Range, and between me and it South Park, a rolling prairie seventy-five miles long and over 10,000 feet high, treeless, bounded by mountains and so rich in sun-cured hay that one might fancy that all the herds of Colorado could find pasture there. Its chief centre is the rough mining town of Fairplay, but there are rumours of great mineral wealth in various quarters. The region has been 'rushed', and mining camps have risen at Alma and elsewhere, so lawless and brutal that vigilance committees are forming as a matter of necessity. South Park is closed, or nearly so, by snow during an ordinary winter; and just now the great freight wagons are carrying up the last supplies of the season, and taking down women and other temporary inhabitants. A great many people come up here in the summer. The rarefied air produces great oppression on the lungs, accompanied with bleeding. It is said that you can tell a new arrival by seeing him go about holding a blood-stained handkerchief to his mouth. But I came down upon it from regions of ice and snow; and as the snow which had fallen on it had all disappeared by evaporation and drifting, it looked to me quite lowland and liveable, though lonely and indescribably mournful, 'silent sea', suggestive of 'the muffled oar'. I cantered across the narrow end of it, delighted to have got through the snow; and when I struck the 'Denver stage road' I supposed that all the difficulties of mountain travel were at an end, but this has not turned out to be exactly the case.

After riding twenty miles, which made the distance for that day fifty, I remounted Birdie to ride six miles farther, to a house which had been mentioned to me as a stopping place. The road ascended to a height of 11,000 feet, and from thence I looked my last at the lonely, uplifted prairie sea. 'Denver stage road!' The worst, rudest, dismallest, darkest road I have yet travelled on, nothing but a winding ravine, the Platte canyon, pine crowded and pine darkened, walled in on both sides for six miles by pine-skirted mountains 12,000 feet high! Along this abyss for fifty miles there are said to be only five houses, and were it not for miners going down, and freight wagons going up, the solitude would be awful. As it was, I did not see a creature. It was four when I left South Park, and between those mountain walls and under the pines it soon became quite dark, a darkness which could be felt. The snow which had melted in the sun had refrozen, and was one sheet of smooth ice. Birdie slipped so alarmingly that I got off and walked, but then neither of us could keep our feet, and in the darkness she seemed so likely to fall upon me that I took out of my pack the man's socks which had been given me at Perry's Park and drew them on over her forefeet – an expedient which for a time succeeded admirably, and which I commend to all travellers similarly circumstanced. It was unutterably dark, and all these operations had to be performed by the sense of touch only. I remounted, allowed her to take her own way, as I could not see even her ears, and though her hind legs slipped badly, we contrived to get along through the narrowest part of the canyon, with a tumbling river close to the road. The pines were very dense, and sighed and creaked mournfully in the severe frost, and there were other eerie noises not easy to explain. At last, when the socks were nearly worn out, I saw the blaze of a campfire, with two hunters sitting by it on the hillside, and at the mouth of a gulch something which looked like buildings. We got across the river partly on ice and partly by fording, and I found that this was the place where, in spite of its somewhat dubious reputation, I had been told that I could put up.

A man came out in the sapient and good-natured stage of intoxication, and, the door being opened, I was confronted by a rough bar and a smoking, blazing kerosene lamp without a chimney. This is the worst place I have put up at as to food, lodging and general character; an old and very dirty log cabin, not chinked, with one dingy room used for cooking and feeding, in which a miner was lying very ill of fever; then a large roofless shed with a canvas side, which is to be an addition, and then the bar. They accounted for the disorder by the building operations. They asked me if I were the English lady written of in the Denver News, and for once I was glad that my fame had preceded me, as it seemed to secure me against being quietly 'put out of the way'. A horrible meal was served – dirty, greasy, disgusting. A celebrated hunter, Bob

Craik, came in to supper with a young man in tow, whom, in spite of his rough hunter's or miner's dress, I at once recognised as an English gentleman. It was their campfire which I had seen on the hillside. This gentleman was lording it in true caricature fashion, with a Lord Dundreary drawl and a general execration of everything; while I sat in the chimney corner, speculating on the reason why many of the upper class of my countrymen – 'High Toners', as they are called out here – make themselves so ludicrously absurd. They neither know how to hold their tongues or to carry their personal pretensions. An American is nationally assumptive, an Englishman personally so. He took no notice of me till something passed which showed him I was English, when his manner at once changed into courtesy, and his drawl was shortened by a half. He took pains to let me know that he was an officer in the Guards, of good family, on four months' leave, which he was spending in slaying buffalo and elk, and also that he had a profound contempt for everything American. I cannot think why Englishmen put on these broad, mouthing tones, and give so many personal details. They retired to their camp, and the landlord having passed into the sodden, sleepy stage of drunkenness, his wife asked if I should be afraid to sleep in the large canvas-sided, unceiled, doorless shed, as they could not move the sick miner. So, I slept there on a shake-down, with the stars winking overhead through the roof, and the mercury showing 30 degrees of frost.

I never told you that I once gave an unwary promise that I would not travel alone in Colorado unarmed, and that in consequence I left Estes Park with a Sharp's revolver loaded with ball cartridge in my pocket, which has been the plague of my life. Its bright ominous barrel peeped out in quiet Denver shops, children pulled it out to play with, or when my riding dress hung up with it in the pocket, pulled the whole from the peg to the floor; and I cannot conceive of any circumstances in which I could feel it right to make any use of it, or in which it could do me any possible good. Last night, however, I took it out, cleaned and oiled it and laid it under my pillow, resolving to keep awake all night. I slept as soon as I lay down, and never woke till the bright morning sun shone through the roof, making me ridicule my own fears and abjure pistols for ever.

ROBERT BYRON
INTRODUCTION

Robert Byron's ambition to visit the architectural treasures of the Middle East in 1933 was, like so many great journeys, spurred on by a doomed love. In this case, his rejection by Desmond Parsons, a fellow student at Oxford. This was the Brideshead generation and Byron was a contemporary of both Evelyn Waugh and Anthony Powell. Both Byron and Waugh were members of the Hypocrites, a high-minded drinking club; Byron was expelled from Oxford, before graduation, for the anti-social behaviour which became his hallmark. Waugh declared him 'the last and finest fruit of the insolent humanism of the 18th century'.

Byron strived to appear unconventional. 'He seems to hate everything ordinary people like,' wrote his friend, Nancy Mitford. It was during a brief spell as a freelance art critic, on assignment to the Byzantine wonders of Ravenna, that his interest in the Islamic architecture of Central Asia was first piqued.

For the journey that was to make his name, he set out from Venice, sailing for Cyprus, then overland to Persia and Afghanistan. He travelled with a friend, Christopher Sykes, son of Sir Percy Sykes, a British diplomat and author who had touched on Islamic architecture in his own work. Sykes senior was, according to Byron, 'the only writer who has noticed the buildings here, and he but shortly'.

The remark, though passing, was well made. Victorian travel writers styled themselves as polymaths, wise and natural explorers who could immediately understand the cultures and conventions of the strange lands through which they passed. Those who followed wore their learning more lightly, sprinkling their prose with knowing flourishes of satire, even comedy.

In Venice, ahead of their departure: '[At] dinner, Bertie mentioned that all whales have syphilis.' Or, at the legendary Harry's Bar: 'Our host regaled us with a drink compounded of champagne and cherry brandy. "To have the right effect," said Harry confidentially, "it must be the worst cherry brandy." It was.' And finally in Persia, where Byron observes 'a medieval tyranny of modern sensibilities,' when a 'Mrs Nicolson told the English public she could buy no marmalade in Teheran'. If there is a whiff of PG Wodehouse, Byron's purpose was deadly serious: to elevate the buildings he encountered to the status of art. In *The Road to Oxiana*, his memoir of the trip published in 1937, he succeeds admirably. Bruce Chatwin has gone so as far as to call it 'a sacred text, beyond criticism'. The American cultural historian Paul Fussell endorsed the claim, suggesting *The Road to Oxiana* is to travel writing what *Ulysses* is to the modern novel, or what *The Waste Land* is to poetry.

It's hard to disagree, unless you read it with your eyes shut. 'I have never encountered splendour of this kind before,' Byron wrote of the architecture of Isfahan. The same might be said of his own writing. In places, Byron's soaring prose is positively transcendent. His description of the Friday Mosque, featured here, seems to conform to Eliot's maxim on poetry, writing that communicates before it is understood. Each reading seems to reveal yet more poise, to yield more beauty.

The Road to Oxiana seems as relevant as ever, given the ongoing cultural sabotage wreaked upon the region by various conflicts. For the modern traveller, Byron's overland route is all but impossible. Byron himself took significant risks. He blackened his face to enter the forbidden mosque of Goharshad; he publicly, and repeatedly, denounced the shah. It is his incident-prone nature that makes him so winning. 'I had a frightful misadventure this morning,' he wrote, on being put up in the room of a British doctor. 'He caught me in an orgy, sitting on his bed over a bottle of wine and a cigar. Knowing I should be out all day, I was lunching early.'

His route ended in Peshawar, in pre-Partition India, today in Pakistan. Byron was happiest in far-flung lands, a fact he acknowledges on his return, aboard the SS *Maloja*, bound for

Marseilles. 'A big boat of 20,000 tons, pitching through an inky sea...salt, sweat and boredom everywhere'. The confinement aboard ship was 'an appalling plenty: a fortnight blotted out of one's life at great expense.' Back in England, Byron endured the bittersweet sensation known to all travellers. 'At Paddington [station] I began to feel dazed, dazed at the prospect of coming to a stop, at the impending collision between eleven months' momentum and the immobility of a beloved home.'

Just 32 when *The Road to Oxiana* was published, he died four years later, in 1941, en route to Alexandria when his ship was sunk by a German torpedo.

THE ROAD TO OXIANA
BY ROBERT BYRON

ISFAHAN, 18TH MARCH

The beauty of Isfahan steals on the mind unawares. You drive about, under avenues of white tree trunks and canopies of shining twigs; past domes of turquoise and spring yellow in a sky of liquid violet-blue; along the river patched with twisting shoals, catching that blue in its muddy silver, and lined with feather groves where the sap calls; across bridges of pale toffee brick, tier on tier of arches breaking into piled pavilions; overlooked by lilac mountains, by the Kuh-i-Sufi shaped like Punch's hump and by other ranges receding to a line of snowy surf; and before you know how, Isfahan has become indelible, has insinuated its image into that gallery of places which everyone privately treasures.

I gave it no help in doing so. The monuments have kept me too busy.

One could explore for months without coming to the end of them. From the eleventh century, architects and craftsmen have recorded the fortunes of the town, its changes of taste, government and belief. The buildings reflect these local circumstances; it is their charm, the charm of most old towns. But a few illustrate the heights of art independently, and rank Isfahan among those rarer places, like Athens or Rome, which are the common refreshment of humanity.

The two dome chambers of the Friday Mosque point this distinction by their difference. Both were built about the same time, at the end of the eleventh century. In the larger, which is the main sanctuary of the mosque, twelve massive piers engage in a Promethean struggle with the weight of the dome. The struggle in fact obscures the victory: to perceive the latter demands a previous interest in mediaeval engineering or the character of the Seljuks. Contrast this with the smaller chamber, which is really a tomb-tower incorporated in the mosque. The inside is roughly thirty feet square and sixty high; its volume is perhaps one third of the other's. But while the larger lacked the experience necessary to its scale, the smaller embodies that precious moment between too little experience and too much, when the elements of construction have been refined of superfluous bulk, yet still withstand the allurements of superfluous grace; so that each element, like the muscles of a trained athlete, performs its function with winged precision, not concealing its effort, as overrefinement will do, but adjusting it to the highest degree of intellectual meaning. This is the perfection of architecture, attained not so much by the form of the elements – for this is a matter of convention – but by their chivalry of balance and proportion. And this small interior comes nearer to that perfection than I would have thought possible outside classical Europe.

The very material is a signal of economy: hard small bricks of mousy grey, which swallow up the ornament of Kufic texts and stucco inlay in their puritan singleness of purpose. In skeleton, the chamber is a system of arches, one broad in the middle of each wall, two narrow beside each corner, four miniature in each squinch, eight in the squinch zone and sixteen above the squinches to receive the dome. The invention of Firuzabad has expanded; and will expand much further before Persian architecture dies in the eighteenth century. Here we catch it in the prime of youth and vigour. Even at this stage, the system is repeated or varied in many other buildings: the tomb-tower at Maragha, for instance. But I doubt if there is another building in Persia, or in the whole of Islam, which offers so tense, so immediate an apparition of pure cubic form.

According to the inscription round the dome, the tomb-tower was built by Abul Ghanaim Marzuban, the Minister of Malek Shah, in 1088. One wonders what circumstance at that moment induced such a flight of genius. Was it the action of a new mind from Central Asia on the old civilisation of the plateau, a procreation by nomadic energy out of Persian aestheticism? The Seljuks were not the only conquerors of Persia to have this effect. The Ghaznavide dynasty before them, the Mongol and Timurid dynasties after them, all came from north of the Oxus, and each produced a new Renascence on Persian soil. Even the Safavids, who inspired the last and most languid phase of Persian art, were Turks originally.

It was this last phase which gave Isfahan the character it has today, and which produced, curiously enough, its other great masterpiece. In 1612, Shah Abbas was occupied with the Royal Mosque at the southwest end of the Maidan, whose huge blue bulk and huge acreage of coarse floral tilework form just that kind of 'oriental' scenery so dear to the Omar Khayam fiends – pretty, if you like, even magnificent, but not important in the general scale of things. In 1618, however, he built another mosque on the southeast side of the Maidan, which was called after his father-in-law Sheikh Lutfullah.

This building stands at the opposite pole of architectural virtue to the small dome chamber in the Friday Mosque. The latter is remarkable because, apart from its unique merit, that merit is of a kind which most people have regarded as the exclusive property of the European mind. The Mosque of Sheikh Lutfullah is Persian in the fabulous sense: the Omar Khayam brigade, to whom rational form is as much anathema as rational action, can wallow in it to their hearts' content. For while the dome chamber is form only, has no colour, and obliterates its ornament by the intentness of its construction, the Mosque of Sheikh Lutfullah hides any symptom of construction or dynamic form beneath a mirage of shallow curved surfaces, the multitudinous offspring of the original squinch. Form there is and must be; but how it is created, and what supports it, are questions of which the casual eye is unconscious, as it is meant to be, lest its attention should wander from the pageant of colour and pattern. Colour and pattern are a commonplace in Persian architecture. But here they have a quality which must astonish the European, not because they infringe what he thought was his own monopoly, but because he can previously have had no idea that abstract pattern was capable of so profound a splendour.

As though to announce these principles as soon as possible, the outside of the mosque is careless of symmetry to a grotesque degree. Only the dome and portal are seen from the front. But owing to the discrepancy between the axis of the mosque and that of the Ali Gapu opposite, the portal, instead of being immediately under the dome, is set slightly to one side of it. Yet such is the character of the dome, so unlike is it to any other dome in Persia or elsewhere, that this deformity is hardly noticeable. Round a flattened hemisphere made of tiny bricks and covered with prawn-coloured wash runs a bold branching rose tree inlaid in black and white. Seen from close to, the design has a hint of William Morris, particularly in its thorns; but as a whole it is more formal than pre-Raphaelite, more comparable to the design of a Genoese brocade immensely magnified. Here and there, at the junction of the branches or in the depths of the foliage, ornaments of ochre and dark blue mitigate the harshness of the black-and-white tracery, and bring it into harmony with the soft golden pink of the background: a process which is continued by a pervading under-foliage of faint light blue. But the genius of the effect is in the play of surfaces. The inlay is glazed. The stucco wash is not. Thus the sun strikes the dome with a broken highlight whose intermittent flash, moving with the time of day, adds a third texture to the pattern, mobile and unforeseen.

If the outside is lyric, the inside is Augustan. Here a still shallower dome, about seventy feet in diameter, swims above a ring of sixteen windows. From the floor to the base of the windows rise eight main arches, four enclosing right angles, four flat wall-space, so that the boundaries of the floor form a square. The space between the tops of the arches is occupied by eight pendentives divided into planes like a bat's wing.

The dome is inset with a network of lemon-shaped compartments, which increase in size as they descend from a formalised peacock at the apex and are surrounded by plain bricks; each is filled with a foliage pattern inlaid on plain stucco. The walls, bordered by broad white inscriptions on dark blue, are similarly inlaid with twirling arabesques or baroque squares on deep ochre stucco. The colours of all this inlay are dark blue, light greenish-blue and a tint of indefinite wealth like wine. Each arch is framed in turquoise corkscrews. The mihrab in the west wall is enamelled with tiny flowers on a deep blue meadow.

Each part of the design, each plane, each repetition, each separate branch or blossom has its own sombre beauty. But the beauty of the whole comes as you move. Again, the highlights are broken by the play of glazed and unglazed surfaces; so that with every step they rearrange themselves in countless shining patterns; while even the pattern of light through the thick window traceries is inconstant, owing to outer traceries which are several feet away and double the variety of each varying silhouette.

I have never encountered splendour of this kind before. Other interiors came into my mind as I stood there, to compare it with: Versailles, or the porcelain rooms at

Schönbrunn, or the Doge's Palace or St Peter's. All are rich; but none so rich. Their richness is three-dimensional; it is attended by all the effort of shadow. In the Mosque of Sheikh Lutfullah, it is a richness of light and surface, of pattern and colour only. The architectural form is unimportant. It is not smothered, as in rococo; it is simply the instrument of a spectacle, as earth is the instrument of a garden. And then I suddenly thought of that unfortunate species, modern interior decorators, who imagine they can make a restaurant, or a cinema or a plutocrat's drawing room look rich if given money enough for gold leaf and looking glass. They little know what amateurs they are. Nor, alas, do their clients.

YEZD (4100FT), 20TH MARCH

The desert between Isfahan and Yezd seemed broader, blacker and bleaker than any, despite the warm spring sun. Its only relief was the ventilation mounds of the karats, strung out like bowler hats in rows of ten and twenty miles, and enormously magnified by the clear shimmering air. I remember Noel's telling me he had calculated that one-third of the adult male population of Persia is perpetually at work on these underground water channels. So developed is the sense of hydrostatics in successive generations that they can construct an incline of forty or fifty miles through almost flat country without any instruments, and at never more than a given number of feet below the ground.

I had a frightful misadventure this morning. Last night, on going to the English mission for an injection, I was thankful to accept their kind suggestion that, since the doctor was away, I should sleep in his bedroom. In the middle of the night the poor man came back unexpectedly, and seeing a strange head on his pillow, was obliged to sleep on a sofa. But worse followed. When at last he did venture into his own room to fetch some clean clothes, he caught me in an orgy, sitting on his bed over a bottle of wine and a cigar. Knowing I should be out all day, I was lunching early. I tried to put a bold face on it by offering him some wine, but he formed an unfavourable impression.

I was worried, on arriving here, that I had no letters of recommendation. 'I shall be your letter', said Ali Asgar gravely, explaining that he had been servant to the present Governor of Yezd for ten years, when the latter was Mayor of Isfahan; in fact, just before I engaged him in Shiraz, the Governor had telegraphed asking him to come back, and he had refused. Now, as we entered the Governor's office, here he was! The Governor jumped out of his chair with a cry. Ali Asgar, who at his brightest has the aspect of an ageing curate, stood with folded hands and sagging knees, smirking and fluttering his eyelids with the modesty of a Victorian miss. Eventually, as he had prophesied, the Governor turned his warmth to me, asking if Ali Asgar might be free to have supper with him and talk over old times.

This settled, I had every facility to explore, accompanied by an intelligent and obliging police officer. The throw-off of a monument hunt in a virgin town like Yezd must take place from a convenient height, whence it is possible to see which domes or minarets, by their form or material, give promise of good work beneath. Today, clue after clue yielded treasure, till at the end of the day we were almost too tired to walk home.

Sir Percy Sykes is the only writer who has noticed the buildings here, and he but shortly. Do people travel blind? It is hard to imagine how the portal of the Friday Mosque could escape anyone's notice. It stands over 100 feet high, and its narrow tapering arch is almost as spectacular as the chancel arch at Beauvais. After this, the court inside is a disappointment, a parochial little enclosure. But not the sanctuary, whose walls, dome and mihrab are covered with fourteenth-century mosaic in perfect condition. This is the best decoration of that kind I have seen since Herat. It differs from the work there. The colours are colder, the designs more lucid and precise, but not so gorgeous.

An extraordinary series of simple, egg-domed mausoleums now lured us across the town – extraordinary in that, being built of a brick that was hardly distinguishable from mud, they might have been expected to contain nothing but wreckage. Yet one after another they revealed walls, vaults and domes painted with bold, plaited Kufic in a style so rich, and at times so distorted, as to lack any known precedent. The most elaborate of them is the Vakht-i-sa'at, which was built in 1324. Some of the others must be earlier. The Shrine of the Twelve Imams, for example, has a frieze of Kufic in the same style as that inside the Pir Alam Dar at Damghan, which dates from the eleventh century.

We came on another curiosity in the bazaar, one of the old city gates known as the Darwaza Mehriz. Its massive wooden door is reinforced by iron plates which are stamped with primitive signs of the Zodiac. Such things have an appearance of incalculable antiquity. But primitive forms make unreliable calendars. They may be just a symptom of artistic ineptitude.

Yezd is unlike other Persian towns. No belt of gardens, no cool blue domes, defend it from the forbidding wastes outside. Town and desert are of one colour, one substance; the first grows out of the second, and the tall wind towers, a witness of the heat, are such a forest as a desert might grow naturally. They give the place a fantastic outline, though not so fantastic as those of Hyderabad in Sind. The wind there always blows from the sea, and the towers project canopies to meet it. The towers of Yezd are square, and catch the wind from all four quarters by means of hollow grooves, which impel it down into chambers beneath. Two such chambers at either end of a house set up a draught through the length of it.

At present, though the Governor has ambitious plans, only

one boulevard has been driven through the old labyrinths. Lovers of the picturesque deplore even this. But it is a boon to the inhabitants, who now have somewhere to walk, breathe, meet each other and survey the distant mountains.

Going to the garage in search of transport to Kirman, I fell into conversation with an ex-deputy, who told me that Kavam-al-Mulk has been in prison, but is now released, while the fate of Sardar Assad and the other Bakhtiari brothers is still unknown. He was bitter against Marjoribanks, and I wondered why, till he recounted how his uncle, an old man of seventy-four and blind in one eye, has been two years in prison for refusing to let Marjoribanks have his rice-growing estates in Mazandaran. That inimitable ruler has been seizing estates all over the country, and making a fortune out of them, since the other Naboths have not been so obstinate. I was astonished at the man's indiscretion. But I suppose he thought I should not betray him. I shan't, I hope. This happened before I got to Yezd, and he wasn't an ex-deputy.

APSLEY CHERRY-GARRARD
INTRODUCTION

Published in 1922, *The Worst Journey in the World* is not, as some might reasonably presume, an explicit reference to Robert Falcon Scott's tragic attempt to be the first man to the South Pole. Rather, it is the story of the search for an egg, an account of Apsley Cherry-Garrard's role in the Terra Nova Expedition (1910–1913) which claimed Scott's life.

In some respects, Cherry-Garrard was fortunate (or not) to win a place in the expedition at all. His initial application was rejected. He applied once more, offering to donate £1,000 to expedition funds. Turned down a second time, he gave the money regardless; his generosity did not go unnoticed. Though Scott was determined to reach the Pole, it was not the Terra Nova's sole aim. Dr Edward 'Bill' Wilson travelled to Antarctica as the expedition's chief scientist. A keen ornithologist, Wilson's principal task was to collect the unhatched eggs of Emperor penguins, to study the embryos within; impressed by Cherry-Garrard's magnanimity, Wilson rewarded him with the position of assistant zoologist.

Born in 1886, Cherry-Garrard was, at 24, the youngest member of Scott's crew. Fit and strong (he had rowed at Oxford), Cherry-Garrard was, by all accounts, eminently likeable. This, despite the fact he was painfully shy and suffered from depression – he was known among the expedition team as 'Cheery'.

In June 1910, Scott's men sailed for Antarctica from Cardiff in Wales, arriving at their Antarctic base, Cape Evans on Ross Island, the following January. They used what remained of the southern hemisphere summer laying supply depots along sections of Scott's proposed route to the Pole, with an attempt planned for November.

In June 1911, Wilson, Cherry-Garrard and another scientist, Henry 'Birdie' Bowers, set out for Cape Crozier, located on the far side of Ross Island and home to a large Emperor penguin colony.

Cherry-Garrard described it as 'the weirdest bird's-nesting expedition that has ever been or ever will be'. They walked in near-total darkness, hauling 750 lbs of supplies in temperatures as low as -78°F. The journey was, in theory, 67 miles each way; in reality, the ice they encountered was so uneven that, in places, progress was only possible by using a relay system; three men moving one sled, returning for another and so on. This meant five miles of walking for every mile gained. Cherry-Garrard also suffered from myopia; in an era before lensed goggles, wearing spectacles proved impossible, making things harder still.

They reached Cape Evans after 19 days' effort. The penguin colony, featured in the extract here, was everything they had hoped for. Wilson acquired three eggs. Then a blizzard struck, forcing them to delay their return. Their tent was carried away by the wind while they slept; with no protection other than sleeping bags and a makeshift igloo, Bowers, Wilson and Cherry-Garrard sang hymns to keep up their spirits. Cherry-Garrard's teeth chattered so severely, a number of them shattered. When the weather abated, they found their tent, snagged on nearby rocks, and headed back, arriving at Cape Evans on 1 August. 'I'll swear there was still a grace about us when we staggered in,' Cherry-Garrard wrote, 'and we kept our tempers, even with God...thus ended the worst journey in the world.' (The title for the book came at the suggestion of a friend, George Bernard Shaw.)

Scott departed Cape Evans on 1 November, bound for the South Pole, although he did not decide his five-man polar party until two months later, on 3 January 1912. In addition to Edgar Evans and Captain Lawrence Oates, the others named were Bowers and Wilson. Their bodies were found, along with that of Scott, on 12 November 1912, one year after setting out. Cherry-Garrard, who was among the search party, helped bury his friends beneath a cairn. 'I do not know how long we were there,' he wrote, 'but when all was finished, and the chapter of Corinthians had been read, it was midnight of some day. The sun was dipping low above the Pole, the Great Ice Barrier was almost in shadow. And the sky was blazing – sheets and sheets of iridescent clouds. The cairn and cross stood dark against a glory of burnished gold.'

The loss of Bowers and Wilson hit their friend hard. His biographer, Sara Wheeler, believes that, in addition to regular dental work required as a result of his time at Cape Crozier, Cherry-Garrard was afflicted by post-traumatic stress.

He was married late in life to Angela Turner in 1939; by now in his fifties, Cherry-Garrard adopted the pebble-sharing ritual used by Gentoo penguins during their courtship.

THE WORST JOURNEY IN THE WORLD
BY APSLEY CHERRY-GARRARD

The disturbed Emperors made a tremendous row, trumpeting with their curious metallic voices. There was no doubt they had eggs, for they tried to shuffle along the ground without losing them off their feet. But when they were hustled, a good many eggs were dropped and left lying on the ice, and some of these were quickly picked up by eggless Emperors who had probably been waiting a long time for the opportunity. In these poor birds the maternal side seems to have necessarily swamped the other functions of life. Such is the struggle for existence that they can only live by a glut of maternity, and it would be interesting to know whether such a life leads to happiness or satisfaction.

I have told how the men of the *Discovery* found this rookery where we now stood. How they made journeys in the early spring but never arrived early enough to get eggs and only found parents and chicks. They concluded that the Emperor was an impossible kind of bird who, for some reason or other, nests in the middle of the Antarctic winter with the temperature anywhere below seventy degrees of frost, and the blizzards blowing, always blowing, against his devoted back. And they found him holding his precious chick balanced upon his big feet, and pressing it maternally, or paternally (for both sexes squabble for the privilege) against a bald patch in his breast. And when at last he simply must go and eat something in the open leads nearby, he just puts the child down on the ice, and twenty chickless Emperors rush to pick it up. And they fight over it, and so tear it that sometimes it will die. And, if it can, it will crawl into any ice crack to escape from so much kindness, and there it will freeze. Likewise many broken and addled eggs were found, and it is clear that the mortality is very great. But some survive, and summer comes; and when a big blizzard is going to blow (they know all about the weather), the parents take the children out for miles across the sea ice, until they reach the threshold of the open sea. And there they sit until the wind comes, and the swell rises, and breaks that ice floe off; and away they go in the blinding drift to join the main pack ice, with a private yacht all to themselves.

You must agree that a bird like this is an interesting beast, and when, seven months ago, we rowed a boat under those great black cliffs, and found a disconsolate Emperor chick still in the down, we knew definitely why the Emperor has to nest in midwinter. For if a June egg was still without feathers in the beginning of January, the same egg laid in the summer would leave its produce without practical covering for the following winter. Thus the Emperor penguin is compelled to undertake all kinds of hardships because his children insist on developing so slowly, very much as we are tied in our human relationships for the same reason. It is of interest that such a primitive bird should have so long a childhood.

But interesting as the life history of these birds must be, we had not travelled for three weeks to see them sitting on their eggs. We wanted the embryos, and we wanted them as young as possible, and fresh and unfrozen that specialists at home might cut them into microscopic sections and learn from them the previous history of birds throughout the evolutionary ages. And so Bill and Birdie rapidly collected five eggs, which we hoped to carry safely in our fur mitts to our igloo upon

Mount Terror, where we could pickle them in the alcohol we had brought for the purpose. We also wanted oil for our blubber stove, and they killed and skinned three birds – an Emperor weighs up to 6½ stones.

The Ross Sea was frozen over, and there were no seal in sight. There were only 100 Emperors as compared with 2000 in 1902 and 1903. Bill reckoned that every fourth or fifth bird had an egg, but this was only a rough estimate, for we did not want to disturb them unnecessarily. It is a mystery why there should have been so few birds, but it certainly looked as though the ice had not formed very long. Were these the first arrivals? Had a previous rookery been blown out to sea and was this the beginning of a second attempt? Is this bay of sea ice becoming unsafe?

Those who previously discovered the Emperors with their chicks saw the penguins nursing dead and frozen chicks if they were unable to obtain a live one. They also found decomposed eggs which they must have incubated after they had been frozen. Now we found that these birds were so anxious to sit on something that some of those which had no eggs were sitting on ice! Several times Bill and Birdie picked up eggs to find them lumps of ice, rounded and about the right size, dirty and hard. Once a bird dropped an ice nest egg as they watched, and again a bird returned and tucked another into itself, immediately forsaking it for a real one, however, when one was offered.

Meanwhile a whole procession of Emperors came round under the cliff on which I stood. The light was already very bad and it was well that my companions were quick in returning: we had to do everything in a great hurry. I hauled up the eggs in their mitts (which we fastened together round our necks with lampwick lanyards) and then the skins, but failed to help Bill at all. 'Pull,' he cried, from the bottom. 'I am pulling,' I said. 'But the line's quite slack down here,' he shouted. And when he had reached the top by climbing up on Bowers' shoulders, and we were both pulling all we knew Birdie's end of the rope was still slack in his hands. Directly we put on a strain the rope cut into the ice edge and jammed – a very common difficulty when working among crevasses. We tried to run the rope over an ice axe without success, and things began to look serious when Birdie, who had been running about prospecting and had meanwhile put one leg through a crack into the sea, found a place where the cliff did not overhang. He cut steps for himself, we hauled and at last we were all together on the top – his foot being by now surrounded by a solid mass of ice.

We legged it back as hard as we could go: five eggs in our fur mitts, Birdie with two skins tied to him and trailing behind and myself with one. We were roped up, and climbing the ridges and getting through the holes was very difficult. In one place where there was a steep rubble and snow slope down I left the ice-axe halfway up; in another it was too dark to see our former ice-axe footsteps, and I could see nothing, and so just let myself go and trusted to luck. With infinite patience Bill said: 'Cherry, you must learn how to use an ice axe.' For the rest of the trip my wind clothes were in rags.

We found the sledge, and none too soon, and now had three eggs left, more or less whole. Both mine had burst in my mitts: the first I emptied out, the second I left in my mitt to put into the cooker; it never got there, but on the return journey I had my mitts far more easily thawed out than Birdie's (Bill had none) and I believe the grease in the egg did them good. When we got into the hollows under the ridge where we had to cross, it was too dark to do anything but feel our way. We did so over many crevasses, found the ridge and crept over it. Higher up we could see more, but to follow our tracks soon became impossible, and we plugged straight ahead and luckily found the slope down which we had come. All day it had been blowing a nasty cold wind with a temperature between -20° and

-30°, which we felt a good deal. Now it began to get worse. The weather was getting thick and things did not look very nice when we started up to find our tent. Soon it was blowing force 4, and soon we missed our way entirely. We got right up above the patch of rocks which marked our igloo and only found it after a good deal of search.

I have heard tell of an English officer at the Dardanelles who was left, blinded, in No Man's Land between the English and Turkish trenches. Moving only at night, and having no sense to tell him which were his own trenches, he was fired at by Turk and English alike as he groped his ghastly way to and from them. Thus he spent days and nights until one night, he crawled towards the English trenches, to be fired at as usual. 'Oh God! what can I do!' someone heard him say, and he was brought in.

Such extremity of suffering cannot be measured: madness or death may give relief. But this I know: we on this journey were already beginning to think of death as a friend. As we groped our way back that night, sleepless, icy and dog tired in the dark and the wind and the drift, a crevasse seemed almost a friendly gift.

'Things must improve,' said Bill next day. 'I think we reached bedrock last night.' We hadn't, by a long way.

It was like this.

We moved into the igloo for the first time, for we had to save oil by using our blubber stove if we were to have any left to travel home with, and we did not wish to cover our tent with the oily black filth which the use of blubber necessitates. The blizzard blew all night, and we were covered with drift which came in through hundreds of leaks: in this windswept place we had found no soft snow with which we could pack our hard snow blocks. As we flensed some blubber from one of our penguin skins, the powdery drift covered everything we had.

Though uncomfortable this was nothing to worry about overmuch. Some of the drift which the blizzard was bringing would collect to leeward of our hut and the rocks below which it was built, and they could be used to make our hut more weatherproof. Then with great difficulty we got the blubber stove to start, and it spouted a blob of boiling oil into Bill's eye. For the rest of the night he lay, quite unable to stifle his groans, obviously in very great pain: he told us afterwards that he thought his eye was gone. We managed to cook a meal somehow, and Birdie got the stove going afterwards, but it was quite useless to try and warm the place. I got out and cut the green canvas outside the door, so as to get the roof cloth in under the stones, and then packed it down as well as I could with snow, and so blocked most of the drift coming in.

It is extraordinary how often angels and fools do the same thing in this life, and I have never been able to settle which we were on this journey. I never heard an angry word: once only (when this same day I could not pull Bill up the cliff out of the penguin rookery) I heard an impatient one: and these groans were the nearest approach to complaint. Most men would have howled. 'I think we reached bedrock last night', was strong language for Bill. 'I was incapacitated for a short time,' he says in his report to Scott. Endurance was tested on this journey under unique circumstances, and always these two men with all the burden of responsibility which did not fall upon myself, displayed that quality which is perhaps the only one which may be said with certainty to make for success, self-control.

We spent the next day – it was 21 July – in collecting every scrap of soft snow we could find and packing it into the crevasses between our hard snow blocks. It was a pitifully small amount, but we could see no cracks when we had finished. To counteract the lifting tendency the wind had on our roof, we cut some great flat hard snow blocks and laid them on the canvas top to steady it against the sledge which formed the ridge support. We also pitched our tent outside the igloo door. Both tent and igloo were therefore eight or nine hundred feet up

Terror: both were below an outcrop of rocks from which the mountain fell steeply to the Barrier behind us, and from this direction came the blizzards. In front of us the slope fell for a mile or more down to the ice cliffs, so windswept that we had to wear crampons to walk upon it. Most of the tent was in the lee of the igloo, but the cap of it came over the igloo roof, while a segment of the tent itself jutted out beyond the igloo wall.

That night we took much of our gear into the tent and lighted the blubber stove. I always mistrusted that stove, and every moment I expected it to flare up and burn the tent. But the heat it gave as it burned furiously, with the double lining of the tent to contain it, was considerable.

It did not matter, except for a routine which we never managed to keep, whether we started to thaw our way into our frozen sleeping bags at 4 in the morning or 4 in the afternoon. I think we must have turned in during the afternoon of that Friday, leaving the cooker, our finnesko, a deal of our footgear, Bowers' bag of personal gear and many other things in the tent. I expect we left the blubber stove there too, for it was quite useless at present to try and warm the igloo. The tent floor cloth was under our sleeping bags in the igloo.

'Things must improve,' said Bill. After all there was much for which to be thankful. I don't think anybody could have made a better igloo with the hard snow blocks and rocks which were all we had: we would get it airtight by degrees. The blubber stove was working, and we had fuel for it: we had also found a way down to the penguins and had three complete, though frozen, eggs: the two which had been in my mitts smashed when I fell about because I could not wear spectacles. Also the twilight given by the sun below the horizon at noon was getting longer.

But already we had been out twice as long in winter as the longest previous journeys in spring. The men who made those journeys had daylight where we had darkness, they had never had such low temperatures, generally nothing approaching them, and they had seldom worked in such difficult country. The nearest approach to healthy sleep we had had for nearly a month was when during blizzards the temperature allowed the warmth of our bodies to thaw some of the ice in our clothing and sleeping bags into water. The wear and tear on our minds was very great. We were certainly weaker. We had a little more than a tin of oil to get back on, and we knew the conditions we had to face on that journey across the Barrier: even with fresh men and fresh gear it had been almost unendurable.

And so we spent half an hour or more getting into our bags. Cirrus cloud was moving across the face of the stars from the north, it looked rather hazy and thick to the south, but it is always difficult to judge weather in the dark. There was little wind and the temperature was in the minus twenties. We felt no particular uneasiness. Our tent was well dug in, and was also held down by rocks and the heavy tank off the sledge which were placed on the skirting as additional security. We felt that no power on earth could move the thick walls of our igloo, or drag the canvas roof from the middle of the embankment into which it was packed and lashed.

'Things must improve,' said Bill.

I do not know what time it was when I woke up. It was calm, with that absolute silence which can be so soothing or so terrible as circumstances dictate. Then there came a sob of wind, and all was still again. Ten minutes and it was blowing as though the world was having a fit of hysterics. The earth was torn in pieces: the indescribable fury and roar of it all cannot be imagined.

'Bill, Bill, the tent has gone', was the next I remember – from Bowers shouting at us again and again through the door. It is always these early morning shocks which hit one hardest: our slow minds suggested that this might mean a peculiarly lingering form of death. Journey after journey Birdie and I fought our way across the few yards which had separated the tent from the igloo door. I have never understood why so much of our gear which was in the tent remained, even in the lee of the igloo. The place where the tent had been was littered with gear, and when we came to reckon up afterwards we had everything except the bottom piece of the cooker, and the top of the outer cooker. We never saw these again. The most wonderful thing of all was that our finnesko were lying where they were left, which happened to be on the ground in the part of the tent which was under the lee of the igloo. Also Birdie's bag of personal gear was there, and a tin of sweets...

...I can well believe that neither of my companions gave up hope for an instant. They must have been frightened, but they were never disturbed. As for me I never had any hope at all; and when the roof went, I felt that this was the end. What else could I think? We had spent days in reaching this place through the darkness in cold such as had never been experienced by human beings. We had been out for four weeks under conditions in which no man had existed previously for more than a few days, if that. During this time we had seldom slept except from sheer physical exhaustion, as men sleep on the rack; and every minute of it we had been fighting for the bedrock necessaries of bare existence, and always in the dark. We had kept ourselves going by enormous care of our feet and hands and bodies, by burning oil and by having plenty of hot, fatty food. Now we had no tent, one tin of oil left out of six and only part of our cooker. When we were lucky and not too cold we could almost wring water from our clothes, and directly we got out of our sleeping bags we were frozen into solid sheets of armoured ice. In cold temperatures with all the advantages of a tent over our heads we were already taking more than an hour of fierce struggling and cramp to get into our sleeping bags – so frozen were they and so long did it take us to thaw our way in. No! Without the tent we were dead men.

JAMES COOK
INTRODUCTION

Cook described himself as a man 'whose ambition leads me not only further than any other man has been before me, but as far as I think it possible for man to go'. The son of a Yorkshire farmer, James Cook might have served out his time as a journeyman officer had he not come to the attention of his Royal Navy superiors during the British siege of Quebec in 1759. His skills in navigation were a product of a rigorous merchant-navy apprenticeship, and Cook's expertise in mapping, specifically the strategically crucial St. Lawrence River, led to the capture of city from the French during the Seven Years' War. Recognising his skills as a surveyor, the Admiralty dispatched him to Newfoundland for five consecutive summers, from 1763 to 1767, during which time he provided the first reliable maps of the coastline.

A year later, Cook was given command of a naval research vessel, HMS *Endeavour*. Of his three round-the-world voyages, it is this one, from 1768 to 1771, for which he is best remembered. The *Endeavour* departed on 26 August 1768 and arrived in Tahiti in April 1769, where Cook observed the transit of Venus, an astronomical phenomenon sufficiently rare enough to draw scientists from many nations. Only then did Cook open his sealed orders from the Admiralty.

The HMS *Endeavour*'s true mission was to locate Terra Australis, a southerly landmass whose existence, though hypothetical, geographers believed necessary to counterbalance the northern hemisphere. On 19 April 1770, Cook found his missing continent. Ten days later, at what is now Cronulla in Sydney, he established the first contact between Europeans and indigenous Australians (whom Cook calls 'Indians'), when he and his crew met members of the Gwiyagal tribe.

The expedition's botanist, a young Joseph Banks, was so excited by the exotic specimens he collected there that Cook named the site Botany Bay. Over the coming months, the *Endeavour* charted Australia's eastern coastline. Cook returned home by way of the Pacific, charting Tonga and Easter Island for good measure.

A second voyage, aboard HMS *Resolution* from 1772 to 1775, brought more achievements of note: a circumnavigation of Antarctica and the loss of only one man to scurvy, a rare occurrence during such a long voyage. Cook was a pioneer. He was greatly aided, for example, by his adoption of a 'Harrison's chronometer'; a device only recently invented by the English clockmaker John Harrison, it allowed for the first time the accurate calculation of positions of longitude at sea. Cook also experimented, as the extract here shows, with the diet of his crew, insisting on fruit and vegetables. His introduction of sauerkraut to the menu was, famously, so successful the stuff had to be rationed.

Cook is often portrayed as the explorer who went and came back again, a peerless navigator who nonetheless made minimal contributions to science. 'I have made no very great discoveries,' Cook wrote after his first voyage, 'yet I have explored more of the Great South Sea than all that have gone before me, so much that little remains now to be done to have a thorough knowledge of that part of the globe.'

It was during a third voyage, departing in 1776 to locate the North-West Passage, that James Cook met his end. Given to fits of temper, it was following the theft of one of his cutters at Kealakekua Bay in Hawaii in 1779 that Cook attempted to apprehend the Hawaiian king, Kalani'ōpu'u. It drew a violent reaction from the king's people, and, in the ensuing altercation, Cook and four of his crew were killed.

THE THREE VOYAGES OF CAPTAIN JAMES COOK AROUND THE WORLD
BY JAMES COOK

FROM CHAPTER IV

The next morning, at low water, I went and sounded and buoyed the bar, the ship being now ready for sea. We saw no Indians this day, but all the hills round us for many miles were on fire, which at night made a most striking and beautiful appearance.

The 21st [June 1770] passed without our getting sight of any of the inhabitants, and indeed without a single incident worth notice. On the 22d we killed a turtle for the day's provision, upon opening which we found a wooden harpoon or turtle-peg about as thick as a man's finger, near fifteen inches long, and bearded at the end, such as we had seen among the natives, sticking through both shoulders: it appeared to have been struck a considerable time, for the wound had perfectly healed up over the weapon.

Early in the morning of the 23d I sent some people into the country to gather a supply of the greens which have been before mentioned by the name of Indian kale; one of them having straggled from the rest suddenly fell in with four Indians, three men and a boy, whom he did not see till, by turning short in the wood, he found himself among them. They had kindled a fire, and were broiling a bird of some kind, and part of a kangaroo, the remainder of which, and a cockatoo, hung at a little distance upon a tree. The man, being unarmed, was at first greatly terrified; but he had the presence of mind not to run away, judging, very rightly, that he was most likely to incur danger by appearing to apprehend it; on the contrary, he went and sat down by them, and, with an air of cheerfulness and good humour, offered them his knife, the only thing he had about him which he thought would be acceptable to them; they received it, and having handed it from one to the other, they gave it him again: he then made an offer to leave them, but this they seemed not disposed to permit; still, however, he dissembled his fears, and sat down again; they considered him with great attention and curiosity, particularly his clothes, and then felt his hands and face, and satisfied themselves that his body was of the same texture with their own. They treated him with the greatest civility, and having kept him about half an hour, they made signs that he might depart: he did not wait for a second dismission, but when he left them, not taking the direct way to the ship, they came from their fire and directed him, so that they well knew whence he came.

In the meantime, Mr Banks, having made an excursion on the other side of the river to gather plants, found the greatest part of the cloth that had been given to the Indians lying in a heap together, probably as useless lumber, not worth carrying away; and perhaps, if he had sought further, he might have found the other trinkets; for they seemed to set very little value upon any thing we had, except our turtle, which was a commodity that we were least able to spare.

The blowing weather, which prevented our attempt to get out to sea, still continuing, Mr Banks and Dr Solander went out again on the 24th to see whether any new plant could be picked up: they traversed the woods all day without success; but as they were returning through a deep valley the sides of which, though almost as perpendicular as a wall, were covered with trees and bushes, they found lying upon the ground several marking nuts, the anacardium orientale; these put them upon a new scent, and they made a most diligent search after the tree that bore them, which perhaps no European botanist ever saw; but to their great mortification they could not find it: so that, after spending much time, and cutting down four or five trees, they returned quite exhausted with fatigue to the ship.

On the 25th, having made an excursion up the river, I found a canoe belonging to our friends the Indians, whom we had not seen since the affair of the turtle; they had left it tied to some mangroves about a mile distant from the ship, and I could see by their fires that they were retired at least six miles directly inland.

As Mr Banks was again gleaning the country for his Natural History, on the 26th he had the good fortune to take an animal of the opossum tribe: it was a female, and with it he took two young ones: it was found much to resemble the remarkable animal of the kind, which Mons. de Buffon has described in his Natural History by the name of Phalanger, but it was not the same. Mons. de Buffon supposes this tribe to be peculiar to America, but in this he is certainly mistaken; and, probably, as Pallas has observed in his Zoology, the Phalanger itself is a native of the East Indies, as the animal which was caught by Mr Banks resembled it in the extraordinary conformation of the feet, in which it differs from animals of every other tribe.

On the 27th Mr Gore shot a kangaroo, which, with the skin, entrails and head, weighed eighty-four pounds. Upon examination, however, we found that this animal was not at its full growth, the innermost grinders not being yet formed. We dressed it for dinner the next day, but to our great disappointment, we found it had a much worse flavour than that we had eaten before.

The wind continued in the same quarter, and with the same violence, till five o'clock in the morning of the 29th, when it fell calm; soon after a light breeze sprung up from the land, and it being about two hours' ebb, I sent a boat to see what water was upon the bar; in the meantime we got the anchor up, and made all ready to put to sea. But when the boat came back, the officer reported that there was only thirteen feet water upon the bar, which was six inches less than the ship drew. We were therefore obliged to come to, and the sea breeze setting in again about eight o'clock, we gave up all hope of sailing that day.

We had fresh gales at S. E., with hazy weather and rain, till two in the morning of the 31st, when the weather being something more moderate, I had thoughts of trying to warp the ship out of the harbour; but upon going out myself first in the boat, I found it still blow too fresh for the attempt. During all this time the pinnace and yawl continued to ply the net and hook with tolerable success; sometimes taking a turtle, and frequently bringing in from two to three hundred weight of fish.

On the 1st of August the carpenter examined the pumps, and, to our great mortification, found them all in a state of decay, owing, as he said, to the sap having been left in the wood; one of them was so rotten as, when hoisted up, to drop to pieces, and the rest were little better; so that our chief trust was now in the soundness of our vessel, which happily did not admit more than one inch of water in an hour.

At six o'clock in the morning of Friday, the 3d, we made another unsuccessful attempt to warp the ship out of the harbour; but at five o'clock in the morning of the 4th, our efforts had a better effect, and about seven we got once more under sail, with a light air from the land, which soon died away, and was followed by the sea breezes from S. E. by S., with which we stood off to sea E. by N., having the pinnace ahead, which was ordered to keep sounding continually. The yawl had been sent to the turtle bank to take up the net which had been left there; but as the wind freshened, we got out before her. A little before noon we anchored in fifteen fathom water, with a sandy bottom; for I did not think it safe to run in among the shoals till I had well viewed them at low water from the masthead, which might determine me which way to steer; for, as yet, I was in doubt whether I should beat back to the southward, round all the shoals, or seek a passage to the eastward or the northward, all which at present appeared to be equally difficult and dangerous. When we were at anchor, the harbour from which we sailed bore S. 70 W., distant about five leagues; the northernmost point of the main in sight, which I named CAPE BEDFORD, and which lies in latitude 15° 16' S., longitude 214° 45' W., bore N. 20 W., distant three leagues and a half; but to the N. E. of this cape we could see land which had the appearance of two high islands: the turtle banks bore east, distant one mile: our latitude, by observation, was 15° 32' S., and our depth of water in standing off from the land was from three and a half to fifteen fathom.

FROM CHAPTER V

To the harbour which we had now left, I gave the name of Endeavour River. It is only a small bar harbour, or creek, which runs in a winding channel three or four leagues inland, and at the head of which there is a small brook of fresh water. There is not depth of water for shipping above a mile within the bar, and at this distance only on the north side, where the bank is so steep for near a quarter of a mile that a ship may lie afloat at low water, so near the shore as to reach it with a stage, and the situation is extremely convenient for heaving down; but at low water, the depth upon the bar is not more than nine or ten feet, nor more than seventeen or eighteen at the height of the tide; the difference between high and low water, at spring tides, being about nine feet. At the new and full of the moon it is high water between nine and ten o'clock. It must also be remembered that this part of the coast is so barricaded with shoals, as to make the harbour still more difficult of access; the safest approach is from the southward, keeping the main land close upon the board all the way. Its situation may always be found by the latitude, which has been very accurately laid down. Over the south point is some high land, but the north point is formed by a low sandy beach, which extends about three miles to the northward, where the land begins again to be high.

The chief refreshment that we procured here was turtle, but as they were not to be had without going five leagues out to sea, and the weather was frequently tempestuous, we did not abound with this dainty: what we caught, as well as the fish, was always equally divided among us all by weight, the meanest person on board having the same share as myself; and I think every commander, in such a voyage as this, will find it his interest to follow the same rule. In several parts of the sandy beaches and sand hills near the sea, we found purslane, and a kind of bean that grows upon a stalk, which creeps along the ground: the purslane we found very good when it was boiled, and the beans are not to be despised, for we found them of great service to our sick: the best greens, however, that could be procured here were the tops of the coccos, which have been mentioned already, as known in the West Indies by the name of Indian kale: these were, in our opinion, not much inferior to spinach, which in taste they somewhat resemble; the roots indeed are not good, but they might probably be meliorated by proper cultivation. They are found here chiefly in boggy ground. The few cabbage palms that we met with were in general small, and yielded so little cabbage, that they were not worth seeking.

Besides the kangaroo, and the opossum that have been already mentioned, and a kind of polecat, there are wolves upon this part of the coast, if we were not deceived by the tracks upon the ground, and several species of serpents: some of the serpents are venomous, and some harmless. There are no tame animals here except dogs, and of these we saw but two or three, which frequently came about the tents to pick up the scraps and bones that happened to lie scattered near them. There does not indeed seem to be many of any animal, except the kangaroo; we scarcely saw any other above once, but this we met with almost every time we went into the woods. Of land fowls we saw crows, kites, hawks, cockatoos of two sorts, one white and the other black, a very beautiful kind of loriquets, some parrots, pigeons of two or three sorts and several small birds not known in Europe. The waterfowls are herns, whistling ducks, which perch, and, I believe, roost upon trees, wild geese, curlieus and a few others; but these do not abound. The face of the country, which has been occasionally mentioned before, is agreeably diversified by hill and valley, lawn and wood. The soil of the hills is hard, dry and stony, yet it produces coarse grass besides wood: the soil of the plains and valleys is in some places sand, and in some clay; in some also it is rocky and stony, like the hills; in general, however, it is well clothed, and has at least the appearance of fertility. The whole country, both hill and valley, wood and plain, abounds with anthills, some of which are six or eight feet high, and twice as much in circumference. The trees here are not of many sorts; the gum tree, which we found on the southern part of the coast, is the most common, but here it is not so large: on each side of the river, through its whole course, there are mangroves in great numbers, which in some places extend a mile within the coast. The country is in all parts well watered, there being several fine rivulets at a small distance from each other, but none in the place where we lay, at least not during the time we were there, which was the dry season; we were, however, well supplied with water by springs, which were not far off.

CHARLES DARWIN
INTRODUCTION

In 1831, when a British naval expedition was proposed to survey
the coast of South America, Charles Darwin was recommended by
a friend for the position of naturalist. It was not uncommon for a
ship's surgeon to fulfil both roles, and Darwin had briefly studied
medicine. He turned the post down. He was talked round by the
ship's captain, Robert FitzRoy. An accomplished sailor and aspiring
meteorologist, FitzRoy lived in fear of madness. The nephew of Lord
Castlereagh, a Tory grandee who, in 1821, committed suicide by
cutting his throat, FitzRoy suffered from depression. Convinced the
malady was genetic, he feared the enforced solitude of years at sea
might lead him to similar action. The company of an amiable,
proactive man of science would be the ideal corrective. FitzRoy
flattered Darwin, maintaining the post was fit only for a gentleman.
Darwin, grandson of Enlightenment philosopher Erasmus Darwin
and porcelain magnate Josiah Wedgwood, was just the man.

The voyage was planned to last two years. Instead, Darwin
travelled for half a decade, setting in motion events that would
transform not just natural science but our very understanding of
humanity. Their vessel, HMS *Beagle*, set sail on 27 December
1831, bound for Tenerife. Unable to put ashore for fear of cholera,
it made for Cape Verde, off West Africa. Darwin began work
almost immediately, making detailed studies of the atmospheric
dusts particular to the region. Though he had been tasked with
making observations primarily on geology, as the voyage
progressed almost everything Darwin saw piqued his interest: the
discolouration of the ocean; the breathing mechanisms of fish;
lightning; slavery; parasites pertaining to spiders; salt pans; birds;
animal husbandry; dinosaur fossils; forms of government; and Inca
culture. The list went on.

Darwin was wracked by acute seasickness and spent almost

three years of the expedition's five-year duration on land. Indeed, *The Voyage of the Beagle*, his account of the trip, contains little of life aboard the ship. Instead Darwin's investigations – in Uruguay, the Falklands, Tierra del Fuego, and the Galapagos Islands – focused on studies of the species on land, in particular the archipelago's giant tortoises, who would help formulate his theory of natural selection.

The homeward leg included stopovers in New Zealand, Australia and Mauritius, and Darwin arrived back in Britain in 1836. The first book to result from the voyage was *The Structures and Distribution of Coral Reefs*, published in 1842. Darwin spent the next two decades poring over his research, bolstering it with new investigations. Then, in June 1858, Darwin received an unsolicited paper from a young specimen hunter named Alfred Russel Wallace. While researching birds of paradise in Malaysia, it occurred to Wallace that the survival of fitter species over those less well physically adapted, particularly in the face of disease, was not a matter of chance. The paper prompted Darwin, who had arrived at similar findings, to publish his own research.

Darwin was a quiet soul, with no appetite to argue his theories in public forums. At his friends' behest, he permitted a draft of his results to be read at a meeting of the Linnaean Society on 1 July 1858. It was met with bored indifference, relegated to other business at the end of a long session. Darwin himself was absent, victim once more to the chronic ill health he suffered.

The greatest legacy of Darwin's voyages, *On the Origin of Species*, was nevertheless published in 1859. The theories Darwin put forward of humanity's evolution from apes divided society. Crucially, Darwin declined to acknowledge the divine hand. Richard Dawkins, albeit with a vested interest, calls it 'the most important thought to occur to a human mind'. In truth, there was no eureka moment, rather the slow, patient acquisition and study of data. And all of it could be traced back to the *Beagle*'s expedition.

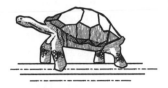

THE VOYAGE OF THE BEAGLE
BY CHARLES DARWIN

September 15th. – This archipelago consists of ten principal islands, of which five exceed the others in size. They are situated under the Equator, and between five and six hundred miles westward of the coast of America. They are all formed of volcanic rocks; a few fragments of granite curiously glazed and altered by the heat, can hardly be considered as an exception. Some of the craters, surmounting the larger islands, are of immense size, and they rise to a height of between three and four thousand feet. Their flanks are studded by innumerable smaller orifices. I scarcely hesitate to affirm that there must be in the whole archipelago at least two thousand craters. These consist either of lava or scoriae, or of finely stratified, sandstone-like tuff. Most of the latter are beautifully symmetrical; they owe their origin to eruptions of volcanic mud without any lava: it is a remarkable circumstance that every one of the twenty-eight tuff craters which were examined had their southern sides either much lower than the other sides, or quite broken down and removed. As all these craters apparently have been formed when standing in the sea, and as the waves from the trade wind and the swell from the open Pacific here unite their forces on the southern coasts of all the islands, this singular uniformity in the broken state of the craters, composed of the soft and yielding tuff, is easily explained.

Considering that these islands are placed directly under the equator, the climate is far from being excessively hot; this seems chiefly caused by the singularly low temperature of the surrounding water, brought here by the great southern polar current. Excepting during one short season, very little rain falls, and even then it is irregular; but the clouds generally hang low. Hence, whilst the lower parts of the islands are very sterile, the upper parts, at a height of a thousand feet and upwards, possess a damp climate and a tolerably luxuriant vegetation. This is especially the case on the windward sides of the islands, which first receive and condense the moisture from the atmosphere. In the morning (*17th*) we landed on Chatham Island, which, like the others, rises with a tame and rounded outline, broken here and there by scattered hillocks, the remains of former craters. Nothing could be less inviting than the first appearance. A broken field of black basaltic lava, thrown into the most rugged waves, and crossed by great fissures, is everywhere covered by stunted, sunburnt brushwood, which shows little signs of life. The dry and parched surface, being heated by the noonday sun, gave to the air a close and sultry feeling, like that from a stove: we fancied even that the bushes smelt unpleasantly. Although I diligently tried to collect as many plants as possible, I succeeded in getting very few; and such wretched-looking little weeds would have better become an arctic than an equatorial Flora. The brushwood appears, from a short distance, as leafless as our trees during winter; and it was some time before I discovered that not only almost every plant was now in full leaf, but that the greater number were in flower. The commonest bush is one of the Euphorbiaceae: an acacia and a great odd-looking cactus are the only trees which afford any shade. After the season of heavy rains, the islands are said to appear for a short time partially green. The volcanic island of Fernando Noronha, placed in many respects under nearly similar conditions, is the only other country where I have seen a vegetation at all like this of the Galapagos Islands.

The *Beagle* sailed round Chatham Island, and anchored in several bays. One night I slept on shore on a part of the island, where black truncated cones were extraordinarily numerous: from one small eminence I counted sixty of them, all surmounted by craters more or less perfect. The greater number consisted merely of a ring of red scoriae or slags, cemented together: and their height above the plain of lava was not more than from fifty to a hundred feet; none had been very lately active. The entire surface of this part of the island seems to have been permeated, like a sieve, by the subterranean vapours: here and there the lava, whilst soft, has been blown into great bubbles; and in other parts, the tops of caverns similarly formed have fallen in, leaving circular pits with steep sides. From the regular form of the many craters, they gave to the country an artificial appearance, which vividly reminded me of those parts of Staffordshire, where the great iron-foundries are most numerous. The day was glowing hot, and the scrambling over the rough surface and through the intricate thickets, was very fatiguing; but I was well repaid by the strange Cyclopean scene. As I was walking along I met two large tortoises, each of which must have weighed at least two hundred pounds: one was eating a piece of cactus, and as I approached, it stared at me and slowly walked away; the other gave a deep hiss, and drew in its head. These huge reptiles, surrounded by the black lava, the leafless shrubs and large cacti, seemed to my fancy like some antediluvian animals. The few dull-coloured birds cared no more for me than they did for the great tortoises.

23rd. – The *Beagle* proceeded to Charles Island. This archipelago has long been frequented, first by the bucaniers, and latterly by whalers, but it is only within the last six years that a small colony has been established here. The inhabitants are between two and three hundred in number; they are

nearly all people of colour, who have been banished for
political crimes from the Republic of the Equator, of which
Quito is the capital. The settlement is placed about four and a
half miles inland, and at a height probably of a thousand feet.
In the first part of the road we passed through leafless thickets,
as in Chatham Island. Higher up, the woods gradually became
greener; and as soon as we crossed the ridge of the island, we
were cooled by a fine southerly breeze, and our sight refreshed
by a green and thriving vegetation. In this upper region coarse
grasses and ferns abound; but there are no tree ferns: I saw
nowhere any member of the palm family, which is the more
singular, as 360 miles northward, Cocos Island takes its name
from the number of coconuts. The houses are irregularly
scattered over a flat space of ground, which is cultivated with
sweet potatoes and bananas. It will not easily be imagined how
pleasant the sight of black mud was to us, after having been so
long accustomed to the parched soil of Peru and northern Chile.
The inhabitants, although complaining of poverty, obtain,
without much trouble, the means of subsistence. In the woods
there are many wild pigs and goats; but the staple article of
animal food is supplied by the tortoises. Their numbers have of
course been greatly reduced in this island, but the people yet
count on two days' hunting giving them food for the rest of the
week. It is said that formerly single vessels have taken away as
many as seven hundred, and that the ship's company of a frigate
some years since brought down in one day two hundred
tortoises to the beach.

The rocks on the coast abounded with great black lizards
between three and four feet long; and on the hills, an ugly
yellowish-brown species was equally common. We saw many of
this latter kind, some clumsily running out of the way, and
others shuffling into their burrows. I shall presently describe
in more detail the habits of both these reptiles. The whole of
this northern part of Albemarle Island is miserably sterile.

October 8th. – We arrived at James Island: this island, as well as Charles Island, were long since thus named after our kings of the Stuart line. Mr Bynoe, myself and our servants were left here for a week, with provisions and a tent, whilst the *Beagle* went for water. We found here a party of Spaniards, who had been sent from Charles Island to dry fish, and to salt tortoise meat. About six miles inland, and at the height of nearly 2000 feet, a hovel had been built in which two men lived, who were employed in catching tortoises, whilst the others were fishing on the coast. I paid this party two visits, and slept there one night. As in the other islands, the lower region was covered by nearly leafless bushes, but the trees were here of a larger growth than elsewhere, several being two feet and some even two feet nine inches in diameter. The upper region being kept damp by the clouds, supports a green and flourishing vegetation. So damp was the ground that there were large beds of a coarse cyperus, in which great numbers of a very small water rail lived and bred. While staying in this upper region, we lived entirely upon tortoise meat: the breastplate roasted (as the Gauchos do carne con cuero), with the flesh on it, is very good; and the young tortoises make excellent soup; but otherwise the meat to my taste is indifferent.

The natural history of these islands is eminently curious, and well deserves attention. Most of the organic productions are aboriginal creations, found nowhere else; there is even a difference between the inhabitants of the different islands; yet all show a marked relationship with those of America, though separated from that continent by an open space of ocean, between 500 and 600 miles in width. The archipelago is a little world within itself, or rather a satellite attached to America, whence it has derived a few stray colonists, and has received the general character of its indigenous productions. Considering the small size of the islands, we feel the more astonished at the number of their aboriginal beings, and at their confined range. Seeing every height crowned with its crater, and the boundaries of most of the lava streams still distinct, we are led to believe that within a period geologically recent the unbroken ocean was here spread out. Hence, both in space and time, we seem to be brought somewhat near to that great fact – that mystery of mysteries – the first appearance of new beings on this earth...

We will now turn to the order of reptiles, which gives the most striking character to the zoology of these islands. The species are not numerous, but the numbers of individuals of each species are extraordinarily great. There is one small lizard belonging to a South American genus, and two species (and probably more) of the Amblyrhynchus – a genus confined to the Galapagos Islands. There is one snake which is numerous; it is identical, as I am informed by M Bibron, with the Psammophis temminckii from Chile. Of sea turtle I believe there are more than one species, and of tortoises there are, as we shall presently show, two or three species or races. Of toads and frogs there are none: I was surprised at this, considering how well suited for them the temperate and damp upper woods appeared to be. It recalled to my mind the remark made by Bory St. Vincent, namely, that none of this family are found on any of the volcanic islands in the great oceans. As far as I can ascertain from various works, this seems to hold good throughout the Pacific, and even in the large islands of the Sandwich archipelago. Mauritius offers an apparent exception, where I saw the Rana mascariensis in abundance: this frog is said now to inhabit the Seychelles, Madagascar and Bourbon; but on the other hand, Du Bois, in his voyage in 1669, states that there were no reptiles in Bourbon except tortoises; and the Officier du Roi asserts that before 1768 it had been attempted, without success, to introduce frogs into Mauritius – I presume for the purpose of eating: hence it may be well doubted whether this frog is an aboriginal of these islands. The absence of the frog family in the oceanic islands is the more remarkable when contrasted with the case of lizards, which swarm on most of the smallest islands. May this difference not be caused by the greater facility with which the eggs of lizards, protected by calcareous shells might be transported through salt water, than could the slimy spawn of frogs?

I will first describe the habits of the tortoise (Testudo nigra, formerly called Indica), which has been so frequently alluded to. These animals are found, I believe, on all the islands of the archipelago; certainly on the greater number. They frequent in preference the high damp parts, but they likewise live in the lower and arid districts. I have already shown, from the numbers which have been caught in a single day, how very numerous they must be. Some grow to an immense size: Mr Lawson, an Englishman, and vice-governor of the colony, told us that he had seen several so large, that it required six or eight men to lift them from the ground; and that some had afforded as much as two hundred pounds of meat. The old males are the largest, the females rarely growing to so great a size: the male can readily be distinguished from the female by the greater length of its tail. The tortoises which live on those islands where there is no water, or in the lower and arid parts of the others, feed chiefly on the succulent cactus. Those which frequent the higher and damp regions, eat the leaves of various trees, a kind of berry (called guayavita) which is acid and austere, and likewise a pale green filamentous lichen (Usnera plicata) that hangs from the boughs of the trees.

The tortoise is very fond of water, drinking large quantities, and wallowing in the mud. The larger islands alone possess springs, and these are always situated towards the central parts, and at a considerable height. The tortoises, therefore, which frequent the lower districts, when thirsty, are obliged to travel from a long distance. Hence broad and well-beaten paths branch off in every direction from the wells down to the sea coast; and the Spaniards by following them up, first discovered the watering places. When I landed at Chatham Island, I could not imagine what animal travelled so methodically along well-chosen tracks. Near the springs it was a curious spectacle to behold many of these huge creatures, one set eagerly travelling onwards with outstretched necks, and another set returning after having drunk their fill. When the tortoise arrives at the spring, quite regardless of any spectator, he buries his head in the water above his eyes, and greedily swallows great mouthfuls, at the rate of about ten in a minute. The inhabitants say each animal stays three or four days in the neighbourhood of the water, and then returns to the lower country; but they differed respecting the frequency of these visits. The animal probably regulates them according to the nature of the food on which it has lived. It is, however, certain, that tortoises can subsist even on these islands where there is no other water than what falls during a few rainy days in the year.

I believe it is well ascertained that the bladder of the frog acts as a reservoir for the moisture necessary to its existence: such seems to be the case with the tortoise. For some time after a visit to the springs, their urinary bladders are distended with fluid, which is said gradually to decrease in volume, and to become less pure. The inhabitants, when walking in the lower district, and overcome with thirst, often take advantage of this circumstance, and drink the contents of the bladder if full: in one I saw killed, the fluid was quite limpid, and had only a very slightly bitter taste. The inhabitants, however, always first drink the water in the pericardium, which is described as being best.

The tortoises, when purposely moving towards any point, travel by night and day, and arrive at their journey's end much sooner than would be expected. The inhabitants, from observing marked individuals, consider that they travel a distance of about eight miles in two or three days. One large tortoise, which I watched, walked at the rate of sixty yards in ten minutes, that is 360 yards in the hour, or four miles a day – allowing a little time for it to eat on the road. During the breeding season, when the male and female are together, the male utters a hoarse roar or bellowing, which, it is said, can be heard at the distance of more than a hundred yards. The female never uses her voice, and the male only at these times; so that when the people hear this noise, they know that the two are together. They were at this time (October) laying their eggs. The female, where the soil is sandy, deposits them together, and covers them up with sand; but where the ground is rocky she drops them indiscriminately in any hole: Mr Bynoe found seven placed in a fissure. The egg is white and spherical; one which I measured was seven inches and three-eighths in circumference, and therefore larger than a hen's egg. The young tortoises, as soon as they are hatched, fall a prey in great numbers to the carrion-feeding buzzard. The old ones seem generally to die from accidents, as from falling down precipices: at least, several of the inhabitants told me that they never found one dead without some evident cause.

The inhabitants believe that these animals are absolutely deaf; certainly they do not overhear a person walking close behind them. I was always amused when overtaking one of these great monsters as it was quietly pacing along, to see how suddenly, the instant I passed, it would draw in its head and legs, and uttering a deep hiss fall to the ground with a heavy sound, as if struck dead. I frequently got on their backs, and then giving a few raps on the hinder part of their shells, they would rise up and walk away – but I found it very difficult to keep my balance. The flesh of this animal is largely employed, both fresh and salted; and a beautifully clear oil is prepared from the fat. When a tortoise is caught, the man makes a slit in the skin near its tail, so as to see inside its body whether the fat under the dorsal plate is thick. If it is not, the animal is liberated and it is said to recover soon from this strange operation. In order to secure the tortoise, it is not sufficient to turn them like turtle, for they are often able to get on their legs again.

There can be little doubt that this tortoise is an aboriginal inhabitant of the Galapagos; for it is found on all, or nearly all, the islands, even on some of the smaller ones where there is no water; had it been an imported species, this would hardly have been the case in a group which has been so little frequented.

CHARLES DICKENS
INTRODUCTION

'My readers have opportunities of judging for themselves whether the influences and tendencies which I distrusted in America had, at that time, any existence but in my imagination.' So wrote Charles Dickens in his preface to *American Notes*, his account, published in October 1842, of a publicity tour to the United States that same year. Dickens already enjoyed a large American readership, his work serialised on both sides of the Atlantic. When Little Nell lay grievously ill towards the end of *The Old Curiosity Shop*, fans on the New York dockside, yet to receive the relevant instalment, called out to arriving ships as to her fate.

Dickens considered himself an honorary American, an admirer of the republican project, and took 'a grateful interest' in a nation that placed such value on individual liberty. When he arrived in Boston, his admirers, Henry Wadsworth Longfellow among them, renamed it 'Boz-town' in his honour. Dickens found the city to his liking, noting an 'intellectual refinement and superiority'.

New York agreed with Dickens too. 'Was there ever such a sunny street as this Broadway,' he noted, 'the pavement stones are polished with the tread of feet until they shine.' A dedicated social commentator, Dickens' itinerary also took in the infamous Five Points. Here things assumed a different tone. The 'hideous tenements' that stood before him 'take their name from robbery and murder: all that is loathsome, drooping and decayed is here'.

This became the lens through which, gradually, he began to view the whole nation. Dickens was certainly unprepared for the level of public attention that followed him, an example, he believed, of America's inherent vulgarity. He considered one fellow traveller 'the most inquisitive...that can possibly be imagined. He never spoke otherwise than interrogatively. He was an embodied inquiry...with a great note of interrogation in each eye, two in his cocked ears, two more in his turned-up nose and chin, at least half a dozen more about the corners of his mouth'.

In Washington, he found the Senate a 'dignified and decorous body...its proceedings conducted with much gravity and order'. Until, that is, he encountered his least favourite American custom, tobacco, and 'the universal disregard of the spittoon... I strongly recommend all strangers not to look at the floor'.

On its publication, *American Notes* received a critical mauling. It was perceived as a condescending rant, the bilious mutterings of old Empire. Edgar Allan Poe described it as 'suicidal'. The American press labelled Dickens a mercenary, concerned more with money – and melodrama – than facts.

Dickens' attitude was cultivated partly from indignation. His books were not covered by international copyright, and, for all the copies that flew off shelves, he made little in royalties. Yet some of his insights, on the deprivations in the prisons he visited in Philadelphia and New York for instance, seem justified. Dickens appended *American Notes* with a coruscating chapter on slavery, 'that most hideous blot and foul disgrace'.

'The problem,' the Harvard historian Jill Lepore has observed, 'wasn't that Dickens' America was inaccurate: it is, and it isn't. The problem was that it was vicious.' US readers concurred, with copies of both *American Notes* and *Martin Chuzzlewit*, whose serialisation began in 1842, burned in the streets.

Dickens was unrepentant. 'I have nothing to defend,' he wrote, 'or to explain away. The truth is the truth; and neither childish absurdities, nor unscrupulous contradictions, can make it otherwise. The earth would still move round the sun, though the whole Catholic Church said no.'

Despite having all the makings of a diplomatic incident, the great man's reputation in the US survived. His novels continued to sell in vast numbers, and Dickens returned to America a quarter of a century later, in 1867, to discover all had been forgiven.

He gave a six-month speaking tour. Many in his audiences were too young to recall his damning assessment of their country. New Yorkers who had sent his work up in flames 25 years previously now queued around the block; some reports claimed, fancifully, for up to a mile. And the royalties improved. From around 80 appearances, Dickens was remunerated to the tune of $228,000, equivalent to $3m today. Mark Twain was among those who paid homage, describing the talks as 'glittering frostwork'.

In April of 1867, at a dinner given by New York's press corps, Dickens set the record straight, announcing he would amend subsequent editions of *American Notes*. This, in turn, came to be known as the official 'Dickens edition'. 'Prejudiced, I am not,' he wrote in the updated version, 'and never have been, otherwise than in favour of the United States.'

AMERICAN NOTES
BY CHARLES DICKENS

We reached Washington at about half past six that evening, and had upon the way a beautiful view of the Capitol, which is a fine building of the Corinthian order, placed upon a noble and commanding eminence. Arrived at the hotel, I saw no more of the place that night; being very tired, and glad to get to bed.

It is sometimes called the City of Magnificent Distances, but it might with greater propriety be termed the City of Magnificent Intentions; for it is only on taking a bird's-eye view of it from the top of the Capitol that one can at all comprehend the vast designs of its projector, an aspiring Frenchman. Spacious avenues that begin in nothing and lead nowhere; streets, mile-long, that only want houses, roads and inhabitants; public buildings that need but a public to be complete; and ornaments of great thoroughfares, which only lack great thoroughfares to ornament – are its leading features. One might fancy the season over, and most of the houses gone out of town forever with their masters. To the admirers of cities it is a Barmecide Feast: a pleasant field for the imagination to rove in; a monument raised to a deceased project, with not even a legible inscription to record its departed greatness.

Such as it is, it is likely to remain. It was originally chosen for the seat of Government, as a means of averting the conflicting jealousies and interests of the different States; and very probably too, as being remote from mobs: a consideration not to be slighted, even in America. It has no trade or commerce of its own: having little or no population beyond the President and his establishment; the members of the legislature who reside there during the session; the Government clerks and officers employed in the various departments; the keepers of the hotels and boarding houses; and the tradesmen who supply their tables. It is very unhealthy. Few people would live in Washington, I take it, who were not obliged to reside there; and the tides of emigration and speculation, those rapid and regardless currents, are little likely to flow at any time towards such dull and sluggish water.

The principal features of the Capitol, are, of course, the two houses of Assembly. But there is, besides, in the centre of the building, a fine rotunda, ninety-six feet in diameter, and ninety-six high, whose circular wall is divided into compartments, ornamented by historical pictures. Four of these have for their subjects prominent events in the revolutionary struggle. They were painted by Colonel Trumbull, himself a member of Washington's staff at the time of their occurrence, from which circumstance they derive a peculiar interest of their own. In this same hall Mr Greenough's large statue of Washington has been lately placed. It has great merits of course, but it struck me as being rather strained and violent for its subject. I could wish, however, to have seen it in a better light than it can ever be viewed in, where it stands.

There is a very pleasant and commodious library in the Capitol; and from a balcony in front, the bird's-eye view, of which I have just spoken, may be had, together with a beautiful prospect of the adjacent country. In one of the ornamented portions of the building, there is a figure of Justice; whereunto the Guide Book says, 'the artist at first contemplated giving more of nudity, but he was warned that the public sentiment in this country would not admit of it, and in his caution he has gone, perhaps, into the opposite extreme'. Poor Justice! she has been made to wear much stranger garments in America than those she pines in, in the Capitol. Let us hope that she has changed her dressmaker since they were fashioned, and that the public sentiment of the country did not cut out the clothes she hides her lovely figure in just now.

The House of Representatives is a beautiful and spacious hall, of semicircular shape, supported by handsome pillars. One part of the gallery is appropriated to the ladies, and there they sit in front rows, and come in, and go out, as at a play or concert. The chair is canopied, and raised considerably above the floor of the House; and every member has an easy chair and a writing desk to himself: which is denounced by some people out of doors as a most unfortunate and injudicious arrangement, tending to long sittings and prosaic speeches. It is an elegant chamber to look at, but a singularly bad one for all purposes of hearing. The Senate, which is smaller, is free from this objection, and is exceedingly well adapted to the uses for which it is designed. The sittings, I need hardly add, take place in the day; and the parliamentary forms are modelled on those of the old country.

I was sometimes asked, in my progress through other places, whether I had not been very much impressed by the heads of the lawmakers at Washington; meaning not their chiefs and leaders, but literally their individual and personal heads, whereon their hair grew, and whereby the phrenological character of each legislator was expressed: and I almost as often struck my questioner dumb with indignant consternation by answering, 'No, that I didn't remember being at all overcome'. As I must, at whatever hazard, repeat the avowal here, I will follow it up by relating my impressions on this subject in as few words as possible.

In the first place – it may be from some imperfect

development of my organ of veneration – I do not remember
having ever fainted away, or having even been moved to tears
of joyful pride, at sight of any legislative body. I have borne
the House of Commons like a man, and have yielded to no
weakness but slumber in the House of Lords. I have seen
elections for borough and county, and have never been
impelled (no matter which party won) to damage my hat by
throwing it up into the air in triumph, or to crack my voice
by shouting forth any reference to our Glorious Constitution,
to the noble purity of our independent voters or the
unimpeachable integrity of our independent members. Having
withstood such strong attacks upon my fortitude, it is
possible that I may be of a cold and insensible temperament,
amounting to iciness, in such matters; and therefore my
impressions of the live pillars of the Capitol at Washington
must be received with such grains of allowance as this free
confession may seem to demand.

Did I see in this public body an assemblage of men bound
together in the sacred names of Liberty and Freedom, and so
asserting the chaste dignity of those twin goddesses in all their
discussions, as to exalt at once the Eternal Principles to which
their names are given, and their own character and the
character of their countrymen, in the admiring eyes of the
whole world?

It was but a week, since an aged, grey-haired man, a lasting
honour to the land that gave him birth, who has done good
service to his country, as his forefathers did, and who will be
remembered scores upon scores of years after the worms bred
in its corruption are but so many grains of dust – it was but a
week since this old man had stood for days upon his trial
before this very body, charged with having dared to assert the
infamy of that traffic, which has for its accursed merchandise
men and women, and their unborn children. Yes. And publicly
exhibited in the same city all the while; gilded, framed and

glazed hung up for general admiration; shown to strangers not with shame, but pride; its face not turned towards the wall, itself not taken down and burned; is the Unanimous Declaration of the Thirteen United States of America, which solemnly declares that All Men are created Equal; and are endowed by their Creator with the Inalienable Rights of Life, Liberty and the Pursuit of Happiness!

It was not a month since this same body had sat calmly by, and heard a man, one of themselves, with oaths which beggars in their drink reject, threaten to cut another's throat from ear to ear. There he sat, among them; not crushed by the general feeling of the assembly, but as good a man as any.

There was but a week to come, and another of that body, for doing his duty to those who sent him there; for claiming in a Republic the Liberty and Freedom of expressing their sentiments, and making known their prayer; would be tried, found guilty and have strong censure passed upon him by the rest. His was a grave offence indeed; for years before, he had risen up and said, 'A gang of male and female slaves for sale, warranted to breed like cattle, linked to each other by iron fetters, are passing now along the open street beneath the windows of your Temple of Equality! Look!' But there are many kinds of hunters engaged in the Pursuit of Happiness, and they go variously armed. It is the Inalienable Right of some among them to take the field after their Happiness equipped with cat and cartwhip, stocks and iron collar, and to shout their view halloa! (always in praise of Liberty) to the music of clanking chains and bloody stripes.

Where sat the many legislators of coarse threats; of words and blows such as coalheavers deal upon each other when they forget their breeding? On every side. Every session had its anecdotes of that kind, and the actors were all there.

Did I recognise in this assembly a body of men, who, applying themselves in a new world to correct some of the

falsehoods and vices of the old, purified the avenues to Public
Life, paved the dirty ways to Place and Power, debated
and made laws for the Common Good and had no party but
their Country?

I saw in them the wheels that move the meanest perversion
of virtuous Political Machinery that the worst tools ever
wrought. Despicable trickery at elections; underhanded
tamperings with public officers; cowardly attacks upon
opponents, with scurrilous newspapers for shields, and hired
pens for daggers; shameful trucklings to mercenary knaves,
whose claim to be considered is that every day and week they
sow new crops of ruin with their venal types, which are the
dragon's teeth of yore, in everything but sharpness; aidings
and abettings of every bad inclination in the popular mind,
and artful suppressions of all its good influences: such things
as these, and in a word, Dishonest Faction in its most
depraved and most unblushing form, stared out from every
corner of the crowded hall.

Did I see among them the intelligence and refinement: the
true, honest, patriotic heart of America? Here and there were
drops of its blood and life, but they scarcely coloured the
stream of desperate adventurers which sets that way for profit
and for pay. It is the game of these men, and of their profligate
organs, to make the strife of politics so fierce and brutal, and
so destructive of all self-respect in worthy men, that sensitive
and delicate-minded persons shall be kept aloof, and they, and
such as they, be left to battle out their selfish views unchecked.
And thus this lowest of all scrambling fights goes on, and they
who in other countries would, from their intelligence and
station, most aspire to make the laws, do here recoil the
furthest from that degradation.

That there are, among the representatives of the people in
both Houses, and among all parties, some men of high
character and great abilities, I need not say. The foremost

among those politicians who are known in Europe have been already described, and I see no reason to depart from the rule I have laid down for my guidance, of abstaining from all mention of individuals. It will be sufficient to add that to the most favourable accounts that have been written of them, I more than fully and most heartily subscribe; and that personal intercourse and free communication have bred within me, not the result predicted in the very doubtful proverb, but increased admiration and respect. They are striking men to look at, hard to deceive, prompt to act, lions in energy, Crichtons in varied accomplishments, Indians in fire of eye and gesture, Americans in strong and generous impulse; and they as well represent the honour and wisdom of their country at home, as the distinguished gentleman who is now its Minister at the British Court sustains its highest character abroad.

I visited both houses nearly every day during my stay in Washington. On my initiatory visit to the House of Representatives, they divided against a decision of the chair; but the chair won. The second time I went, the member who was speaking, being interrupted by a laugh, mimicked it, as one child would in quarrelling with another, and added, 'that he would make honourable gentlemen opposite sing out a little more on the other side of their mouths presently'. But interruptions are rare; the speaker being usually heard in silence. There are more quarrels than with us, and more threatenings than gentlemen are accustomed to exchange in any civilised society of which we have record: but farmyard imitations have not as yet been imported from the Parliament of the United Kingdom. The feature in oratory which appears to be the most practised, and most relished, is the constant repetition of the same idea or shadow of an idea in fresh words; and the inquiry out of doors is not, 'What did he say?' but, 'How long did he speak?' These, however, are but enlargements of a principle which prevails elsewhere.

The Senate is a dignified and decorous body, and its proceedings are conducted with much gravity and order. Both houses are handsomely carpeted; but the state to which these carpets are reduced by the universal disregard of the spittoon with which every honourable member is accommodated, and the extraordinary improvements on the pattern which are squirted and dabbled upon it in every direction, do not admit of being described. I will merely observe that I strongly recommend all strangers not to look at the floor; and if they happen to drop anything, though it be their purse, not to pick it up with an ungloved hand on any account.

It is somewhat remarkable too at first, to say the least, to see so many honourable members with swelled faces; and it is scarcely less remarkable to discover that this appearance is caused by the quantity of tobacco they contrive to stow within the hollow of the cheek. It is strange enough too to see an honourable gentleman leaning back in his tilted chair with his legs on the desk before him, shaping a convenient 'plug' with his penknife, and when it is quite ready for use, shooting the old one from his mouth, as from a pop-gun, and clapping the new one in its place.

I was surprised to observe that even steady old chewers of great experience are not always good marksmen, which has rather inclined me to doubt that general proficiency with the rifle, of which we have heard so much in England. Several gentlemen called upon me, who, in the course of conversation, frequently missed the spittoon at five paces; and one (but he was certainly shortsighted) mistook the closed sash for the open window at three. On another occasion, when I dined out, and was sitting with two ladies and some gentlemen round a fire before dinner, one of the company fell short of the fireplace six distinct times. I am disposed to think, however, that this was occasioned by his not aiming at that object, as there was a white marble hearth before the fender, which was more convenient, and may have suited his purpose better.

The Patent Office at Washington furnishes an extraordinary example of American enterprise and ingenuity; for the immense number of models it contains are the accumulated inventions of only five years; the whole of the previous collection having been destroyed by fire. The elegant structure in which they are arranged is one of design rather than execution, for there is but one side erected out of four, though the works are stopped. The Post Office is a very compact and very beautiful building. In one of the departments, among a collection of rare and curious articles, are deposited the presents which have been made from time to time to the American ambassadors at foreign courts by the various potentates to whom they were the accredited agents of the Republic; gifts which by the law they are not permitted to retain. I confess that I looked upon this as a very painful exhibition, and one by no means flattering to the national standard of honesty and honour. That can scarcely be a high state of moral feeling which imagines a gentleman of repute and station likely to be corrupted in the discharge of his duty by the present of a snuffbox, or a richly mounted sword or an Eastern shawl; and surely the Nation who reposes confidence in her appointed servants is likely to be better served than she who makes them the subject of such very mean and paltry suspicions.

The President's mansion is more like an English clubhouse, both within and without, than any other kind of establishment with which I can compare it. The ornamental ground about it has been laid out in garden walks; they are pretty, and agreeable to the eye; though they have that uncomfortable air of having been made yesterday, which is far from favourable to the display of such beauties.

My first visit to this house was on the morning after my arrival, when I was carried thither by an official gentleman, who was so kind as to charge himself with my presentation to the President.

We entered a large hall, and having twice or thrice rung a bell which nobody answered, walked without further ceremony through the rooms on the ground floor, as divers other gentlemen (mostly with their hats on, and their hands in their pockets) were doing very leisurely. Some of these had ladies with them, to whom they were showing the premises; others were lounging on the chairs and sofas; others, in a perfect state of exhaustion from listlessness, were yawning drearily. The greater portion of this assemblage were rather asserting their supremacy than doing anything else, as they had no particular business there that anybody knew of. A few were closely eyeing the movables, as if to make quite sure that the President (who was far from popular) had not made away with any of the furniture, or sold the fixtures for his private benefit.

We had previously looked into another chamber fitted all round with a great, bare, wooden desk or counter, whereon lay files of newspapers to which sundry gentlemen were referring. But there were no such means of beguiling the time in this apartment, which was as unpromising and tiresome as any waiting room in one of our public establishments, or any physician's dining room during his hours of consultation at home.

There were some fifteen or twenty persons in the room. One, a tall, wiry, muscular old man from the west; sunburnt and swarthy; with a brown white hat on his knees, and a giant umbrella resting between his legs; who sat bolt upright in his chair, frowning steadily at the carpet, and twitching the hard lines about his mouth, as if he had made up his mind 'to fix' the President on what he had to say, and wouldn't bate him a grain. Another, a Kentucky farmer, six feet six in height, with his hat on, and his hands under his coattails, who leaned against the wall and kicked the floor with his heel, as though he had Time's head under his shoe and were literally 'killing' him. A third, an oval-faced, bilious-looking man with sleek black hair cropped close, and whiskers and beard shaved down to blue dots, who sucked the head of a thick stick, and from time to time took it out of his mouth to see how it was getting on. A fourth did nothing but whistle. A fifth did nothing but spit. And indeed all these gentlemen were so very persevering and energetic in this latter particular, and bestowed their favours so abundantly upon the carpet, that I take it for granted the Presidential housemaids have high wages, or, to speak more genteelly, an ample amount of 'compensation': which is the American word for salary, in the case of all public servants.

At a businesslike table covered with papers sat the President himself. He looked somewhat worn and anxious, and well he might; being at war with everybody – but the expression of his face was mild and pleasant, and his manner was remarkably unaffected, gentlemanly and agreeable. I thought that in his whole carriage and demeanour, he became his station singularly well.

Being advised that the sensible etiquette of the republican court, admitted of a traveller, like myself, declining, without any impropriety, an invitation to dinner, which did not reach me until I had concluded my arrangements for leaving Washington some days before that to which it referred, I only returned to this house once. It was on the occasion of one of those general assemblies which are held on certain nights, between the hours of nine and twelve o'clock, and are called, rather oddly, Levees.

I went with my wife at about ten. There was a pretty dense crowd of carriages and people in the courtyard, and so far as I could make out, there were no very clear regulations for the taking up or setting down of company. There were certainly no policemen to soothe startled horses, either by sawing at their bridles or flourishing truncheons in their eyes; and I am ready to make oath that no inoffensive persons were knocked

violently on the head, or poked acutely in their backs or
stomachs; or brought to a standstill by any such gentle
means, and then taken into custody for not moving on. But
there was no confusion or disorder. Our carriage reached the
porch in its turn, without any blustering, swearing, shouting,
backing or other disturbance: and we dismounted with as
much ease and comfort as though we had been escorted by
the whole Metropolitan Force from A to Z inclusive.

The great drawing room, which I have already mentioned,
and the other chambers on the ground floor, were crowded
to excess. The company was not, in our sense of the term,
select, for it comprehended persons of very many grades
and classes; nor was there any great display of costly attire:
indeed, some of the costumes may have been, for aught
I know, grotesque enough.

HENRY FIELDING
INTRODUCTION

Henry Fielding was a progenitor of the modern novel. A key figure in Augustan literature, that movement which ran for roughly the first half of the 18th century, his contemporaries included Alexander Pope, Jonathan Swift and Samuel Johnson. Fielding's speciality was satire, making him a superb chronicler of character and base appetites. It is a style Fielding deploys in *The Journal of a Voyage to Lisbon*, published in 1755 as his swansong.

Fielding found his fictional exemplar in *Tom Jones*, published in 1749, and whose habitually amorous hero rises from the foundling's hospital to make his fortune by way of numerous ribald encounters. Fielding's own life was colourful. He had five children with his first wife, Charlotte Craddock. On her death in 1744, and to the consternation of polite society, he married her maid, Mary Daniel, who bore him five more.

By April 1754, Fielding's health had begun to fail dramatically. Aged 47, he was suffering from asthma (a consequence of the poor London air), from gout (rich London food) and from cirrhosis of the liver (a well-stocked wine cellar). It was advised he take a trip to Lisbon, where the warmer, cleaner climate might alleviate his symptoms. Fielding was unable to walk, his stomach by now much distended, and thus suffered the indignity of being hoisted aboard ship, the *Queen of Portugal*. 'I ran the gauntlope,' he wrote, 'through rows of sailors and watermen, few of whom failed of paying their compliments to me by all manner of jests and insults on my misery.'

The bulk of the narrative concerns the voyage itself. The ship's captain, Veale, was in no hurry to set sail, waiting for more passengers and cargo. Several weeks in, Fielding found himself no further south than the Isle of Wight, barely a mile off the English coast. Once underway, the wind deserted them frequently, such that Veale believed himself bewitched, 'contemptible in the wind's eye'. The idea grew when, moving once more, one of the ship's kittens was swept overboard. Veale sent his crew to retrieve it, only to crush the poor creature to death in his own quarters as it hid beneath a pile of cushions. The bilious Fielding was in grave discomfort throughout. He was forced to share a cabin with a companion who snored loudly, but not loudly enough to drown out the women next door who were violently seasick, even when the ship was at anchor.

Most of *The Journal of a Voyage to Lisbon* concerns the voyage itself. Fielding was more interested in thinking of his literary forbears than his contemporaries, and the Portuguese capital barely features. Fielding died two months after his arrival in Lisbon and is buried in the English cemetery there, a final cruel twist, given that, by all accounts, Fielding hated the place. Yet it is also poignant and moving, a meditation on ageing by a great artist writing in full knowledge of his own decline. 'A lamp almost burnt out does not give so steady and uniform a light as when it blazes in full vigour,' his publishers wrote in their dedication, yet it 'sometimes darts a ray as bright as ever.' Indeed, one of the book's highlights is an illuminating essay, featured here, on the nature of travel writing itself. It is Fielding in full and vigorous voice.

The book was published posthumously and its release was timely. On the morning of 1 November 1755, All Saints' Day, Lisbon's churches were packed with worshippers. The earthquake that struck destroyed most of the city's buildings, and the estimates of those killed vary wildly, between 10,000 and 100,000. Scientists and philosophers were sent into a tailspin. Immanuel Kant claimed it had been caused by gasses beneath the Earth's surface. Jean-Jacques Rousseau said the disaster had been exacerbated by the close proximity of city living, while Voltaire deemed it nothing less than divine judgement, all of which served to increase interest in Fielding's book. Some historians suggest the cost of rebuilding the city ran to 50% of Portugal's GDP. One of the few structures to survive was Henry Fielding's grave.

THE JOURNAL OF A VOYAGE TO LISBON
BY HENRY FIELDING

There would not, perhaps, be a more pleasant or profitable study among those which have their principal end in amusement than that of travels or voyages, if they were writ, as they might be and ought to be, with a joint view to the entertainment and information of mankind. If the conversation of travellers be so eagerly sought after as it is, we may believe their books will be still more agreeable company, as they will in general be more instructive and more entertaining.

But when I say the conversation of travellers is usually so welcome, I must be understood to mean that only of such as have had good sense enough to apply their peregrinations to a proper use, so as to acquire from them a real and valuable knowledge of men and things, both which are best known by comparison. If the customs and manners of men were everywhere the same, there would be no office so dull as that of a traveller, for the difference of hills, valleys, rivers, in short, the various views of which we may see the face of the earth, would scarce afford him a pleasure worthy of his labour; and surely it would give him very little opportunity of communicating any kind of entertainment or improvement to others.

To make a traveller an agreeable companion to a man of sense, it is necessary, not only that he should have seen much, but that he should have overlooked much of what he hath seen. Nature is not, any more than a great genius, always admirable in her productions, and therefore the traveller, who may be called her commentator, should not expect to find everywhere subjects worthy of his notice.

It is certain, indeed, that one may be guilty of omission, as well as of the opposite extreme; but a fault on that side will be more easily pardoned, as it is better to be hungry than surfeited; and to miss your dessert at the table of a man whose gardens abound with the choicest fruits, than to have your taste affronted with every sort of trash that can be picked up at the green-stall or the wheelbarrow.

If we should carry on the analogy between the traveller and the commentator, it is impossible to keep one's eye a moment off from the laborious much-read Doctor Zachary Gray, of whose redundant notes on Hudibras I shall only say that it is, I am confident, the single book extant in which above five hundred authors are quoted, not one of which could be found in the collection of the late Doctor Mead.

As there are few things which a traveller is to record, there are fewer on which he is to offer his observations: this is the office of the reader; and it is so pleasant a one, that he seldom chooses to have it taken from him, under the pretence of lending him assistance. Some occasions, indeed, there are when proper observations are pertinent, and others when they are necessary; but good sense alone must point them out. I shall lay down only one general rule; which I believe to be of universal truth between relator and hearer, as it is between author and reader; this is that the latter never forgive any observation of the former which doth not convey some knowledge that they are sensible they could not possibly have attained of themselves.

But all his pains in collecting knowledge, all his judgment in selecting and all his art in communicating it, will not suffice unless he can make himself, in some degree, an agreeable as well as an instructive companion. The highest instruction we can derive from the tedious tale of a dull fellow scarce ever pays us for our attention. There is nothing, I think, half so valuable as knowledge, and yet there is nothing which men will give themselves so little trouble to attain; unless it be, perhaps, that lowest degree of it which is the object of curiosity, and which hath therefore that active passion constantly employed in its service. This, indeed, it is in the power of every traveller to gratify; but it is the leading principle in weak minds only.

To render his relation agreeable to the man of sense, it is therefore necessary that the voyager should possess several eminent and rare talents; so rare indeed that it is almost wonderful to see them ever united in the same person.

And if all these talents must concur in the relator, they are certainly in a more eminent degree necessary to the writer; for here the narration admits of higher ornaments of style, and every fact and sentiment offers itself to the fullest and most deliberate examination.

It would appear, therefore, I think, somewhat strange if such writers as these should be found extremely common; since nature hath been a most parsimonious distributor of her richest talents, and hath seldom bestowed many on the same person. But, on the other hand, why there should scarce exist a single writer of this kind worthy our regard; and, whilst there is no other branch of history (for this is history) which hath not exercised the greatest pens, why this alone should be overlooked by all men of great genius and erudition, and delivered up to the Goths and Vandals as their lawful property, is altogether as difficult to determine.

And yet that this is the case, with some very few exceptions, is most manifest. Of these I shall willingly admit Burnet and Addison; if the former was not, perhaps, to be considered as a political essayist, and the latter as a commentator on the classics, rather than as a writer of travels; which last title, perhaps, they would both of them have been least ambitious to affect.

Indeed, if these two and two or three more should be removed from the mass, there would remain such a heap of dullness behind, that the appellation of voyage writer would not appear very desirable.

I am not here unapprised that old Homer himself is by some considered as a voyage writer; and, indeed, the beginning of his *Odyssey* may be urged to countenance that opinion, which I shall not controvert. But, whatever species of writing the *Odyssey* is of, it is surely at the head of that species, as much as the *Iliad* is of another; and so far the excellent Longinus would allow, I believe, at this day.

But, in reality, the *Odyssey*, the Telemachus, and all of that kind, are to the voyage writing I here intend, what romance is to true history, the former being the confounder and corrupter of the latter. I am far from supposing that Homer, Hesiod and the other ancient poets and mythologists had any settled design to pervert and confuse the records of antiquity; but it is certain they have effected it; and for my part I must confess I should have honoured and loved Homer more had he written a true history of his own times in humble prose than those noble poems that have so justly collected the praise of all ages; for, though I read these with more admiration and astonishment, I still read Herodotus, Thucydides and Xenophon with more amusement and more satisfaction.

The original poets were not, however, without excuse. They found the limits of nature too strait for the immensity of their genius, which they had not room to exert without extending fact by fiction: and that especially at a time when the manners of men were too simple to afford that variety which they have since offered in vain to the choice of the meanest writers. In doing this they are again excusable for the manner in which they have done it.

They are not, indeed, so properly said to turn reality into fiction, as fiction into reality. Their paintings are so bold, their colours so strong, that everything they touch seems to exist in the very manner they represent it; their portraits are so just, and their landscapes so beautiful, that we acknowledge the strokes of nature in both without enquiring whether Nature herself, or her journeyman the poet, formed the first pattern of the piece.

But other writers (I will put Pliny at their head) have no such pretensions to indulgence; they lie for lying's sake, or in order insolently to impose the most monstrous improbabilities and absurdities upon their readers on their own authority; treating them as some fathers treat children, and as other fathers do laymen, exacting their belief of whatever they relate, on no other foundation than their own authority, without ever taking the pains of adapting their lies to human credulity, and of calculating them for the meridian of a common understanding; but, with as much weakness as wickedness, and with more impudence often than either, they assert facts contrary to the honour of God, to the visible order of the creation, to the known laws of nature, to the histories of former ages and to the experience of our own, and which no man can at once understand and believe.

If it should be objected (and it can nowhere be objected better than where I now write, in Lisbon, as there is nowhere more pomp of bigotry) that whole nations have been firm believers in such most absurd suppositions, I reply, the fact is not true. They have known nothing of the matter, and have believed they knew not what. It is, indeed, with me no matter of doubt but that the pope and his clergy might teach any of those Christian heterodoxies, the tenets of which are the most diametrically opposite to their own; nay, all the doctrines of Zoroaster, Confucius and Mahomet, not only with certain and immediate success, but without one Catholic in a thousand knowing he had changed his religion.

What motive a man can have to sit down and to draw forth a list of stupid, senseless, incredible lies upon paper, would be difficult to determine, did not Vanity present herself so immediately as the adequate cause. The vanity of knowing more than other men is, perhaps, besides hunger, the only inducement to writing, at least to publishing, at all. Why then should not the voyage writer be inflamed with the glory of having seen what no man ever did or will see but himself? This is the true source of the wonderful in the discourse and writings, and sometimes, I believe, in the actions of men. There is another fault, of a kind directly opposite to this, to which these writers are sometimes liable, when, instead of filling their pages with monsters which nobody hath ever seen, and with adventures which never have, nor could possibly have, happened to them, waste their time and paper with recording things and facts of so common a kind that they challenge no other right of being remembered than as they had the honour of having happened to the author, to whom nothing seems trivial that in any manner happens to himself. Of such consequence do his own actions appear to one of this kind that he would probably think himself guilty of infidelity should he omit the minutest thing in the detail of his journal. That the fact is true is sufficient to give it a place there, without any consideration whether it is capable of pleasing or surprising, of diverting or informing, the reader.

I have seen a play (if I mistake not it is one of Mrs Behn's or of Mrs Centlivre's) where this vice in a voyage writer is finely ridiculed. An ignorant pedant to whose government, for I know not what reason, the conduct of a young nobleman in his travels is committed, and who is sent abroad to show my lord the world, of which he knows nothing himself, before his departure from a town, calls for his journal to record the goodness of the wine and tobacco, with other articles of the same importance, which are to furnish the materials of a voyage at his return home. The humour, it is true, is here carried very far; and yet, perhaps, very little beyond what is to be found in writers who profess no intention of dealing in humour at all.

Of one or other, or both of these kinds, are, I conceive, all that vast pile of books which pass under the names of voyages, travels, adventures, lives, memoirs, histories, etc., some of which a single traveller sends into the world in many volumes, and others are, by judicious booksellers, collected into vast bodies in folio and inscribed with their own names, as if they were indeed their own travels: thus unjustly attributing to themselves the merit of others.

Now, from both these faults we have endeavoured to steer clear in the following narrative; which, however the contrary may be insinuated by ignorant, unlearned and freshwater critics, who have never travelled either in books or ships, I do solemnly declare doth, in my own impartial opinion, deviate less from truth than any other voyage extant; my lord Anson's alone being, perhaps, excepted.

Some few embellishments must be allowed to every historian; for we are not to conceive that the speeches in Livy, Sallust or Thucydides were literally spoken in the very words in which we now read them. It is sufficient that every fact hath its foundation in truth, as I do seriously aver is the case in the ensuing pages; and when it is so, a good critic will be so far from denying all kind of ornament of style or diction, or even of circumstance, to his author, that he would be rather sorry if he omitted it; for he could hence derive no other advantage than the loss of an additional pleasure in the perusal.

MARGARET FULLER
INTRODUCTION

Margaret Fuller is widely regarded as America's first feminist. A pioneering thinker, she also holds the honours of being the country's first full-time female literary critic, first foreign correspondent and first war reporter. All that lay in her future when, in 1843, she undertook a tour of America's Great Lakes. Born in 1810, in Cambridge, Massachusetts, Margaret had the good fortune to be not only the daughter of a congressman, Timothy Fuller, but of an enlightened one. It was her father's ambition that Margaret, who was fiercely bright, get the best education.

In 1836 she met Ralph Waldo Emerson, who invited her to join the Transcendental Club, a quasi-spiritual movement for leading New England intellectuals. Emerson also persuaded Fuller to write for, as well as edit, the Club's magazine, *The Dial*. The title brought her a large readership, and it followed her to Boston, where she moved in 1839. It was in a bookshop there that Fuller hosted her 'conversations', workshops to educate women on subjects such as history and the classics, and whose aim was to empower women to become more active in business and politics. 'Today a reader, tomorrow a leader,' Fuller wrote in her most well-known work, *Woman in the Nineteenth Century*, published in 1845.

Her trip to the Great Lakes was conceived in the same spirit, a kind of high-minded reader's tour, during which she would cast her intellectual – and female – eye over the rapidly changing frontier. Her plan was to follow a circular route, from Niagara Falls to Paw Paw, Illinois, and she arrived at Niagara in early June 1843. On her hotel nightstand was Thomas Carlyle's *Past and Present*, published just two months previously, in which the Scottish philosopher bemoaned the lack of men of talent in Britain at a time of great technological change. Fuller drew parallels with the development of the American frontier and believed the solution lay in female emancipation. 'We have waited here long in the dust,' she wrote. 'We are tired and hungry; but the triumphal procession must appear at last.' She published her account of the trip, *Summer on the Lakes*, the following year.

For all Fuller's gravitas, her writing is not without light touches. Approaching a pier in Illinois, for example, her steamboat 'made a bend, and seemed to do obeisance in the heavy style of some dowager duchess entering a circle she wishes to treat with especial respect'. The wilds of Illinois impressed her. 'I do believe Rome and Florence are suburbs compared to this capital of nature's art,' she wrote, being sure to name-drop Rhesus of Thrace, who appears in Homer's *Iliad*.

Following her return, in 1844 Fuller was commissioned to write a column on politics for *The New York Tribune*. The subsequent pieces became the foundation of *Woman in the Nineteenth Century*. Fuller's work for the *Tribune* so impressed her publisher, Horace Greeley, that in 1846, he sent her to England, where she met the likes of George Sand and Thomas Carlyle himself. Aware too of the ongoing political discord in Italy during the Risorgimento, Fuller travelled to Rome as correspondent for the *Tribune*. She fell in love with an activist, Marchese Giovanni Ossoli, with whom she had a son, Angelo.

The family returned to America in early 1850. They had reached New York when their ship sank, off Fire Island, just 100 yards from shore. All three were drowned, and so devastated was Emerson, he dispatched no lesser a lieutenant than Henry David Thoreau to search the shoreline.

SUMMER ON THE LAKES
BY MARGARET FULLER

In the afternoon of this day we reached the Rock River, in whose neighbourhood we proposed to make some stay, and crossed at Dixon's ferry.

This beautiful stream flows full and wide over a bed of rocks, traversing a distance of near two hundred miles, to reach the Mississippi. Great part of the country along its banks is the finest region of Illinois, and the scene of some of the latest romance of Indian warfare. To these beautiful regions Black Hawk returned with his band 'to pass the summer', when he drew upon himself the warfare in which he was finally vanquished. No wonder he could not resist the longing, unwise though its indulgence might be, to return in summer to this home of beauty.

Of Illinois in general, it has often been remarked that it bears the character of country which has been inhabited by a nation skilled like the English in all the ornamental arts of life, especially in landscape gardening. That the villas and castles seem to have been burnt, the enclosures taken down, but the velvet lawns, the flower gardens, the stately parks, scattered at graceful intervals by the decorous hand of art, the frequent deer and the peaceful herd of cattle that make picture of the plain, all suggest more of the masterly mind of man than the prodigal, but careless, motherly love of nature. Especially is this true of the Rock River country. The river flows sometimes through these parks and lawns, then betwixt high bluffs, whose grassy ridges are covered with fine trees, or broken with crumbling stone that easily assumes the forms of buttress, arch and clustered columns. Along the face of such crumbling rocks, swallows' nests are clustered, thick as cities, and eagles and deer do not disdain their summits. One morning, out in the boat along the base of these rocks, it was amusing, and affecting too, to see these swallows put their heads out to look at us. There was something very hospitable about it, as if man had never shown himself a tyrant near them. What a morning that was! Every sight is worth twice as much by the early morning light. We borrow something of the spirit of the hour to look upon them.

The first place, where we stopped was one of singular beauty, a beauty of soft, luxuriant wildness. It was on the bend of the river, a place chosen by an Irish gentleman, whose absenteeship seems of the wisest kind, since for a sum which would have been but a drop of water to the thirsty fever of his native land, he commands a residence which has all that is desirable, in its independence, its beautiful retirement and means of benefit to others.

His park, his deer-chase, he found already prepared; he had only to make an avenue through it. This brought us by a drive, which in the heat of noon seemed long, though afterwards, in the cool of morning and evening, delightful, to the house. This is, for that part of the world, a large and commodious dwelling. Near it stands the log cabin where its master lived while it was building, a very ornamental accessory.

In front of the house was a lawn, adorned by the most graceful trees. A few of these had been taken out to give a full view of the river, gliding through banks such as I have described. On this bend the bank is high and bold, so from the house or the lawn the view was very rich and commanding.

But if you descended a ravine at the side to the water's edge, you found there a long walk on the narrow shore, with a wall above of the richest hanging wood, in which they said the deer lay hid. I never saw one, but often fancied that I heard them rustling, at daybreak, by these bright clear waters, stretching out in such smiling promise, where no sound broke the deep and blissful seclusion, unless now and then this rustling, or the plash of some fish a little gayer than the others; it seemed not necessary to have any better heaven, or fuller expression of love and freedom than in the mood of nature here.

Then, leaving the bank, you would walk far and far through long grassy paths, full of the most brilliant – also the most delicate – flowers. The brilliant are more common on the prairie, but both kinds loved this place.

Amid the grass of the lawn, with a profusion of wild strawberries, we greeted also a familiar love, the Scottish harebell, the gentlest, and most touching form of the flower world.

The master of the house was absent, but with a kindness beyond thanks had offered us a resting place there. Here we were taken care of by a deputy, who would, for his youth, have been assigned the place of a page in former times, but in the Young West, it seems he was old enough for a steward. Whatever be called his function, he did the honours of the place so much in harmony with it, as to leave the guests free to imagine themselves in Elysium. And the three days passed here were days of unalloyed, spotless happiness.

There was a peculiar charm in coming here, where the choice of location, and the unobtrusive good taste of all the arrangements, showed such intelligent appreciation of the spirit of the scene, after seeing so many dwellings of the new settlers, which showed plainly that they had no thought beyond satisfying the grossest material wants. Sometimes they looked attractive, the little brown houses, the natural architecture of the country, in the edge of the timber. But almost always when you came near, the slovenliness of the dwelling and the rude way in which objects around it were treated, when so little care would have presented a charming whole, were very repulsive. Seeing the traces of the Indians, who chose the most beautiful sites for their dwellings, and whose habits do not break in on that aspect of nature under which they were born, we feel as if they were the rightful lords of a beauty they forbore to deform. But most of these settlers do not see it at all; it breathes, it speaks in vain to those who are rushing into its sphere. Their progress is Gothic, not Roman, and their mode of cultivation will, in the course of twenty, perhaps ten, years, obliterate the natural expression of the country... While we were here we had one grand thunderstorm, which added new glory to the scene.

One beautiful feature was the return of the pigeons every afternoon to their home. Every afternoon they came sweeping across the lawn, positively in clouds, and with a swiftness and softness of winged motion, more beautiful than anything of the kind I ever knew. Had I been a musician such as Mendelssohn, I felt that I could have improvised a music quite peculiar from the sound they made, which should have indicated all the beauty over which their wings bore them.

The only really rustic feature was of the many coops of poultry near the house, which I understood it to be one of the chief pleasures of the master to feed.

Leaving this place, we proceeded a day's journey along the beautiful stream, to a little town named Oregon. We called at a cabin from whose door looked out one of those faces which, once seen, are never forgotten; young, yet touched with many traces of feeling, not only possible, but endured; spirited too, like the gleam of a finely tempered blade. It was a face that suggested a history, and many histories, but whose scene would have been in courts and camps. At this moment their

circles are dull for want of that life, which is waning
unexcited in this solitary recess.

The master of the house proposed to show us a 'short cut',
by which we might, to especial advantage, pursue our journey.
This proved to be almost perpendicular down a hill, studded
with young trees and stumps. From these he proposed, with a
hospitality of service, to free our wheels whenever they should
get entangled, also, to be himself the drag, to prevent our too
rapid descent. Such generosity deserved trust; however, we
women could not be persuaded to render it. We got out and
admired, from afar, the process. Left by our guide – and prop!
we found ourselves in a wide field, where, by playful quips and
turns, an endless 'creek' seemed to divert itself with our
attempts to cross it. Failing in this, the next best was to whirl
down a steep bank, which feat our charioteer performed with
an air not unlike that of Rhesus, had he but been as suitably
furnished with chariot and steeds!

At last, after wasting some two or three hours on the 'short
cut', we got out by following an Indian trail – Black Hawk's!
How fair the scene through which it led! How could they let
themselves be conquered, with such a country to fight for!

Afterwards, in the wide prairie, we saw a lively picture of
nonchalance (to speak in the fashion of dear Ireland). There,
in the wide sunny field, with neither tree nor umbrella above
his head, sat a peddler with his pack, waiting apparently for
customers. He was not disappointed. We bought what hold in
regard to the human world as unmarked, as mysterious, and
as important an existence, as the infusoria to the natural, to
wit, pins. This incident would have delighted those modern
sages, who, in imitation of the sitting philosophers of ancient
India, prefer silence to speech, waiting to going and scornfully
smile in answer to the motions of earnest life.

However, it seemed to me today, as formerly on these
sublime occasions, obvious that nothing would come unless

something would go; now, if we had been as sublimely still as the peddler, his pins would have tarried in the pack, and his pockets sustained an aching void of pence!

Passing through one of the fine, parklike woods, almost clear from underbrush and carpeted with thick grasses and flowers, we met (for it was Sunday) a little congregation just returning from their service, which had been performed in a rude house in its midst. It had a sweet and peaceful air, as if such words and thoughts were very dear to them. The parents had with them all their little children; but we saw no old people; that charm was wanting, which exists in such scenes in older settlements, of seeing the silver bent in reverence beside the flaxen head.

At Oregon, the beauty of the scene was of even a more sumptuous character than at our former 'stopping place'. Here swelled the river in its boldest course, interspersed by halcyon isles on which nature had lavished all her prodigality in tree, vine and flower, banked by noble bluffs three hundred feet high, their sharp ridges as exquisitely definite as the edge of a shell; their summits adorned with those same beautiful trees, and with buttresses of rich rock, crested with old hemlocks, which wore a touching and antique grace amid the softer and more luxuriant vegetation. Lofty natural mounds rose amidst the rest, with the same lovely and sweeping outline, showing everywhere the plastic power of water – water, mother of beauty, which, by its sweet and eager flow, had left such lineaments as human genius never dreamt of.

Not far from the river was a high crag, called the Pine Rock, which looks out, as our guide observed, like a helmet above the brow of the country. It seems as if the water left here and there a vestige of forms and materials that preceded its course, just to set off its new and richer designs.

The aspect of this country was to me enchanting, beyond any I have ever seen, from its fullness of expression, its bold and impassioned sweetness. Here the flood of emotion has passed over and marked everywhere its course by a smile. The fragments of rock touch it with a wildness and liberality which give just the needed relief. I should never be tired here, though I have elsewhere seen country of more secret and alluring charms, better calculated to stimulate and suggest. Here the eye and heart are filled.

How happy the Indians must have been here! It is not long since they were driven away, and the ground, above and below, is full of their traces.

'The earth is full of men.'

You have only to turn up the sod to find arrowheads and Indian pottery. On an island belonging to our host, and nearly opposite his house, they loved to stay, and, no doubt, enjoyed its lavish beauty as much as the myriad wild pigeons that now haunt its flower-filled shades. Here are still the marks of their tomahawks, the troughs in which they prepared their corn, their caches.

A little way down the river is the site of an ancient Indian village, with its regularly arranged mounds. As usual, they had chosen with the finest taste. It was one of those soft, shadowy afternoons when we went there, when nature seems ready to weep, not from grief, but from an overfull heart... They may blacken Indian life as they will, talk of its dirt, its brutality; I will ever believe that the men who chose that dwelling place were able to feel emotions of noble happiness as they returned to it, and so were the women that received them. Neither were the children sad or dull, who lived so familiarly with the deer and the birds, and swam that clear wave in the shadow of the Seven Sisters. The whole scene suggested to me a Greek splendour, a Greek sweetness.

HERODOTUS
INTRODUCTION

Dubbed 'the father of history' by Cicero, Herodotus was born in 485 BC in Halicarnassus, in what is now Turkey. A contemporary of Socrates, he travelled throughout ancient Greece and beyond, and the account he produced, *The Histories*, represents the work of a remarkable lifetime.

Written around 440 BC, *The Histories* chronicles the rise of the Persian Empire and its expansion into Ionian Greece. Indeed, the Greco-Persian wars of 499–449 BC, when the valiant Greek city states rose up against their Asiatic occupiers, constitutes about half of *The Histories'* nine sections, each named after one of the Greek muses. (For the record, they are Clio, Euterpe, Thalia, Melpomene, Terpsichore, Erato, Polymnia, Urania and Calliope.)

Living at a time when history was recounted orally, Herodotus was the first to give it written form. If he 'invented' history as a genre, it's also fair to claim he invented travel writing. Alongside reports on exotic wildlife and local customs, Herodotus holds forth on the architectural wonders of Egypt, the nomadic impulses of the Scythians and the beauty of Ethiopian women. *The Histories* also serves as a parable on the evils of expansionism. It pits the agents of enslavement (the Persians) against those of freedom (Greeks), and concludes that war can sometimes be just, and that hubris, ultimately, will turn empires to dust.

Herodotus' place in the canon of great travel writing is not uncontested. His detractors point out that some of his observations are fabricated. (The extract featured here concerns the migratory habits of the phoenix.) Herodotus is also charged with taking the word of local guides too easily, evidenced by his claim that the hieroglyphics adorning the pyramids were a tally of the garlic and onions the workers ate during construction. In his defence, *The Histories* is the work of one man, relying perhaps not even on notes, but on his powers of recall and of oral history at that.

What is beyond dispute is that Herodotus invented the prose style; the ancient Greeks preferred the ethereal beauty of poetry. The critic Daniel Mendelssohn highlights the fact that psilos logos, or 'naked language', as a descriptor for the Herodotean style, only came into being long after Herodotus' death. George Rawlinson, his most notable translator, concurs, explaining that Herodotus' techniques greatly informed those pillars of ancient Greek literature who followed, Thucydides and Xenophon.

Aspects of *The Histories* have found their way into common usage. The first book, Clio, recounts the fate of Croesus of Lydia, whose name is now a synonym for wealth. The term 'barbarian' is Herodotus' own, for non-Greek speakers. The following extract displays such typically Herodotean quirks. That which he has not witnessed personally, and which we now know to be false, he covers briefly; events seen with his own eyes enjoy a freer rein.

In Michael Ondaatje's *The English Patient*, a pathologically well-thumbed copy of *The Histories* serves as both guide and consolation to the book's eponymous antihero. His tribute to Herodotus is perhaps as apposite as any: 'I have seen editions of *The Histories* with a sculpted portrait on the cover. Some statue in a French museum. But I never imagine Herodotus this way. I see him more as one of those spare men of the desert who travel from oasis to oasis trading legends as if it is the exchange of seals, consuming everything without suspicion, piercing together a mirage.'

THE HISTORIES
BY HERODOTUS

TRANSLATED BY GEORGE RAWLINSON

The Egyptians have a sacred bird called the phoenix which I myself have never seen, except in pictures. Indeed, it is a great rarity even in Egypt, only coming there (according to the accounts of the people of Heliopolis) once in five hundred years, when the old phoenix dies. Its size and appearance, if it is like the pictures, are as follows. The plumage is partly red, partly golden, while the general make and size are almost exactly that of the eagle. They tell a story of what this bird does, which does not seem to me to be credible, that he comes all the way from Arabia, and brings the parent bird, all plastered over with myrrh, to the temple of the Sun and there buries the body. In order to bring him, they say, he first forms a ball of myrrh as big as he finds that he can carry; then he hollows out the ball and puts his parent inside, after which he covers over the opening with fresh myrrh, and the ball is then of exactly the same weight as at first; so he brings it to Egypt, plastered over as I have said, and deposits it in the temple of the Sun. Such is the story they tell of the doings of this bird.

In the neighbourhood of Thebes there are some sacred serpents which are perfectly harmless. They are of small size, and have two horns growing out of the top of the head. These snakes, when they die, are buried in the temple of Jupiter, the god to whom they are sacred.

I went once to a certain place in Arabia, almost exactly opposite the city of Buto, to make inquiries concerning the winged serpents. On my arrival, I saw the backbones and ribs of serpents in such numbers as it is impossible to describe. Of the ribs there were a multitude of heaps, some great, some small, some middle sized. The place where the bones lie is at the entrance of a narrow gorge between steep mountains, which there open upon a spacious plain communicating with the great plain of Egypt. The story goes that with the spring, the winged snakes come flying from Arabia towards Egypt, but are met in this gorge by the birds called ibises, who forbid their entrance and destroy them all. The Arabians assert, and the Egyptians also admit, that it is on account of the service thus rendered that the Egyptians hold the ibis in so much reverence.

The ibis is a bird of a deep black colour, with legs like a crane; its beak is strongly hooked, and its size is about that of the land rail. This is a description of the black ibis which contends with the serpents. The commoner sort, for there are two quite distinct species, has the head and the whole throat bare of feathers; its general plumage is white, but the head and neck are jet black, as also are the tips of the wings and the extremity of the tail; in its beak and legs it resembles the other species. The winged serpent is shaped like the water snake. Its wings are not feathered, but resemble very closely those of the bat. And thus I conclude the subject of the sacred animals.

With respect to the Egyptians themselves, it is to be remarked that those who live in the corn country, devoting themselves, as they do, far more than any other people in the world, to the preservation of the memory of past actions, are the best skilled in history of any men that I have ever met. The following is the mode of life habitual to them. For three successive days in each month, they purge the body by means

of emetics and clysters, which is done out of a regard for their
health, since they have a persuasion that every disease to
which men are liable is occasioned by the substances whereon
they feed. Apart from any such precautions, they are, I believe,
next to the Libyans, the healthiest people in the world – an
effect of their climate, in my opinion, which has no sudden
changes. Diseases almost always attack men when they are
exposed to a change, and never more than during changes of
the weather. They live on bread made of spelt, which they form
into loaves called in their own tongue cyllestis. Their drink is a
wine which they obtain from barley, as they have no vines in
their country. Many kinds of fish they eat raw, either salted or
dried in the sun. Quails also, and ducks and small birds, they
eat uncooked, merely first salting them. All other birds and
fishes, excepting those which are set apart as sacred, are eaten
either roasted or boiled.

In social meetings among the rich, when the banquet is
ended, a servant carries round to the several guests a coffin, in
which there is a wooden image of a corpse, carved and painted
to resemble nature as nearly as possible, about a cubit or two
cubits in length. As he shows it to each guest in turn, the
servant says, 'Gaze here, and drink and be merry; for when you
die, such will you be'.

The Egyptians adhere to their own national customs, and
adopt no foreign usages. Many of these customs are worthy of
note, among others their song, the Linus, which is sung under
various names not only in Egypt but in Phoenicia, in Cyprus
and in other places; and which seems to be exactly the same as
that in use among the Greeks, and by them called Linus. There
were very many things in Egypt which filled me with
astonishment, and this was one of them. Whence could the
Egyptians have got the Linus? It appears to have been sung by
them from the very earliest times. For the Linus in Egyptian is
called Maneros; and they told me that Maneros was the only

son of their first king, and that on his untimely death he was honoured by the Egyptians with these dirgelike strains, and in this way they got their first and only melody.

There is another custom in which the Egyptians resemble a particular Greek people, namely the Lacedaemonians. Their young men, when they meet their elders in the streets, give way to them and step aside; and if an elder come in where young men are present, these latter rise from their seats. In a third point they differ entirely from all the nations of Greece. Instead of speaking to each other when they meet in the streets, they make an obeisance, sinking the hand to the knee.

They wear a linen tunic fringed about the legs, and called calasiris; over this they have a white woollen garment thrown on afterwards. Nothing of woollen, however, is taken into their temples or buried with them, as their religion forbids it. Here their practice resembles the rites called Orphic and Bacchic, but which are in reality Egyptian and Pythagorean; for no one initiated in these mysteries can be buried in a woollen shroud, a religious reason being assigned for the observance.

The Egyptians likewise discovered to which of the gods each month and day is sacred; and found out from the day of a man's birth what he will meet with in the course of his life, and how he will end his days, and what sort of man he will be – discoveries whereof the Greeks engaged in poetry have made a use. The Egyptians have also discovered more prognostics than all the rest of mankind besides. Whenever a prodigy takes place, they watch and record the result; then, if anything similar ever happens again, they expect the same consequences.

With respect to divination, they hold that it is a gift which no mortal possesses, but only certain of the gods; thus they have an oracle of Hercules, one of Apollo, of Minerva, of Diana, of Mars and of Jupiter. Besides these, there is the oracle of Latona at Buto, which is held in much higher repute than any of the rest. The mode of delivering the oracles is not uniform, but varies at the different shrines.

Medicine is practised among them on a plan of separation; each physician treats a single disorder, and no more, thus the country swarms with medical practitioners, some undertaking to cure diseases of the eye, others of the head, others again of the teeth, others of the intestines and some those which are not local.

The following is the way in which they conduct their mournings and their funerals. On the death in any house of a man of consequence, forthwith the women of the family beplaster their heads, and sometimes even their faces, with mud; and then, leaving the body indoors, sally forth and wander through the city, with their dress fastened by a band, and their bosoms bare, beating themselves as they walk. All the female relations join them and do the same. The men too, similarly begirt, beat their breasts separately. When these ceremonies are over, the body is carried away to be embalmed.

There are a set of men in Egypt who practice the art of embalming, and make it their proper business. These persons, when a body is brought to them, show the bearers various models of corpses, made in wood, and painted so as to resemble nature. The most perfect is said to be after the manner of him whom I do not think it religious to name in connection with such a matter; the second sort is inferior to the first, and less costly; the third is the cheapest of all. All this the embalmers explain, and then ask in which way it is wished that the corpse should be prepared. The bearers tell them, and having concluded their bargain, take their departure, while the embalmers, left to themselves, proceed to their task. The mode of embalming, according to the most perfect process, is the following. They take first a crooked piece of iron, and with it draw out the brain through the nostrils, thus getting rid of a portion, while the skull is cleared of the rest by rinsing with drugs; next they make a cut along the flank with a sharp Ethiopian stone, and take out the whole contents of the abdomen, which they then cleanse, washing it thoroughly with palm wine, and again frequently with an infusion of pounded aromatics. After this they fill the cavity with the purest bruised myrrh, with cassia and every other sort of spicery except frankincense, and sew up the opening. Then the body is placed in natrum for seventy days, and covered entirely over. After the expiration of that space of time, which must not be exceeded, the body is washed and wrapped round, from head to foot, with bandages of fine linen cloth, smeared over with gum, which is used generally by the Egyptians in the place of glue, and in this state it is given back to the relations, who enclose it in a wooden case which they have had made for the purpose, shaped into the figure of a man. Then fastening the case, they place it in a sepulchral chamber, upright against the wall. Such is the most costly way of embalming the dead.

If persons wish to avoid expense, and choose the second process, the following is the method pursued. Syringes are filled with oil made from the cedar tree, which is then, without any incision or disembowelling, injected into the abdomen. The passage by which it might be likely to return is stopped, and the body laid in natrum the prescribed number of days. At the end of the time the cedar oil is allowed to make its escape; and such is its power that it brings with it the whole stomach and intestines in a liquid state. The natrum meanwhile has dissolved the flesh, and so nothing is left of the dead body but the skin and the bones. It is returned in this condition to the relatives, without any further trouble being bestowed upon it.

The third method of embalming, which is practised in the case of the poorer classes, is to clear out the intestines with a clyster, and let the body lie in natrum the seventy days, after which it is at once given to those who come to fetch it away.

The wives of men of rank are not given to be embalmed immediately after death, nor indeed are any of the more beautiful and valued women. It is not till they have been dead three or four days that they are carried to the embalmers. This is done to prevent indignities from being offered them. It is said that once a case of this kind occurred. The man was detected by the information of his fellow workmen.

Whensoever anyone, Egyptian or foreigner, has lost his life by falling a prey to a crocodile, or by drowning in the river, the law compels the inhabitants of the city near which the body is cast up to have it embalmed, and to bury it in one of the sacred repositories with all possible magnificence. No one may touch the corpse, not even any of the friends or relatives, but only the priests of the Nile, who prepare it for burial with their own hands – regarding it as something more than the mere body of a man – and themselves lay it in the tomb.

WASHINGTON IRVING
INTRODUCTION

Washington Irving made his name penning short stories and tall tales. 1820's *The Legend of Sleepy Hollow* made Irving an international celebrity, a first for a US writer.

By 1828 he was a wealthy man, able to afford a base in Madrid, where he wrote his biography of Christopher Columbus. Among his dramatis personae were, naturally, King Ferdinand and Queen Isabella, the 15th-century Spanish monarchs who not only sent Columbus to the new world, but who drove the Moors from Spain. The Nasrids, whom they defeated, were the last Islamic dynasty to preside over the Caliphate of Cordoba, a vast area that spanned from Zaragoza in the north to Gibraltar in the south, and whose western extent was Lisbon in Portugal. In its pomp, Cordoba was a seat of Islamic power to rival Damascus and Baghdad. The jewel in its crown was the city of Granada and, by Irving's time, its long-abandoned royal palace, the Alhambra. Irving was a romantic, and likely a fantasist in the way all novelists must be. Reading of the Alhambra's treasures, he was stirred by tales of adventure. The Alhambra was out there, and, in 1829, Irving set out to find it.

As Irving made his way south, the landscape enchanted him. 'Many are apt to picture Spain...as a soft southern region,' he wrote, 'decked out with the luxuriant charms of voluptuous Italy. On the contrary...it is a stern, melancholy country.' Irving employed a local guide, Mateo Ximenes. Aged just 17, from the outset Irving cast him as a Sancho Panza to his own Don Quixote. Ximenes fuelled the fire, passing the time with legends he himself had heard of the Alhambra, tales of buried treasure, of ghosts and captured princesses. This doubtless helps explain why the account Irving wrote of the trip, 1832's *Tales of the Alhambra*, blends architectural reviews with fantastical folk tales.

The Alhambra (al hamra means 'red castle') is located on a hill, al-Sabika. An Arabic fastness in the heart of Andalucía, it looks down imperiously over Granada and the Darro River. Built in the 13th century by a Nasrid emir, Mohammed ben al-Ahmar, its fortified complex of gardens and palaces was intended as a paradise on earth, verdant and cool against the Andalusian heat. In fact, the Alhambra dates back to the 9th century, with records of Roman ruins. It was not until the 14th century that it gained the status of a royal palace, with the addition of a watchtower (Torre de la Vela), and a keep (Torre de la Homenaje).

Irving arrived to find it closed to visitors. 'The gardens were destroyed,' he wrote, 'the fountains ceased to play.' The palace was abandoned in the 18th century, yet such was Irving's celebrity, he was able to gain access. A whole month, in fact, to wander its delights. The Alhambra is a gem of medieval Islamic architecture, boasting elaborate arches and ceilings in intricate, honeycomb craftsmanship that reaches its apogee in the Sala de las Dos Hermanas ('Hall of Two Sisters'), and the Sala de los Abencerrajes.

At the heart of the complex is the Patio de los Leones ('Court of the Lions'), named for a magnificent vast basin supported by 12 leonine marbles. It is surrounded, in turn, by carved colonnades bearing epigraphic Arabic poems, and it is here Irving encountered a 'turbaned Moor' who regaled him with tales of the Alhambra's glorious past. 'Ah, Señor,' the gentleman tells Irving, 'when the Moors held Granada, they were a gayer people than they are nowadays. They thought only of love, music and poetry.'

Today the Alhambra is the most popular visitor attraction in Spain. Albaicín, the district that runs beneath the Alhambra's walls, remains the Arab quarter of Granada. The Alhambra's importance was recognised by Spanish royal decree in 1872, and again in 1943. Restoration continued throughout, and it was added to the Unesco World Heritage List in 1984. Irving's book is not only widely available in the city but regarded as a default primer.

TALES OF THE ALHAMBRA
BY WASHINGTON IRVIING

I have often observed that the more proudly a mansion has been tenanted in the day of its prosperity, the humbler are its inhabitants in the day of its decline, and that the palace of a king commonly ends in being the nestling place of the beggar.

The Alhambra is in a rapid state of similar transition. Whenever a tower falls to decay, it is seized upon by some tatterdemalion family, who become joint tenants with the bats and owls of its gilded halls; and hang their rags, those standards of poverty, out of its windows and loopholes.

I have amused myself with remarking some of the motley characters that have thus usurped the ancient abode of royalty, and who seem as if placed here to give a farcical termination to the drama of human pride. One of these even bears the mockery of a regal title. It is a little old woman named Maria Antonia Sabonea, but who goes by the appellation of la Reyna Coquina, or the Cockle-queen. She is small enough to be a fairy; and a fairy she may be for aught I can find out, for no one seems to know her origin. Her habitation is in a kind of closet under the outer staircase of the palace, and she sits in the cool stone corridor, plying her needle and singing from morning till night, with a ready joke for every one that passes; for though one of the poorest, she is one of the merriest little women breathing. Her great merit is a gift for storytelling, having, I verily believe, as many stories at her command as the inexhaustible Scheherezade of the *Thousand and One Nights*. Some of these I have heard her relate in the evening tertulias of Dame Antonia, at which she is occasionally a humble attendant.

That there must be some fairy gift about this mysterious little old woman would appear from her extraordinary luck, since, notwithstanding her being very little, very ugly and very poor, she has had, according to her own account, five husbands and a half, reckoning as a half one a young dragoon who died during courtship. A rival personage to this little fairy queen is a portly old fellow with a bottle-nose, who goes about in a rusty garb, with a cocked hat of oilskin and a red cockade. He is one of the legitimate sons of the Alhambra, and has lived here all his life, filling various offices, such as deputy alguazil, sexton of the parochial church and marker of a fives-court established at the foot of one of the towers. He is as poor as a rat, but as proud as he is ragged, boasting of his descent from the illustrious house of Aguilar, from which sprang Gonzalvo of Cordova, the grand captain. Nay, he actually bears the name of Alonzo de Aguilar, so renowned in the history of the Conquest; though the graceless wags of the fortress have given him the title of el padre santo, or the holy father, the usual appellation of the Pope, which I had thought too sacred in the eyes of true Catholics to be thus ludicrously applied. It is a whimsical caprice of fortune to present, in the grotesque person of this tatterdemalion, a namesake and descendant of the proud Alonzo de Aguilar, the mirror of Andalusian chivalry, leading an almost mendicant existence about this once haughty fortress, which his ancestor aided to reduce; yet such might have been the lot of the descendants of Agamemnon and Achilles, had they lingered about the ruins of Troy!

Of this motley community, I find the family of my gossiping squire, Mateo Ximenes, to form, from their numbers at least, a very important part. His boast of being a son of the Alhambra is not unfounded. His family has inhabited the fortress ever since the time of the Conquest, handing down a hereditary poverty from father to son; not one of them having ever been known to be worth a maravedi. His father, by trade a ribbon weaver, and who succeeded the historical tailor as the head of the family, is now near seventy years of age, and lives in a hovel of reeds and plaster, built by his own hands, just above the iron gate. The furniture consists of a crazy bed, a table and two or three chairs; a wooden chest, containing, besides his scanty clothing, the 'archives of the family'. These are nothing more nor less than the papers of various lawsuits sustained by different generations; by which it would seem that, with all their apparent carelessness and good humour, they are a litigious brood. Most of the suits have been brought against gossiping neighbours for questioning the purity of their blood, and denying their being Christianos viejos, ie old Christians, without Jewish or Moorish taint. In fact, I doubt whether this jealousy about their blood has not kept them so poor in purse: spending all their earnings on escribanos and alguazils. The pride of the hovel is an escutcheon suspended against the wall, in which are emblazoned quarterings of the arms of the Marquis of Caiesedo, and of various other noble houses, with which this poverty-stricken brood claim affinity.

As to Mateo himself, who is now about thirty-five years of age, he has done his utmost to perpetuate his line and continue the poverty of the family, having a wife and a numerous progeny, who inhabit an almost dismantled hovel in the hamlet. How they manage to subsist, he only who sees into all mysteries can tell; the subsistence of a Spanish family of the kind is always a riddle to me; yet they do subsist, and what is more, appear to enjoy their existence. The wife takes her holiday stroll on the Paseo of Granada, with a child in her arms and half a dozen at her heels; and the eldest daughter, now verging into womanhood, dresses her hair with flowers and dances gayly to the castanets.

There are two classes of people to whom life seems one long holiday – the very rich and the very poor; one, because they need do nothing; the other, because they have nothing to do; but there are none who understand the art of doing nothing and living upon nothing better than the poor classes of Spain. Climate does one half, and temperament the rest. Give a Spaniard the shade in summer and the sun in winter, a little bread, garlic, oil and garbances, an old brown cloak and a guitar, and let the world roll on as it pleases. Talk of poverty! With him it has no disgrace. It sits upon him with a grandiose style, like his ragged cloak. He is a hidalgo, even when in rags.

The 'sons of the Alhambra' are an eminent illustration of this practical philosophy. As the Moors imagined that the celestial paradise hung over this favoured spot, so I am inclined at times to fancy that a gleam of the golden age still lingers about this ragged community. They possess nothing, they do nothing, they care for nothing. Yet, though apparently idle all the week, they are as observant of all holy days and saints' days as the most laborious artisan. They attend all fêtes and dancings in Granada and its vicinity, light bonfires on the hills on St. John's Eve, and dance away the moonlight nights on the harvest home of a small field within the precincts of the fortress, which yield a few bushels of wheat.

Before concluding these remarks, I must mention one of the amusements of the place, which has particularly struck me. I had repeatedly observed a long lean fellow perched on the top of one of the towers, manoeuvring two or three fishing rods, as though he were angling for the stars. I was for some time perplexed by the evolutions of this aërial fisherman, and my perplexity increased on observing others employed in like manner on different parts of the battlements and bastions; it was not until I consulted Mateo Ximenes that I solved the mystery.

It seems that the pure and airy situation of this fortress has rendered it, like the castle of Macbeth, a prolific breeding place for swallows and martlets, who sport about its towers in myriads, with the holiday glee of urchins just let loose from school. To entrap these birds in their giddy circlings with hooks baited with flies is one of the favourite amusements of the ragged 'sons of the Alhambra', who, with the good-for-nothing ingenuity of arrant idlers, have thus invented the art of angling in the sky.

THE HALL OF AMBASSADORS

In one of my visits to the old Moorish chamber where the good Tia Antonia cooks her dinner and receives her company, I observed a mysterious door in one corner, leading apparently into the ancient part of the edifice. My curiosity being aroused, I opened it and found myself in a narrow, blind corridor, groping along which I came to the head of a dark winding staircase, leading down an angle of the Tower of Comares. Down this staircase I descended darkling, guiding myself by the wall until I came to a small door at the bottom, throwing which open, I was suddenly dazzled by emerging into the brilliant antechamber of the Hall of Ambassadors; with the fountain of the Court of the Alberca sparkling before me. The antechamber is separated from the court by an elegant gallery, supported by slender columns with spandrels of open work in the Morisco style. At each end of the antechamber are alcoves, and its ceiling is richly stuccoed and painted. Passing through a magnificent portal, I found myself in the far-famed Hall of Ambassadors, the audience chamber of the Moslem monarchs. It is said to be thirty-seven feet square, and sixty feet high; occupies the whole interior of the Tower of Comares; and still bears the traces of past magnificence. The walls are beautifully stuccoed and decorated with Morisco fancifulness; the lofty ceiling was originally of the same favourite material, with the usual frostwork and pensile ornaments or stalactites; which, with the embellishments of vivid colouring and gilding, must have been gorgeous in the extreme. Unfortunately it gave way during an earthquake, and brought down with it an immense arch which traversed the hall. It was replaced by the present vault or dome of larch or cedar, with intersecting ribs, the whole curiously wrought and richly coloured; still Oriental in its character, reminding one of 'those ceilings of cedar and vermilion that we read of in the Prophets and the Arabian Nights'.

From the great height of the vault above the windows, the upper part of the hall is almost lost in obscurity; yet there is a magnificence as well as solemnity in the gloom, as through it we have gleams of rich gilding and the brilliant tints of the Moorish pencil.

The royal throne was placed opposite the entrance in a recess, which still bears an inscription intimating that Yusef I (the monarch who completed the Alhambra) made this the throne of his empire. Everything in this noble hall seems to have been calculated to surround the throne with impressive dignity and splendour; there was none of the elegant voluptuousness which reigns in other parts of the palace. The tower is of massive strength, domineering over the whole edifice and overhanging the steep hillside. On three sides of the Hall of Ambassadors are windows cut through the immense thickness of the walls, and commanding extensive prospects. The balcony of the central window especially looks down upon the verdant valley of the Darro, with its walks, its groves and gardens. To the left it enjoys a distant prospect of the Vega; while directly in front rises the rival height of the Albaycin, with its medley of streets, and terraces and gardens, and once crowned by a fortress that vied in power with the Alhambra. 'Ill fated the man who lost all this!' exclaimed Charles V, as he looked forth from this window upon the enchanting scenery it commands.

The balcony of the window where this royal exclamation was made has of late become one of my favourite resorts. I have just been seated there, enjoying the close of a long brilliant day. The sun, as he sank behind the purple mountains of Alhama, sent a stream of effulgence up the valley of the Darro that spread a melancholy pomp over the ruddy towers of the Alhambra; while the Vega, covered with a slight sultry vapour that caught the setting ray, seemed spread out in the distance like a golden sea. Not a breath of air disturbed the stillness of the hour, and though the faint sound of music and merriment now and then rose from the gardens of the Darro, it but rendered more impressive the monumental silence of the pile which overshadowed me. It was one of those hours and scenes in which memory asserts an almost magical power, and, like the evening sun beaming on these mouldering towers, sends back her retrospective rays to light up the glories of the past.

As I sat watching the effect of the declining daylight upon this Moorish pile, I was led into a consideration of the light, elegant and voluptuous character prevalent throughout its internal architecture, and to contrast it with the grand but gloomy solemnity of the Gothic edifices reared by the Spanish conquerors. The very architecture thus bespeaks the opposite and irreconcilable natures of the two warlike people who so long battled here for the mastery of the Peninsula. By degrees I fell into a course of musing upon the singular fortunes of the Arabian or Morisco-Spaniards, whose whole existence is as a tale that is told, and certainly forms one of the most anomalous yet splendid episodes in history. Potent and durable as was their dominion, we scarcely know how to call them. They were a nation without a legitimate country or name. A remote wave of the great Arabian inundation, cast upon the shores of Europe, they seem to have all the impetus of the first rush of the torrent. Their career of conquest, from the rock of Gibraltar to the cliffs of the Pyrenees, was as rapid and brilliant as the Moslem victories of Syria and Egypt. Nay, had they not been checked on the plains of Tours, all France, all Europe, might have been overrun with the same facility as the empires of the East, and the Crescent at this day have glittered on the fanes of Paris and London.

Repelled within the limits of the Pyrenees, the mixed hordes of Asia and Africa that formed this great irruption gave up the Moslem principle of conquest, and sought to establish in Spain a peaceful and permanent dominion. As conquerors, their heroism was only equalled by their moderation; and in both, for a time, they excelled the nations with whom they contended. Severed from their native homes, they loved the land given them as they supposed by Allah, and strove to embellish it with everything that could administer to the happiness of man. Laying the foundations of their power in a system of wise and equitable laws, diligently cultivating the arts and sciences and promoting agriculture, manufactures and commerce, they gradually formed an empire unrivalled for its prosperity by any of the empires of Christendom; and diligently drawing round them the graces and refinements which marked the Arabian empire in the East at the time of its greatest civilisation, they diffused the light of Oriental knowledge through the western regions of benighted Europe.

The cities of Arabian Spain became the resort of Christian artisans to instruct themselves in the useful arts. The universities of Toledo, Cordova, Seville and Granada were sought by the pale student from other lands to acquaint himself with the sciences of the Arabs and the treasured lore of antiquity; the lovers of the gay science resorted to Cordova and Granada to imbibe the poetry and music of the East; and the steel-clad warriors of the North hastened thither to accomplish themselves in the graceful exercises and courteous usages of chivalry.

If the Moslem monuments in Spain, if the Mosque of

Cordova, the Alcazar of Seville and the Alhambra of Granada still bear inscriptions fondly boasting of the power and permanency of their dominion, can the boast be derided as arrogant and vain? Generation after generation, century after century, passed away, and still they maintained possession of the land. A period elapsed longer than that which has passed since England was subjugated by the Norman Conqueror, and the descendants of Musa and Taric might as little anticipate being driven into exile across the same straits traversed by their triumphant ancestors, as the descendants of Rollo and William, and their veteran peers, may dream of being driven back to the shores of Normandy.

With all this, however, the Moslem empire in Spain was but a brilliant exotic that took no permanent root in the soil it embellished. Severed from all their neighbours in the West by impassable barriers of faith and manners, and separated by seas and deserts from their kindred of the East, the Morisco-Spaniards were an isolated people. Their whole existence was a prolonged, though gallant and chivalric, struggle for a foothold in a usurped land.

They were the outposts and frontiers of Islamism. The Peninsula was the great battleground where the Gothic conquerors of the North and the Moslem conquerors of the East met and strove for mastery; and the fiery courage of the Arab was at length subdued by the obstinate and persevering valour of the Goth.

Never was the annihilation of a people more complete than that of the Morisco-Spaniards. Where are they? Ask the shores of Barbary and its desert places. The exiled remnant of their once-powerful empire disappeared among the barbarians of Africa and ceased to be a nation. They have not even left a distinct name behind them, though for nearly eight centuries they were a distinct people. The home of their adoption, and of their occupation for ages, refuses to acknowledge them, except as invaders and usurpers. A few broken monuments are all that remain to bear witness to their power and dominion, as solitary rocks, left far in the interior, bear testimony to the extent of some vast inundation. Such is the Alhambra – a Moslem pile in the midst of a Christian land; an Oriental palace amidst the Gothic edifices of the West; an elegant memento of a brave, intelligent and graceful people, who conquered, ruled, flourished and passed away.

HENRY JAMES
INTRODUCTION

English Hours, a collection of essays drawn from Henry James' travels around that country, was first published in 1905. The great man of American letters was already well acquainted with the nation he would eventually call home, although James' experience is far from the typical story of the artist in exile. He first visited England as a child when, between 1855 and 1860, the James family toured widely throughout Europe. As a young man, James went on to study at university in Geneva, and was an avowed Francophile. And though Paris held a special place in James' affections – he was, later, a regular correspondent with Gustave Flaubert, Guy de Maupassant and Émile Zola – there was, in truth, only one city for him: London.

From his first sight of it, Henry James was transfixed by the sheer bustle of the great city, in thrall to the idea of it as a repository of all human natures. Travel, after all, is not just about pretty views. 'It is difficult to speak adequately or justly of London,' James wrote. 'It is not a pleasant place; it is not agreeable, or cheerful, or easy or exempt from reproach. It is only magnificent.'

It was in 1869, on a vacation to England on his doctor's advice, that James met George Eliot, whose work he greatly admired, along with other leading cultural figures of the day. He settled in London that same year, aged 26, aware the city was hardly a standard-bearer for health tourism. 'The fogs, the smoke, the dirt,' he noted, 'the darkness, the wet, the distances, the ugliness, the brutal size of the place, the horrible numerosity of society, the manner in which this senseless bigness is fatal to amenity, to convenience, to conversation, to good manners – all this and much more you may expatiate upon.'

There were consolations. London offered whirls of every kind; literary, social and artistic. James was a regular, and high-profile, visitor to the Royal Academy and a generous patron, notably of the artist John Singer Sargent, another American transplant. His role as a champion of art for its own sake led to his most famous literary spat, with HG Wells. The creator of *The War of the Worlds* and *The Time Machine* considered himself as much a journalist as a novelist, and believed writing to be useful only if it shone a light on the truth. It was the view of James, an advocate of Wells' early work, that art was the end in itself, a form of magic, a way of distilling those unseen forces that shape our lives. In his novel *Boon*, published in 1915, Wells ridiculed James' creative process, likening it, in terms of practicality, to a hippopotamus attempting to pick up a pea. 'It is art that makes life, makes interest, makes importance,' James thundered in response, 'and I know of no substitute for the force and beauty of its process.' That he published his riposte with war raging in Europe was brave or foolish, or possibly both.

What makes *English Hours* all the more interesting is the fact James writes about London in a composite style, one that characterised his travel writing, and which blends reportage, almost journalistic in detail, with Jamesian flair. In London, in fact, for all the old-new world subtexts played out in his fiction, James recognises a brashness not entirely un-American, forthright and demanding in nature. 'London doesn't love the latent or the lurking, has neither time, nor taste nor sense for anything less discernible than the red flag in front of the steamroller. It wants cash over the counter and letters ten feet high.'

James became a British national in July 1915, his application countersigned by Herbert Asquith, the British prime minister. Given his attachment to London in all its gritty, complex detail, it is hard not to conclude the die had long been cast.

ENGLISH HOURS
BY HENRY JAMES

A day or two later, in the afternoon, I found myself staring at my fire, in a lodging of which I had taken possession on foreseeing that I should spend some weeks in London. I had just come in, and, having attended to the distribution of my luggage, sat down to consider my habitation. It was on the ground floor, and the fading daylight reached it in a sadly damaged condition. It struck me as stuffy and unsocial, with its mouldy smell and its decoration of lithographs and wax flowers – an impersonal black hole in the huge general blackness. The uproar of Piccadilly hummed away at the end of the street, and the rattle of a heartless hansom passed close to my ears. A sudden horror of the whole place came over me, like a tiger pounce of homesickness which had been watching its moment. London was hideous, vicious, cruel and above all overwhelming; whether or no she was 'careful of the type', she was as indifferent as Nature herself to the single life. In the course of an hour I should have to go out to my dinner, which was not supplied on the premises, and that effort assumed the form of a desperate and dangerous quest. It appeared to me that I would rather remain dinnerless, would rather even starve, than sally forth into the infernal town, where the natural fate of an obscure stranger would be to be trampled to death in Piccadilly and have his carcass thrown into the

Thames. I did not starve, however, and I eventually attached myself by a hundred human links to the dreadful, delightful city. That momentary vision of its smeared face and stony heart has remained memorable to me, but I am happy to say that I can easily summon up others.

It is, no doubt, not the taste of everyone, but for the real London lover the mere immensity of the place is a large part of its savour. A small London would be an abomination, as it fortunately is an impossibility, for the idea and the name are beyond everything an expression of extent and number. Practically, of course, one lives in a quarter, in a plot; but in imagination and by a constant mental act of reference the accommodated haunter enjoys the whole – and it is only of him that I deem it worthwhile to speak. He fancies himself, as they say, for being a particle in so unequalled an aggregation; and its immeasurable circumference, even though unvisited and lost in smoke, gives him the sense of a social, an intellectual margin. There is a luxury in the knowledge that he may come and go without being noticed, even when his comings and goings have no nefarious end. I don't mean by this that the tongue of London is not a very active member; the tongue of London would indeed be worthy of a chapter by itself. But the eyes which at least in some measure feed its activity are fortunately for the common advantage solicited at any moment by a thousand different objects. If the place is big, everything it contains is certainly not so; but this may at least be said – that if small questions play a part there, they play it without illusions about its importance. There are too many questions, small or great; and each day, as it arrives, leads its children, like a kind of mendicant mother, by the hand. Therefore perhaps the most general characteristic is the absence of insistence. Habits and inclinations flourish and fall, but intensity is never one of them. The spirit of the great city is not analytic, and, as they come up, subjects rarely receive at its hands a treatment drearily earnest or tastelessly thorough. There are not many – of those of which London disposes with the assurance begotten of its large experience – that wouldn't lend themselves to a tenderer manipulation elsewhere. It takes a very great affair, a turn of the Irish screw or a divorce case lasting many days, to be fully threshed out. The mind of Mayfair, when it aspires to show what it really can do, lives in the hope of a new divorce case, and an indulgent providence – London is positively in certain ways the spoiled child of the world – abundantly recognises this particular aptitude and humours the whim.

The compensation is that material does arise; that there is a great variety, if not morbid subtlety; and that the whole of the procession of events and topics passes across your stage. For the moment I am speaking of the inspiration there may be in the sense of far frontiers; the London lover loses himself in this swelling consciousness, delights in the idea that the town which encloses him is after all only a paved country, a state by itself. This is his condition of mind quite as much if he be an adoptive as if he be a matter-of-course son. I am by no means sure even that he need be of Anglo-Saxon race and have inherited the birthright of English speech; though, on the other hand, I make no doubt that these advantages minister greatly to closeness of allegiance. The great city spreads her dusky mantle over innumerable races and creeds, and I believe there is scarcely a known form of worship that has not some temple there (have I not attended at the Church of Humanity, in Lamb's Conduit, in company with an American lady, a vague old gentleman and several seamstresses?) or any communion of men that has not some club or guild. London is indeed an epitome of the round world, and just as it is a commonplace to say that there is nothing one can't 'get' there, so it is equally true that there is nothing one may not study at firsthand.

One doesn't test these truths every day, but they form part

of the air one breathes (and welcome, says the London hater –
for there be such perverse reasoners – to the pestilent
compound). They colour the thick, dim distances, which in my
opinion are the most romantic town vistas in the world; they
mingle with the troubled light to which the straight,
ungarnished aperture in one's dull, undistinctive house front
affords a passage and which makes an interior of friendly
comers, mysterious tones and unbetrayed ingenuities, as well
as with the low, magnificent medium of the sky, where the
smoke and fog and the weather in general, the strangely
undefined hour of the day and season of the year, the
emanations of industries and the reflection of furnaces, the
red gleams and blurs that may or may not be of sunset – as you
never see any source of radiance, you can't in the least tell – all
hang together in a confusion, a complication, a shifting but
irremovable canopy. They form the undertone of the deep,
perpetual voice of the place. One remembers them when one's
loyalty is on the defensive; when it is a question of introducing
as many striking features as possible into the list of fine
reasons one has sometimes to draw up, that eloquent
catalogue with which one confronts the hostile indictment –
the array of other reasons which may easily be as long as one's
arm. According to these other reasons it plausibly and
conclusively stands that, as a place to be happy in, London will
never do. I don't say it is necessary to meet so absurd an
allegation except for one's personal complacency. If indifference,
in so gorged an organism, is still livelier than curiosity, you may
avail yourself of your own share in it simply to feel that since
such and such a person doesn't care for real richness, so much
the worse for such and such a person. But once in a while the
best believer recognises the impulse to set his religion in order,
to sweep the temple of his thoughts and trim the sacred lamp.
It is at such hours as this that he reflects with elation that the
British capital is the particular spot in the world which

communicates the greatest sense of life.

The reader will perceive that I do not shrink even from the extreme concession of speaking of our capital as British, and this in a shameless connection with the question of loyalty on the part of an adoptive son. For I hasten to explain that if half the source of one's interest in it comes from feeling that it is the property and even the home of the human race – Hawthorne, that best of Americans, says so somewhere, and places it in this sense side by side with Rome – one's appreciation of it is really a large sympathy, a comprehensive love of humanity. For the sake of such a charity as this one may stretch one's allegiance; and the most alien of the cockneyfied, though he may bristle with every protest at the intimation that England has set its stamp upon him, is free to admit with conscious pride that he has submitted to Londonisation. It is a real stroke of luck for a particular country that the capital of the human race happens to be British. Surely every other people would have it theirs if they could. Whether the English deserve to hold it any longer might be an interesting field of enquiry; but as they have not yet let it slip, the writer of these lines professes without scruple that the arrangement is to his personal taste. For, after all, if the sense of life is greatest there, it is a sense of the life of people of our consecrated English speech. It is the headquarters of that strangely elastic tongue; and I make this remark with a full sense of the terrible way in which the idiom is misused by the populace in general, than whom it has been given to few races to impart to conversation less of the charm of tone. For a man of letters who endeavours to cultivate, however modestly, the medium of Shakespeare and Milton, of Hawthorne and Emerson, who cherishes the notion of what it has achieved and what it may even yet achieve, London must ever have a great illustrative and suggestive value, and indeed a kind of sanctity. It is the single place in which most readers, most possible lovers, are gathered together; it is the most inclusive public and the largest social incarnation of the language, of the tradition. Such a personage may well let it go for this, and leave the German and the Greek to speak for themselves, to express the grounds of their predilection, presumably very different.

When a social product is so vast and various, it may be approached on a thousand different sides, and liked and disliked for a thousand different reasons. The reasons of Piccadilly are not those of Camden Town, nor are the curiosities and discouragements of Kilburn the same as those of Westminster and Lambeth. The reasons of Piccadilly – I mean the friendly ones – are those of which, as a general thing, the rooted visitor remains most conscious; but it must be confessed that even these, for the most part, do not lie upon the surface. The absence of style, or rather of the intention of style, is certainly the most general characteristic of the face of London. To cross to Paris under this impression is to find one's self surrounded with far other standards. There everything reminds you that the idea of beautiful and stately arrangement has never been out of fashion, that the art of composition has always been at work or at play. Avenues and squares, gardens and quays, have been distributed for effect, and today the splendid city reaps the accumulation of all this ingenuity. The result is not in every quarter interesting, and there is a tiresome monotony of the 'fine' and the symmetrical, above all, of the deathly passion for making things 'to match'. On the other hand the whole air of the place is architectural. On the banks of the Thames it is a tremendous chapter of accidents – the London lover has to confess to the existence of miles upon miles of the dreariest, stodgiest commonness. Thousands of acres are covered by low black houses of the cheapest construction, without ornament, without grace, without character or even identity. In fact there are many, even in the best quarters, in all the region of Mayfair and Belgravia, of so paltry and inconvenient, especially of so diminutive a type (those that are let in lodgings – such poor lodgings as they make – may serve as an example), that you wonder what peculiarly limited domestic need they were constructed to meet. The great misfortune of London to the eye (it is true that this remark applies much less to the City) is the want of elevation. There is no architectural impression without a certain degree of height, and the London street vista has none of that sort of pride.

All the same, if there be not the intention, there is at least the accident of style, which, if one looks at it in a friendly way, appears to proceed from three sources. One of these is simply the general greatness, and the manner in which that makes a difference for the better in any particular spot; so that, though you may often perceive yourself to be in a shabby comer, it never occurs to you that this is the end of it. Another is the atmosphere, with its magnificent mystifications, which flatters and superfuses, makes everything brown, rich, dim, vague, magnifies distances and minimises details, confirms the inference of vastness by suggesting that, as the great city makes everything, it makes its own system of weather and its own optical laws. The last is the congregation of the parks, which constitute an ornament not elsewhere to be matched, and give the place a superiority that none of its uglinesses overcome. They spread themselves with such a luxury of space in the centre of the town that they form a part of the impression of any walk, of almost any view, and, with an audacity altogether their own, make a pastoral landscape under the smoky sky. There is no mood of the rich London climate that is not becoming to them – I have seen them look delightfully romantic, like parks in novels, in the wettest winter – and there is scarcely a mood of the appreciative resident to which they have not something to say. The high things of London, which here and there peep over them, only make the spaces vaster by reminding you that you are, after all, not in Kent or Yorkshire; and these things, whatever they be – rows of 'eligible' dwellings, towers of churches, domes of institutions – take such an effective grey-blue tint that a clever watercolourist would seem to have put them in for pictorial reasons.

The view from the bridge over the Serpentine has an extraordinary nobleness, and it has often seemed to me that the Londoner, twitted with his low standard, may point to it with every confidence. In all the town scenery of Europe there can be few things so fine; the only reproach it is open to is that it begs the question by seeming – in spite of its being the pride of five millions of people – not to belong to a town at all. The towers of Notre Dame, as they rise in Paris from the island that divides the Seine, present themselves no more impressively than those of Westminster as you see them looking doubly far beyond the shining stretch of Hyde Park water. Equally delectable is the large riverlike manner in which the Serpentine opens away between its wooded shores. Just after you have crossed the bridge (whose very banisters, old and ornamental, of yellowish-brown stone, I am particularly fond of), you enjoy on your left, through the gate of Kensington Gardens as you go towards Bayswater, an altogether enchanting vista – a footpath over the grass, which loses itself beneath the scattered oaks and elms exactly as if the place were a 'chase'. There could be nothing less like London in general than this particular morsel, and yet it takes London, of all cities, to give you such an impression of the country.

It takes London to put you in the way of a purely rustic walk from Notting Hill to Whitehall. You may traverse this immense distance – a most comprehensive diagonal – altogether on soft, fine turf, amid the song of birds, the bleat of lambs, the ripple of ponds, the rustle of admirable trees. Frequently have I wished that, for the sake of such a daily luxury and of exercise made romantic, I were a Government clerk living, in snug domestic conditions, in a Pembridge villa – let me suppose – and having my matutinal desk in Westminster. I should turn into Kensington Gardens at their northwest limit, and I should have my choice of a hundred pleasant paths to the gates of Hyde Park. In Hyde Park I should follow the waterside, or the Row or any other fancy of the occasion; liking best, perhaps, after all, the Row in its morning mood, with the mist hanging over the dark-red course, and the scattered early riders taking an identity as the soundless gallop brings them nearer. I am free to admit that in the Season, at the conventional hours, the Row becomes a weariness (save perhaps just for a glimpse once a year, to remind one's self how much it is like Du Maurier); the preoccupied citizen eschews it and leaves it for the most part to the gaping barbarian. I speak of it now from the point of view of the pedestrian; but for the rider as well it is at its best when he passes either too early or too late. Then, if he be not bent on comparing it to its disadvantage with the bluer and boskier alleys of the Bois de Boulogne, it will not be spoiled by the fact that, with its surface that looks like tan, its barriers like those of the ring on which the clown stands to hold up the hoop to the young lady, its empty benches and chairs, its occasional orange peel, its mounted policemen patrolling at intervals like expectant supernumeraries, it offers points of real contact with a circus whose lamps are out. The sky that bends over it is frequently not a bad imitation of the dingy tent of such an establishment. The ghosts of past cavalcades seem to haunt the foggy arena, and somehow they are better company than the mashers and elongated beauties of current seasons. It is not without interest to remember that most of the salient figures of English society during the present century – and English society means, or rather has hitherto meant, in a large degree, English history – have bobbed in the

saddle between Apsley House and Queen's Gate. You may call
the roll if you care to, and the air will be thick with dumb voices
and dead names, like that of some Roman amphitheatre.

It is doubtless a signal proof of being a London lover quand
même that one should undertake an apology for so bungled an
attempt at a great public place as Hyde Park Corner. It is
certain that the improvements and embellishments recently
enacted there have only served to call further attention to the
poverty of the elements and to the fact that this poverty is
terribly illustrative of general conditions. The place is the
beating heart of the great West End, yet its main features are a
shabby, stuccoed hospital, the low park gates, in their neat but
unimposing frame, the drawing-room windows of Apsley
House and of the commonplace frontages on the little terrace
beside it; to which must be added, of course, the only item in
the whole prospect that is in the least monumental – the arch
spanning the private road beside the gardens of Buckingham
Palace. This structure is now bereaved of the rueful effigy
which used to surmount it – the Iron Duke in the guise of a tin
soldier – and has not been enriched by the transaction as much
as might have been expected. There is a fine view of Piccadilly
and Knightsbridge, and of the noble mansions, as the house
agents call them, of Grosvenor Place, together with a sense
of generous space beyond the vulgar little railing of the Green
Park; but, except for the impression that there would be
room for something better, there is nothing in all this that
speaks to the imagination: almost as much as the grimy
desert of Trafalgar Square the prospect conveys the idea of an
opportunity wasted.

Nonetheless has it on a fine day in spring an expressiveness
of which I shall not pretend to explain the source further than
by saying that the flood of life and luxury is immeasurably
great there. The edifices are mean, but the social stream itself
is monumental, and to an observer not purely stolid there is

more excitement and suggestion than I can give a reason for in the long, distributed waves of traffic, with the steady policemen marking their rhythm, which roll together and apart for so many hours. Then the great, dim city becomes bright and kind, the pall of smoke turns into a veil of haze carelessly worn, the air is coloured and almost scented by the presence of the biggest society in the world, and most of the things that meet the eye – or perhaps I should say more of them, for the most in London is, no doubt, ever the realm of the dingy – present themselves as 'well appointed'. Everything shines, more or less, from the windowpanes to the dog collars. So it all looks, with its myriad variations and qualifications, to one who surveys it over the apron of a hansom, while that vehicle of vantage, better than any box at the opera, spurts and slackens with the current.

SAMUEL JOHNSON
INTRODUCTION

'When a man is tired of London, he is tired of life,' wrote Samuel Johnson. This may help explain why, by the age of 61, he had barely travelled beyond the city's limits. His trip to Scotland in 1773 to the far-flung Hebrides islands seems somewhat out of character. In keeping with Johnson's principal interests, he went on matters social, the plight of the Highlanders under English oppression, as well as literary.

The quintessential man of letters – rarely a moment of Johnson's waking life went unrecorded – it was inevitable he would produce a book on the subject. *A Journey to the Western Islands of Scotland* (1775), tells of the three months he spent travelling the Highlands and islands. His companion was James Boswell, Johnson's perennial acolyte, who would go on to become his celebrated biographer.

It was a period when English gentlemen north of the border might exercise a certain discretion. The Jacobite rebellion of 1745, in which Charles Edward Stuart had sought to capture the throne, was fresh in the national – and nationalist – consciousness. The consequences of the uprising were severe. At the time of Johnson's visit, the Highland clearances, a heavy-handed English tactic forcing tenant farmers off their lands, had been underway for more than a decade. The subsequent 'enclosures', enclosing common pasture into private fields to deny peasants access to grazing, continued to create significant depopulation.

Discretion is not a word readily associated with Johnson, and yet he struggled with the bluff nature of his hosts. 'The Highlander,' Johnson wrote, 'gives to every question an answer so prompt and peremptory that skepticism itself is dared into silence, and the mind sinks before the bold reporter in unresisting credulity...such is the laxity of Highland conversation that the inquirer is kept in continual suspense, and by a kind of intellectual retrogradation, knows less as he hears more.'

If Johnson viewed the Scots with condescension – he arranged accommodation only with the English gentry – he was not immune from the repercussions of English occupation. 'The loss of an inhabitant leaves a lasting vacuity,' he wrote of the many Scots leaving for England and America, 'for nobody born in any other parts of the world will choose this country for his residence, and an island once depopulated will remain a desert.' And while he found the weather vexing – 'Three dry days [are] not to be expected for many months' – he was aware that 'winter comes with its cold and its scarcity upon families very slenderly provided'.

In the western Highlands, Johnson hoped to locate traditional Scotsmen, at least a tourist's approximation. English foreign policy extended to dismantling Scotland's indigenous social structure, removing power from clan chiefs; it was illegal to wear tartan or to distil whisky. Johnson sought a Scottish incarnation of Rousseau's noble savage, a defiant, claymore-wielding, bagpipe-playing warrior. He was disappointed: 'In the islands the plaid is rarely worn. The law by which the Highlanders have been obliged to change the form of their dress, has, in all the places that we have visited, been universally obeyed.'

Perhaps they had seen him coming; despite the remoteness of the location, Johnson was still a celebrity. 'I know not whether we touched at any corner,' he observed, 'where fame had not already prepared us a reception.' A known gourmand, there was much that pleased Johnson in the Hebrides, not least the food.

A JOURNEY TO THE
WESTERN ISLANDS OF SCOTLAND
BY SAMUEL JOHNSON

The third or fourth day after our arrival at Armidel brought us an invitation to the isle of Raasay, which lies east of Sky. It is incredible how soon the account of any event is propagated in these narrow countries by the love of talk, which much leisure produces, and the relief given to the mind in the penury of insular conversation by a new topic. The arrival of strangers at a place so rarely visited excites rumour and quickens curiosity. I know not whether we touched at any corner where fame had not already prepared us a reception.

To gain a commodious passage to Raasay, it was necessary to pass over a large part of Sky. We were furnished therefore with horses and a guide. In the Islands there are no roads, nor any marks by which a stranger may find his way. The horseman has always at his side a native of the place who, by pursuing game, or tending cattle or being often employed in messages or conduct, has learned where the ridge of the hill has breadth sufficient to allow a horse and his rider a passage, and where the moss or bog is hard enough to bear them. The bogs are avoided as toilsome at least, if not unsafe, and therefore the journey is made generally from precipice to precipice; from which if the eye ventures to look down, it sees below a gloomy cavity, whence the rush of water is sometimes heard.

But there seems to be in all this more alarm than danger. The Highlander walks carefully before, and the horse, accustomed to the ground, follows him with little deviation. Sometimes the hill is too steep for the horseman to keep his seat, and sometimes the moss is too tremulous to bear the double weight of horse and man. The rider then dismounts, and all shift as they can.

Journeys made in this manner are rather tedious than long. A very few miles require several hours. From Armidel we came at night to Coriatachan, a house very pleasantly situated between two brooks, with one of the highest hills of the island behind it. It is the residence of Mr. Mackinnon, by whom we were treated with very liberal hospitality among a more numerous and elegant company than it could have been supposed easy to collect.

The hill behind the house we did not climb. The weather was rough, and the height and steepness discouraged us. We were told that there is a cairn upon it. A cairn is a heap of stones thrown upon the grave of one eminent for dignity of birth, or splendour of achievements. It is said that by digging, an urn is always found under these cairns: they must therefore have been thus piled by a people whose custom was to burn the dead. To pile stones is, I believe, a northern custom, and to burn the body was the Roman practice; nor do I know when it was that these two acts of sepulture were united.

The weather was next day too violent for the continuation of our journey; but we had no reason to complain of the interruption. We saw in every place what we chiefly desired to know, the manners of the people. We had company, and, if we had chosen retirement, we might have had books.

I never was in any house of the Islands where I did not find books in more languages than one, if I stayed long enough to want them, except one from which the family was removed. Literature is not neglected by the higher rank of the Hebridians.

It need not, I suppose, be mentioned, that in countries so little frequented as the Islands, there are no houses where travellers are entertained for money. He that wanders about these wilds either procures recommendations to those whose habitations lie near his way, or, when night and weariness come upon him, takes the chance of general hospitality. If he finds only a cottage, he can expect little more than shelter; for the cottagers have little more for themselves: but if his good fortune brings him to the residence of a gentleman, he will be glad of a storm to prolong his stay. There is, however, one inn by the seaside at Sconsor, in Sky, where the post office is kept.

At the tables where a stranger is received, neither plenty nor delicacy is wanting. A tract of land so thinly inhabited, must have much wild fowl; and I scarcely remember to have seen a dinner without them. The moor game is everywhere to be had. That the sea abounds with fish needs not be told, for it supplies a great part of Europe. The Isle of Sky has stags and roebucks, but no hares. They sell very numerous droves of oxen yearly to England, and therefore cannot be supposed to want beef at home. Sheep and goats are in great numbers, and they have the common domestic fowls.

But as here is nothing to be bought, every family must kill its own meat, and roast part of it somewhat sooner than Apicius would prescribe. Every kind of flesh is undoubtedly excelled by the variety and emulation of English markets; but that which is not best may be yet very far from bad, and he that shall complain of his fare in the Hebrides has improved his delicacy more than his manhood.

Their fowls are not like those plumped for sale by the poulterers of London, but they are as good as other places commonly afford, except that the geese, by feeding in the sea, have universally a fishy rankness.

These geese seem to be of a middle race, between the wild and domestic kinds. They are so tame as to own a home, and so wild as sometimes to fly quite away.

Their native bread is made of oats, or barley. Of oatmeal they spread very thin cakes, coarse and hard, to which unaccustomed palates are not easily reconciled. The barley cakes are thicker and softer; I began to eat them without unwillingness; the blackness of their colour raises some dislike, but the taste is not disagreeable. In most houses there is wheat flour, with which we were sure to be treated, if we stayed long enough to have it kneaded and baked. As neither yeast nor leaven are used among them, their bread of every kind is unfermented. They make only cakes, and never mould a loaf.

A man of the Hebrides, for of the women's diet I can give no account, as soon as he appears in the morning swallows a glass of whisky; yet they are not a drunken race, at least I never was present at much intemperance; but no man is so abstemious as to refuse the morning dram, which they call a skalk.

The word whisky signifies water, and is applied by way of eminence to strong water, or distilled liquor. The spirit drunk in the North is drawn from barley. I never tasted it, except once for experiment at the inn in Inverary, when I thought it preferable to any English malt brandy. It was strong, but not pungent, and was free from the empyreumatic taste or smell. What was the process I had no opportunity of inquiring, nor do I wish to improve the art of making poison pleasant.

Not long after the dram, may be expected the breakfast. The tea and coffee are accompanied not only with butter, but with honey, conserves and marmalades. If an epicure could remove by a wish, in quest of sensual gratifications, wherever he had supped, he would breakfast in Scotland.

In the Islands, however, they do what I found it not very easy to endure. They pollute the tea table by plates piled with large slices of Cheshire cheese, which mingles its less grateful odours with the fragrance of the tea.

Where many questions are to be asked, some will be

omitted. I forgot to inquire how they were supplied with so much exotic luxury. Perhaps the French may bring them wine for wool, and the Dutch give them tea and coffee at the fishing season in exchange for fresh provision. Their trade is unconstrained; they pay no customs, for there is no officer to demand them; whatever therefore is made dear only by impost is obtained here at an easy rate.

A dinner in the Western Islands differs very little from a dinner in England, except that in the place of tarts, there are always set different preparations of milk. This part of their diet will admit some improvement. Though they have milk, and eggs and sugar, few of them know how to compound them in a custard. Their gardens afford them no great variety, but they have always some vegetables on the table. Potatoes at least are never wanting, which, though they have not known them long, are now one of the principal parts of their food. They are not of the mealy, but the viscous kind.

Their more elaborate cookery, or made dishes, an Englishman at the first taste is not likely to approve, but the culinary compositions of every country are often such as become grateful to other nations only by degrees; though I have read a French author who, in the elation of his heart, says, that French cookery pleases all foreigners, but foreign cookery never satisfies a Frenchman.

DH LAWRENCE
INTRODUCTION

Sea and Sardinia is perhaps the definition of a literary curiosity when compared with the other creations of its author: the Oedipal complexity of *Sons and Lovers* (1913); the anticapitalist, sexual progressiveness of *The Rainbow* (1915); and *Lady Chatterley's Lover* (1928), one of the most controversial novels printed in the English language.

An account of Lawrence's holiday on the island in 1921, its opening lines appear a paean to possibility: 'Comes over one an absolute necessity to move,' Lawrence wrote, 'and what is more, to move in some particular direction. A double necessity then: to get on the move, and to know whither.' It is also the chronicle of a petty, rootless curmudgeon, forced into exile from his homeland.

Lawrence was infamously cantankerous, a sufferer, he claimed, of 'spiritual dyspepsia'. Gracelessness was his default setting. And yet *Sea and Sardinia* is a repository of such wit, as well as spite, you needn't share the sentiments to appreciate the writing. Lawrence visited Sardinia with his wife Frieda. Their choice of destination owed something to proximity (Lawrence was living in Sicily and boats sailed regularly from Palermo), but also to some rogue element Lawrence identified in the island.

'Sardinia...is like nowhere,' he wrote in his introduction. 'Sardinia, which has no history, no date, no race, no offering. Let it be Sardinia. They say neither Romans nor Phoenicians, Greeks nor Arabs ever subdued Sardinia. It lies outside; outside the circuit of civilisation.'

That Lawrence himself lived outside 'the circuit' was vital to his art. When TS Eliot offered him a column in his prestigious magazine, *The Criterion*, Lawrence turned it down, although they remained friends. Ezra Pound was a contemporary, EM Forster another notable ally. And Lawrence needed them. His work courted controversy as a matter of principle, challenging views on sex and class. The British establishment considered Lawrence little more than a highbrow pornographer. Those publishers who rejected his work were 'jelly-boned swines... belly-wriggling invertebrates'. Of society in general, Lawrence went further when the mood took him. 'Death, noble, unstainable death,' he wrote, 'smash the glassy rind of humanity, as one would smash the brittle hide of the insulated bug.'

Lawrence and his wife Frieda were married in 1913. She was a von Richthofen, a minor German aristocrat and distantly related to Manfred, the infamous Red Baron. The outbreak of World War One put Lawrence in a bind. The couple escaped to the village of Zennor in Cornwall, but suspicion dogged their every move. Neighbours whispered in the street, and, under direction from the British government in Whitehall, the local police kept checks on the couple's movements. In 1917 they were expelled for spying under the Defence of the Realm Act. So began what Lawrence termed his 'savage exile', a period that took the Lawrences to Italy and the south of France, as well as to America, Sri Lanka and Australia.

On their Sardinian sojourn, the Lawrences made land in Cagliari, travelling on by train through the Trexenta hills to the small town of Mandas and on to Sorgono. The journey features in the extract here, and Frieda Lawrence, who appears in the book as 'q-b' (Queen Bee), clearly loved the place, despite her husband's determination to be miserable. The poet Richard Aldington, a contemporary, noted DH Lawrence possessed 'a wounding capacity for not adapting himself to others'. It seems a shame Lawrence did not enjoy Sardinia more, some light relief from his routine wrestles for the mortal soul of man. There were clearly moments when the beauty of the island overcame him. Sardinia remains an island where 'the life level is high as the golden-lit plateau', just as in Lawrence's account of it.

SEA AND SARDINIA
BY DH LAWRENCE

Out of the sun it was cold, nevertheless. We went into the streets to try and get warm. The sun was powerful. But alas, as in southern towns generally, the streets are sunless as wells.

So the q-b [Mrs Lawrence] and I creep slowly along the sunny bits, and then perforce are swallowed by shadow. We look at the shops. But there is not much to see. Little, frowsy provincial shops, on the whole.

But a fair number of peasants in the streets, and peasant women in rather ordinary costume: tight-bodiced, volume-skirted dresses of handwoven linen or thickish cotton. The prettiest is of dark-blue-and-red stripes and lines, intermingled, so made that the dark blue gathers round the waist into one colour, the myriad pleats hiding all the rosy red. But when she walks, the full-petticoated peasant woman, then the red goes flash-flash-flash, like a bird showing its colours. Pretty that looks in the sombre street. She has a plain, light bodice with a peak: sometimes a little vest, and great full white sleeves, and usually a handkerchief or shawl loose knotted. It is charming the way they walk, with quick, short steps. When all is said and done, the most attractive costume for women in my eye is the tight little bodice and the many-pleated skirt, full and vibrating with movement. It has a charm which modern elegance lacks completely – a birdlike play in movement.

They are amusing, these peasant girls and women: so brisk and defiant. They have straight backs, like little walls, and decided, well-drawn brows. And they are amusingly on the alert. There is no eastern creeping. Like sharp, brisk birds they dart along the streets, and you feel they would fetch you a bang over the head as leave as look at you. Tenderness, thank heaven, does not seem to be a Sardinian quality. Italy is so tender – like cooked macaroni – yards and yards of soft tenderness ravelled round everything. Here men don't idealise women, by the looks of things. Here they don't make these great leering eyes, the inevitable yours-to-command look of Italian males. When the men from the country look at these women, then it is Mind yourself, my lady. I should think the grovelling Madonna worship is not much of a Sardinian feature. These women must look out for themselves, keep their own backbone stiff and their knuckles hard. Man is going to be male Lord if he can. And woman isn't going to give him too much of his own way, either. So there you have it, the fine old martial split between the sexes. It is tonic and splendid, really, after so much sticky intermingling and backbone-less Madonna worship. The Sardinian isn't looking for the 'noble woman nobly planned'. No, thank you. He wants that young madam over there, a young, stiff-necked generation that she is. Far better sport than with the nobly planned sort: hollow frauds that they are. Better sport too than with a Carmen, who gives herself away too much. In these women there is something shy and defiant and un-get-atable. The defiant, splendid split between the sexes, each absolutely determined to defend his side, her side, from assault. So the meeting has a certain wild, salty savour, each the deadly unknown to the other. And at the same time, each his own, her own native pride and courage, taking the dangerous leap and scrambling back.

Give me the old, salty way of love. How I am nauseated with sentiment and nobility, the macaroni slithery-slobbery mess of modern adorations.

One sees a few fascinating faces in Cagliari: those great dark, unlighted eyes. There are fascinating dark eyes in Sicily, bright, big, with an impudent point of light, and a curious roll, and long lashes: the eyes of old Greece, surely. But here one sees eyes of soft, blank darkness, all velvet, with no imp looking out of them. And they strike a stranger, older note: before the soul became self-conscious; before the mentality of Greece appeared in the world. Remote, always remote, as if the intelligence lay deep within the cave, and never came forward. One searches into the gloom for one second, while the glance lasts. But without being able to penetrate to the reality. It recedes, like some unknown creature deeper into its lair. There is a creature, dark and potent. But what?

Sometimes Velázquez, and sometimes Goya gives us a suggestion of these large, dark, unlighted eyes. And they go with fine, fleecy black hair – almost as fine as fur. I have not seen them north of Cagliari.

The q-b spies some of the blue-and-red stripe-and-line cotton stuff of which the peasants make their dress: a large roll in the doorway of a dark shop. In we go, and begin to feel it. It is just soft, thickish cotton stuff – twelve francs a metre. Like most peasant patterns, it is much more complicated and subtle than appears: the curious placing of the stripes, the subtle proportion and a white thread left down one side only of each broad blue block. The stripes, moreover, run across the cloth, not lengthwise with it. But the width would be just long enough for a skirt – though the peasant skirts have almost all a band at the bottom with the stripes running round-ways.

The man – simple, frank and amiable – says the stuff is made in France, and this the first roll since the war. It is the old, old pattern, quite correct – but the material not quite so good. The q-b takes enough for a dress.

He shows us also cashmeres, orange, scarlet, sky blue, royal blue: good, pure-wool cashmeres that were being sent to

India, and were captured from a German mercantile submarine. So he says. Fifty francs a metre – very, very wide. But they are too much trouble to carry in a knapsack, though their brilliance fascinates.

So we stroll and look at the shops, at the filigree gold jewelling of the peasants, at a good bookshop. But there is little to see and therefore the question is, shall we go on? Shall we go forward?

There are two ways of leaving Cagliari for the north: the State railway that runs up the west side of the island, and the narrow-gauge secondary railway that pierces the centre. But we are too late for the big trains. So we will go by the secondary railway, wherever it goes.

There is a train at 2.30, and we can get as far as Mandas, some fifty miles in the interior. When we tell the queer little waiter at the hotel, he says he comes from Mandas, and there are two inns. So after lunch – a strictly fish menu – we pay our bill. It comes to sixty odd francs – for three good meals each, with wine, and the night's lodging; this is cheap, as prices now are in Italy.

Pleased with the simple and friendly Scala di Ferre, I shoulder my sack, and we walk off to the second station. The sun is shining hot this afternoon – burning hot, by the sea. The road and the buildings look dry and desiccated, the harbour rather weary and end of the world.

There is a great crowd of peasants at the little station. And almost every man has a pair of woven saddlebags – a great flat strip of coarse-woven wool, with flat pockets at either end, stuffed with purchases. These are almost the only carrying bags. The men sling them over their shoulder, so that one great pocket hangs in front, one behind.

These saddle bags are most fascinating. They are coarsely woven in bands of raw black-rusty wool, with varying bands of raw white wool or hemp or cotton – the bands and stripes of varying widths going crosswise. And on the pale bands are woven sometimes flowers in most lovely colours, rose red and blue and green, peasant patterns – and sometimes fantastic animals, beasts, in dark wool again. So that these striped zebra bags, some wonderful gay with flowery colours on their stripes, some weird with fantastic, griffinlike animals, are a whole landscape in themselves.

The train has only first and third class. It costs about thirty francs for the two of us, third class to Mantas, which is some sixty miles. In we crowd with the joyful saddlebags, into the wooden carriage with its many seats.

And, wonder of wonders, punctually to the second, off we go, out of Cagliari. End route again.

The coach was fairly full of people returning from market. On these railways the third class coaches are not divided into compartments. They are left open, so that one sees everybody, as down a room. The attractive saddlebags, bercole, were disposed anywhere, and the bulk of the people settled down to a lively conversazione. It is much nicest, on the whole, to travel third class on the railway. There is space, there is air and it is like being in a lively inn, everybody in good spirits.

At our end was plenty of room. Just across the gangway was an elderly couple, like two children, coming home very happily. He was fat, fat all over, with a white moustache and a little not-unamiable frown. She was a tall, lean brown woman, in a brown full-skirted dress and black apron with a huge pocket. She wore no head covering, and her iron-grey hair was parted smoothly. They were rather pleased and excited being in the train. She took all her money out of her big pocket, and counted it and gave it to him: all the ten-lira notes, and the five lira and the two and the one, peering at the dirty scraps of pink-backed one-lira notes to see if they were good. Then she gave him her half-pennies. And he stowed them away in his trouser pocket, standing up to push them down his fat leg.

And then one saw, to one's amazement, that the whole of his shirt tail was left out behind, like a sort of apron worn backwards. Why – a mystery. He was one of those fat, good-natured, unheeding men with a little masterful frown, such as usually have tall, lean, hard-faced, obedient wives.

They were very happy. With amazement he watched us taking hot tea from the Thermos flask. I think he too had suspected it might be a bomb. He had blue eyes and standing-up white eyebrows.

'Beautiful hot–!' he said, seeing the tea steam. It is the inevitable exclamation. 'Does it do you good?'

'Yes,' said the q-b. 'Much good.' And they both nodded complacently. They were going home.

The train was running over the malarial-looking sea plain – past the down-at-heel palm trees, past the mosque-looking buildings. At a level crossing the woman crossing-keeper darted out vigorously with her red flag. And we rambled into the first village. It was built of sun-dried brick-adobe houses, thick adobe garden walls, with tile ridges to keep off the rain. In the enclosures were dark orange trees. But the clay-coloured villages, clay dry, looked foreign: the next thing to mere earth they seem, like foxholes or coyote colonies.

Looking back, one sees Cagliari bluff on her rock, rather fine, with the thin edge of the sea's blade curving round. It is rather hard to believe in the real sea, on this sort of clay-pale plain.

But soon we begin to climb to the hills. And soon the cultivation begins to be intermittent. Extraordinary how the heathy, moorlike hills come near the sea: extraordinary how scrubby and uninhabited the great spaces of Sardinia are. It is wild, with heath and arbutus scrub and a sort of myrtle, breast-high. Sometimes one sees a few head of cattle. And then again come the greyish arable patches, where the corn is grown. It is like Cornwall, like the Land's End region. Here and there, in the distance, are peasants working on the lonely landscape. Sometimes it is one man alone in the distance, showing so vividly in his black-and-white costume, small and far-off like a solitary magpie, and curiously distinct. All the strange magic of Sardinia is in this sight. Among the low, moorlike hills, away in a hollow of the wide landscape one solitary figure, small but vivid black and white, working alone, as if eternally. There are patches and hollows of grey arable land, good for corn. Sardinia was once a great granary.

Usually, however, the peasants of the South have left off the costume. Usually it is the invisible soldiers' grey-green cloth, the Italian khaki. Wherever you go, wherever you be, you see this khaki, this grey-green war clothing. How many millions of yards of the thick, excellent but hateful material the Italian government must have provided I don't know: but enough to cover Italy with a felt carpet, I should think. It is everywhere. It cases the tiny children in stiff and neutral frocks and coats, it covers their extinguished fathers, and sometimes it even encloses the women in its warmth. It is symbolic of the universal grey mist that has come over men, the extinguishing of all bright individuality, the blotting out of all wild singleness. Oh democracy! Oh khaki democracy!

This is very different from Italian landscape. Italy is almost always dramatic, and perhaps invariably romantic. There is drama in the plains of Lombardy, and romance in the Venetian lagoons and sheer scenic excitement in nearly all the hilly parts of the peninsula. Perhaps it is the natural floridity of limestone formations. But Italian landscape is really eighteenth-century landscape, to be represented in that romantic-classic manner which makes everything rather marvellous and very topical: aqueducts, and ruins upon sugarloaf mountains, and craggy ravines and Wilhelm Meister waterfalls: all up and down.

Sardinia is another thing. Much wider, much more ordinary, not up and down at all, but running away into the distance. Unremarkable ridges of moorlike hills running away, perhaps to a bunch of dramatic peaks on the southwest. This gives a sense of space, which is so lacking in Italy. Lovely space about one, and travelling distances – nothing finished, nothing final. It is like liberty itself, after the peaky confinement of Sicily. Room – give me room – give me room for my spirit, and you can have all the toppling crags of romance.

So we ran on through the gold of the afternoon, across a wide, almost Celtic landscape of hills, our little train winding and puffing away very nimbly. Only the heath and scrub, breast-high, man-high, is too big and brigandlike for a Celtic land. The horns of black, wild-looking cattle show sometimes.

After a long pull, we come to a station after a stretch of loneliness. Each time, it looks as if there were nothing beyond – no more habitations. And each time we come to a station.

Most of the people have left the train. And as with men driving in a gig who get down at every public house, so the passengers usually alight for an airing at each station. Our old fat friend stands up and tucks his shirt tail comfortably in his trousers; which trousers all the time make one hold one's breath, for they seem at each very moment to be just dropping right down; and he clambers out, followed by the long brown stalk of a wife.

So the train sits comfortably for five or ten minutes, in the way the trains have. At last we hear whistles and horns, and our old fat friend running and clinging like a fat crab to the very end of the train as it sets off. At the same instant a loud shriek and a bunch of shouts from outside. We all jump up. There, down the line, is the long brown stork of a wife. She had just walked back to a house some hundred yards off, for a few words, and has now seen the train moving.

Now behold her with her hands thrown to heaven, and hear the wild shriek 'Madonna!' through all the hubbub. But she picks up her two skirt-knees, and with her thin legs in grey stockings starts with a mad rush after the train. In vain. The train inexorably pursues its course. Prancing, she reaches one end of the platform as we leave the other end. Then she realises it is not going to stop for her. And then, oh horror, her long arms thrown out in wild supplication after the retreating train; then flung aloft to God; then brought down in absolute despair on her head. And this is the last sight we have of her, clutching her poor head in agony and doubling forward. She is left – she is abandoned.

The poor fat husband has been all the time on the little outside platform at the end of the carriage, holding out his hand to her and shouting frenzied scolding to her and frenzied yells for the train to stop. And the train has not stopped. And she is left – left on that God-forsaken station in the waning light.

So, his face all bright, his eyes round and bright as two stars, absolutely transfigured by dismay, chagrin, anger and distress, he comes and sits in his seat, ablaze, stiff, speechless. His face is almost beautiful in its blaze of conflicting emotions. For some time he is as if unconscious in the midst of his feelings. Then anger and resentment crop out of his consternation. He turns with a flash to the long-nosed, insidious, Phoenician-looking guard. Why couldn't they stop the train for her! And immediately, as if someone had set fire to him, off flares the guard. Heh! – the train can't stop for every person's convenience! The train is a train – the timetable is a timetable. What did the old woman want to take her trips down the line for? Heh! She pays the penalty for her own inconsidcrateness. Had she paid for the train – heh? And the fat man all the time firing off his unheeding and unheeded answers. One minute – only one minute – if he, the conductor had told the driver! if he, the conductor, had shouted! A poor woman! Not another train! What was she going to do! Her ticket? And no money. A poor woman –

There was a train back to Cagliari that night, said the

conductor, at which the fat man nearly burst out of his clothing like a bursting seedpod. He bounced on his seat. What good was that? What good was a train back to Cagliari when their home was in Snelli! Making matters worse –

So they bounced and jerked and argued at one another to their hearts' content. Then the conductor retired, smiling subtly in a way they have. Our fat friend looked at us with hot, angry, ashamed, grieved eyes and said it was a shame. Yes, we chimed, it was a shame. Whereupon a self-important miss who said she came from some Collegio at Cagliari advanced and asked a number of impertinent questions in a tone of pert sympathy. After which our fat friend, left alone, covered his clouded face with his hand, turned his back on the world and gloomed.

It had all been so dramatic that in spite of ourselves we laughed, even while the q-b shed a few tears.

DAVID LIVINGSTONE
INTRODUCTION

The missionary and explorer David Livingstone is best known for
the encounter that took place at Ujiji on Lake Tanganyika on 10
November 1871. Henry Morton Stanley was the *New York
Herald* reporter charged with finding the great man of Africa, from
whom nothing had been heard for the previous six years. 'Dr
Livingstone, I presume?' was, for contemporary readers, a thrilling
moment. He first travelled to Africa in 1841, aged 28, to work as
a missionary in South Africa and Botswana, then the British
protectorate of Bechuanaland. Here he served under Richard
Moffat, a cleric he met through the London Missionary Society
(LMS), a multidenominational organisation dedicated to spreading
the gospel throughout Britain's colonies.

Livingstone's account of that first expedition, *Missionary Travels
and Researches in South Africa*, published in 1857, made him an
international celebrity (at 70,000 copies, it became one of the
bestselling books of the 19th century), a de facto authority. The
first meeting with Stanley paints Livingstone as a solitary figure, an
anchorite bearing the lonely cross of righteousness. In fact,
Livingstone was a married father of four, having wed Moffat's
daughter, Mary, in 1845. The family would join him in Africa on
several occasions, at least until 1853, after which Livingstone
deemed it unsafe.

It was in 1858 that he travelled to the region in and around the
Zambezi River, and with which he was to become synonymous.
(Two towns were named for him: Blantyre in Malawi, and
Livingstone in Zambia, renamed Maramba in 2012.) Livingstone
went not at the behest of the LMS, but in the service of the British
government, as an official ambassador briefed with exploring the
interior for the purposes of trade.

Livingstone's lifelong obsession with charting Africa's rivers betrayed wider motives. By making navigable the continent's waterways, the great powers of Europe would, Livingstone believed, civilise the continent. And softening up the people through commerce, part of the so-called 'scramble for Africa', would in turn create thoroughfares for evangelising. (Livingstone found those local tribes indifferent to his preaching particularly frustrating.) While Livingstone's expeditions can be read as the flexing of Christianity's muscle at the height of the colonial era, he also believed they served a nobler aim: to eradicate the reprehensible human bondage of East Africa. 'Slavery and the slave trade,' Livingstone wrote, 'are insuperable obstacles to any permanence inland.' To him, slavery was the 'great open sore on the world'.

It was during his years mapping the Zambezi that, in 1855, Livingstone became the first European to witness the river's spectacular waterfalls, the Mosi oa Tunya ('smoke that thunders'), and which he named in honour of Queen Victoria. 'Scenes so lovely,' Livingstone wrote of the now Victoria Falls, 'must have been gazed upon by angels in their flight.' Though with little commercial benefit, the falls were to prove the highlight of the trip.

Nothing if not determined, Livingstone made his final trip to Africa in 1865. His employer on this occasion was the Royal Geographical Society, who tasked him with settling a long-running debate around the source of the great river Nile.

When, following their historic meeting, Stanley returned to America, Livingstone stayed on despite persistent ill health, adamant he would find the source of the Nile himself. 'The Nile sources,' he wrote, 'are valuable only as a means of opening my mouth with power...to remedy an immense evil.' Livingstone died the year after the Nile riddle was solved. In May 1873, in the village of Chitambo, he was found, quite dead, crouched in prayer. Henry Morton Stanley was a pallbearer at his funeral.

MISSIONARY TRAVELS AND RESEARCHES IN SOUTH AFRICA
BY DAVID LIVINGSTONE

That the fear of man often remains excessively strong in the carnivora is proved from well-authenticated cases in which the lioness, in the vicinity of towns where the large game had been unexpectedly driven away by firearms, has been known to assuage the paroxysms of hunger by devouring her own young. It must be added, that, though the effluvium which is left by the footsteps of man is in general sufficient to induce lions to avoid a village, there are exceptions; so many came about our half-deserted houses at Chonuane while we were in the act of removing to Kolobeng that the natives who remained with Mrs Livingstone were terrified to stir out of doors in the evenings. Bitches also have been known to be guilty of the horridly unnatural act of eating their own young, probably from the great desire for animal food, which is experienced by the inhabitants as well.

When a lion is met in the daytime, a circumstance by no means unfrequent to travellers in these parts, if preconceived notions do not lead them to expect something very 'noble' or 'majestic', they will see merely an animal somewhat larger than the biggest dog they ever saw, and partaking very strongly of the canine features; the face is not much like the usual drawings of a lion, the nose being prolonged like a dog's; not exactly such as our painters make it – though they might learn better at the Zoological Gardens – their ideas of majesty being usually shown by making their lions' faces like old women in nightcaps. When encountered in the daytime, the lion stands a second or two, gazing, then turns slowly round, and walks as slowly away for a dozen paces, looking over his shoulder; then begins to trot, and when he thinks himself out of sight, bounds off like a greyhound. By day there is not, as a rule, the smallest danger of lions which are not molested attacking man, nor even on a clear moonlight night, except when they possess the breeding storgh* (natural affection); this makes them brave almost any danger; and if a man happens to cross to the windward of them, both lion and lioness will rush at him, in the manner of a bitch with whelps. This does not often happen, as I only became aware of two or three instances of it. In one case a man, passing where the wind blew from him to the animals, was bitten before he could climb a tree; and occasionally a man on horseback has been caught by the leg under the same circumstances. So general, however, is the sense of security on moonlight nights that we seldom tied up our oxen, but let them lie loose by the wagons; while on a dark, rainy night, if a lion is in the neighbourhood, he is almost sure to venture to kill an ox. His approach is always stealthy, except when wounded; and any appearance of a trap is enough to cause him to refrain from making the last spring. This seems characteristic of the feline species; when a goat is picketed in India for the purpose of enabling the huntsmen to shoot a tiger by night, if on a plain, he would whip off the animal so quickly by a stroke of the paw that no one could take aim; to obviate this, a small pit is dug, and the goat is picketed to a stake in the bottom; a small stone is tied in the ear of the goat, which makes him cry the whole night. When the tiger sees the appearance of a trap, he walks round and round the pit, and allows the hunter, who is lying in wait, to have a fair shot.

When a lion is very hungry, and lying in wait, the sight of an animal may make him commence stalking it. In one case a man, while stealthily crawling towards a rhinoceros, happened to glance behind him, and found to his horror a lion stalking him; he only escaped by springing up a tree like a cat. At Lopepe a lioness sprang on the after quarter of Mr Oswell's horse, and when we came up to him we found the marks of the claws on the horse, and a scratch on Mr O's hand. The horse, on feeling the lion on him, sprang away, and the rider, caught by a wait-a-bit thorn, was brought to the ground and rendered insensible. His dogs saved him. Another English gentleman (Captain Codrington) was surprised in the same way, though not hunting the lion at the time, but turning round he shot him dead in the neck. By accident a horse belonging to Codrington ran away, but was stopped by the bridle catching a stump; there he remained a prisoner two days, and when found the whole space around was marked by the footprints of lions. They had evidently been afraid to attack the haltered horse from fear that it was a trap. Two lions came up by night to within three yards of oxen tied to a wagon, and a sheep tied to a tree, and stood roaring, but afraid to make a spring. On another occasion one of our party was lying sound asleep and unconscious of danger between two natives behind a bush at Mashue; the fire was nearly out at their feet in consequence of all being completely tired out by the fatigues of the previous day; a lion came up to within three yards of the fire, and there commenced roaring instead of making a spring: the fact of their riding-ox being tied to the bush was the only reason the lion had for not following his instinct, and making a meal of flesh. He then stood on a knoll three hundred yards distant, and roared all night and continued his growling as the party moved off by daylight next morning.

Nothing that I ever learned of the lion would lead me to attribute to it either the ferocious or noble character ascribed to it elsewhere. It possesses none of the nobility of the Newfoundland or St Bernard dogs. With respect to its great strength there can be no doubt. The immense masses of muscle around its jaws, shoulders and forearms proclaim tremendous force. They would seem, however, to be inferior in power to those of the Indian tiger. Most of those feats of strength that I have seen performed by lions, such as the taking away of an ox, were not carrying, but dragging or trailing the carcass along the ground: they have sprung on some occasions onto the hindquarters of a horse, but no one has ever seen them on the withers of a giraffe. They do not mount on the hindquarters of an eland even, but try to tear him down with their claws. Messrs Oswell and Vardon once saw three lions endeavouring to drag down a buffalo, and they were unable to do so for a time, though he was then mortally wounded by a two-ounce ball.

In general the lion seizes the animal he is attacking by the flank near the hind leg, or by the throat below the jaw. It is questionable whether he ever attempts to seize an animal by the withers. The flank is the most common point of attack, and that is the part he begins to feast on first. The natives and lions are very similar in their tastes in the selection of tit-bits: an eland may be seen disembowelled by a lion so completely that he scarcely seems cut up at all. The bowels and fatty parts form a full meal for even the largest lion. The jackal comes sniffing about, and sometimes suffers for his temerity by a stroke from the lion's paw laying him dead. When gorged, the lion falls fast asleep, and is then easily dispatched. Hunting a lion with dogs involves very little danger as compared with hunting the Indian tiger, because the dogs bring him out of cover and make him stand at bay, giving the hunter plenty of time for a good deliberate shot.

Where game is abundant, there you may expect lions in proportionately large numbers. They are never seen in herds, but six or eight, probably one family, occasionally hunt together.

One is in much more danger of being run over when walking in the streets of London than he is of being devoured by lions in Africa, unless engaged in hunting the animal. Indeed, nothing that I have seen or heard about lions would constitute a barrier in the way of men of ordinary courage and enterprise.

The same feeling which has induced the modern painter to caricature the lion has led the sentimentalist to consider the lion's roar the most terrific of all earthly sounds. We hear of the 'majestic roar of the king of beasts'. It is, indeed, well calculated to inspire fear if you hear it in combination with the tremendously loud thunder of that country, on a night so pitchy dark that every flash of the intensely vivid lightning leaves you with the impression of stone-blindness, while the rain pours down so fast that your fire goes out, leaving you without the protection of even a tree, or the chance of your gun going off. But when you are in a comfortable house or wagon, the case is very different, and you hear the roar of the lion without any awe or alarm. The silly ostrich makes a noise as loud, yet he never was feared by man. To talk of the majestic roar of the lion is mere majestic twaddle. On my mentioning this fact some years ago, the assertion was doubted, so I have been careful ever since to inquire the opinions of Europeans, who have heard both, if they could detect any difference between the roar of a lion and that of an ostrich; the invariable answer was that they could not when the animal was at any distance. The natives assert that they can detect a variation between the commencement of the noise of each. There is, it must be admitted, considerable difference between the singing noise of a lion when full, and his deep, gruff growl when hungry. In general the lion's voice seems to come deeper from the chest than that of the ostrich, but to this day I can distinguish between them with certainty only by knowing that the ostrich roars by day and the lion by night.

The African lion is of a tawny colour, like that of some

mastiffs. The mane in the male is large, and gives the idea of great power. In some lions the ends of the hair of the mane are black; these go by the name of black-maned lions, though as a whole all look of the yellow tawny colour. At the time of the discovery of the lake, Messrs Oswell and Wilson shot two specimens of another variety. One was an old lion, whose teeth were mere stumps, and his claws worn quite blunt; the other was full grown, in the prime of life, with white, perfect teeth; both were entirely destitute of mane. The lions in the country near the lake give tongue less than those further south. We scarcely ever heard them roar at all.

The lion has other checks on inordinate increase besides man. He seldom attacks full-grown animals; but frequently, when a buffalo calf is caught by him, the cow rushes to the rescue, and a toss from her often kills him. One we found was killed thus; and on the Leeambye another, which died near Sesheke, had all the appearance of having received his death-blow from a buffalo. It is questionable if a single lion ever attacks a full-grown buffalo. The amount of roaring heard at night on occasions when a buffalo is killed seems to indicate there are always more than one lion engaged in the onslaught.

On the plain, south of Sebituane's ford, a herd of buffaloes kept a number of lions from their young by the males turning their heads to the enemy. The young and the cows were in the rear. One toss from a bull would kill the strongest lion that ever breathed. I have been informed that in one part of India even the tame buffaloes feel their superiority to some wild animals, for they have been seen to chase a tiger up the hills, bellowing as if they enjoyed the sport. Lions never go near any elephants except the calves, which, when young, are sometimes torn by them; every living thing retires before the lordly elephant, yet a full-grown one would be an easier prey than the rhinoceros; the lion rushes off at the mere sight of this latter beast.

JACK LONDON
INTRODUCTION

'It began in the swimming pool in Glen Ellen,' Jack London recalled of his 1907 voyage from San Francisco to Australia. Glen Ellen, London's sprawling Sonoma County ranch, was a rich man's obsession; the *Snark*, the 40ft ketch he constructed for the expedition, became another.

The build (the boat took its name from Lewis Carroll's *The Hunting of the Snark*) began in 1906, and London, a wealthy man, spared no expense. 'The bathroom,' he wrote, 'is small and compact but a beautiful dream of schemes and devices, pumps and levers.' Of the lifeboat, 'ours...was stipulated to cost one hundred and fifty dollars, and when I came to pay the bill, it turned out to be three hundred and ninety-five dollars.' Nautical largesse, he concluded, 'beats life insurance'. He even contemplated installing an ice machine. 'Ice in the tropics,' London said, 'is more necessary than bread.'

The *Snark* departed San Francisco on 23 April, with London, his wife Charmian and a small crew on board. London's pedigree as a sailor was genuine. In 1889, aged just 13, he bought a sloop with borrowed money and, briefly, became an 'oyster pirate', a term he coined to describe poaching in the Bay Area. The young London was incensed by the state's sale of previously public fisheries, an early example of his social activism. A few years later, London signed on with the California Fish Patrol, now the California Department of Fish and Wildlife. In 1893, aged 17, he piloted a schooner through a typhoon off the coast of Japan. In *Snark*, London calls that 'the proudest achievement of my life, my moment of highest living...with my own hands I had done my trick at the wheel and guided a hundred tons of wood and iron through a few million tonnes of wind and waves'.

The Cruise of the Snark is compelling despite its truncated plot, a result of the mishaps that bedevilled the journey. Money, it seemed, was no guarantee of quality. 'Seventy horsepower our engine is,' London boasted of the specification, 'and we do not know of a river with a current strong enough to defy us.' Once in the open ocean, however, said engine 'broke away from its shattered foundations, reared up in the air and smashed all connections and fastenings'. Repairs were costly.

At sea once more, it transpired that the seafaring skills of Roscoe Eames, Charmian's uncle and the navigator on the trip, were not as advertised. 'He was a San Francisco Bay yachtsman,' London discovered, 'where land is always only several miles away and the art of navigation is never employed.' That they made it as far as Hawaii was a minor miracle. Hounded once more by creditors, it was at Waikiki beach that London turned to 'surf-riding' to unwind. His account, featured in the extract here, is a call to arms, an encouragement to the everyman and -woman to seize new experiences.

The *Snark* docked next at Molokai, where London spent a week's residence at the island's leper colony. His report on the humane conditions did much to alter perceptions of the disease. Then on to Tahiti, south of the Marquesas Islands, then Bora Bora, in search of bonefish. In the Solomon Islands, their next port of call, London contracted yaws, a bacterial skin infection that caused the crew, by going ashore, to break local quarantine laws – and which necessitated the Londons' premature return to the US in 1909. The press framed the voyage as a folly. For all the upsets, however, both London and Charmian adored the *Snark*, and the voyage captures perfectly London's dedication to adventure.

THE CRUISE OF THE SNARK
BY JACK LONDON

That is what it is, a royal sport for the natural kings of earth. The grass grows right down to the water at Waikiki Beach, and within fifty feet of the everlasting sea. The trees also grow down to the salty edge of things, and one sits in their shade and looks seaward at a majestic surf thundering in on the beach to one's very feet. Half a mile out, where is the reef, the white-headed combers thrust suddenly skyward out of the placid turquoise blue and come rolling in to shore. One after another they come, a mile long, with smoking crests, the white battalions of the infinite army of the sea. And one sits and listens to the perpetual roar, and watches the unending procession and feels tiny and fragile before this tremendous force expressing itself in fury and foam and sound. Indeed, one feels microscopically small, and the thought that one may wrestle with this sea raises in one's imagination a thrill of apprehension, almost of fear. Why, they are a mile long, these bull-mouthed monsters, and they weigh a thousand tons, and they charge in to shore faster than a man can run. What chance? No chance at all, is the verdict of the shrinking ego; and one sits, and looks, and listens and thinks the grass and the shade are a pretty good place in which to be.

And suddenly, out there where a big smoker lifts skyward, rising like a sea god from out of the welter of spume and churning white, on the giddy, toppling, overhanging and downfalling, precarious crest appears the dark head of a man. Swiftly he rises through the rushing white. His black shoulders, his chest, his loins, his limbs – all is abruptly projected on one's vision. Where but the moment before was only the wide desolation and invincible roar is now a man, erect, full statured, not struggling frantically in that wild movement, not buried and crushed and buffeted by those mighty monsters, but standing above them all, calm and superb, poised on the giddy summit, his feet buried in the churning foam, the salt smoke rising to his knees, and all the rest of him in the free air and flashing sunlight, and he is flying through the air, flying forward, flying fast as the surge on which he stands. He is a Mercury – a brown Mercury. His heels are winged, and in them is the swiftness of the sea. In truth, from out of the sea he has leaped upon the back of the sea, and he is riding the sea that roars and bellows and cannot shake him from its back. But no frantic outreaching and balancing is his. He is impassive, motionless as a statue carved suddenly by some miracle out of the sea's depth from which he rose. And straight on toward shore he flies on his winged heels and the white crest of the breaker. There is a wild burst of foam, a long tumultuous rushing sound as the breaker falls futile and spent on the beach at your feet; and there at your feet steps calmly ashore a Kanaka, burnt, golden and brown by the tropic sun. Several minutes ago he was a speck a quarter of a mile away. He has 'bitted the bull-mouthed breaker' and ridden it in, and the pride in the feat shows in the carriage of his magnificent body as he glances for a moment carelessly at you who sit in the shade of the shore. He is a Kanaka – and more, he is a man, a member of the kingly species that has mastered matter and the brutes and lorded it over creation.

It is all very well sitting here in cool shade of the beach, but you are a man, one of the kingly species, and what that Kanaka can do, you can do yourself. Go to. Strip off your clothes that are a nuisance in this mellow clime. Get in and wrestle with the sea; wing your heels with the skill and power that reside in you; bit the sea's breakers, master them and ride upon their backs as a king should.

And that is how it came about that I tackled surf-riding. And now that I have tackled it, more than ever do I hold it to be a royal sport. But first let me explain the physics of it. A wave is a communicated agitation. The water that composes the body of a wave does not move. If it did, when a stone is thrown into a pond and the ripples spread away in an ever-widening circle, there would appear at the centre an ever-increasing hole. No, the water that composes the body of a wave is stationary. Thus, you may watch a particular portion of the ocean's surface and you will see the sane water rise and fall a thousand times to the agitation communicated by a thousand successive waves. Now imagine this communicated agitation moving shoreward. As the bottom shoals, the lower portion of the wave strikes land first and is stopped. But water is fluid, and the upper portion has not struck anything, wherefore it keeps on communicating its agitation, keeps on going. And when the top of the wave keeps on going, while the bottom of it lags behind, something is bound to happen. The bottom of the wave drops out from under and the top of the wave falls over, forward and down, curling and cresting and roaring as it does so. It is the bottom of a wave striking against the top of the land that is the cause of all surfs.

But the transformation from a smooth undulation to a breaker is not abrupt except where the bottom shoals abruptly. Say the bottom shoals gradually for from quarter of a mile to a mile, then an equal distance will be occupied by the transformation. Such a bottom is that off the beach of Waikiki, and it produces a splendid surf-riding surf. One leaps upon the back of a breaker just as it begins to break, and stays on it as it continues to break all the way in to shore.

And now to the particular physics of surf-riding. Get out on a flat board, six feet long, two feet wide, and roughly oval in shape. Lie down upon it like a small boy on a coaster and paddle with your hands out to deep water, where the waves begin to crest. Lie out there quietly on the board. Sea after sea breaks before, behind, and under and over you, and rushes in to shore, leaving you behind. When a wave crests, it gets steeper. Imagine yourself, on your board, on the face of that steep slope. If it stood still, you would slide down just as a boy slides down a hill on his coaster. 'But,' you object, 'the wave doesn't stand still.' Very true, but the water composing the wave stands still, and there you have the secret. If ever you start sliding down the face of that wave, you'll keep on sliding and you'll never reach the bottom. Please don't laugh. The face of that wave may be only six feet, yet you can slide down it a quarter of a mile, or half a mile, and not reach the bottom. For, see, since a wave is only a communicated agitation or impetus, and since the water that composes a wave is changing every instant, new water is rising into the wave as fast as the wave travels. You slide down this new water, and yet remain in your old position on the wave, sliding down the still newer water that is rising and forming the wave. You slide precisely as fast as the wave travels. If it travels fifteen miles an hour, you slide fifteen miles an hour. Between you and shore stretches a quarter of mile of water. As the wave travels, this water obligingly heaps itself into the wave, gravity does the rest and down you go, sliding the whole length of it. If you still cherish the notion, while sliding, that the water is moving with you, thrust your arms into it and attempt to paddle; you will find that you have to be remarkably quick to get a stroke, for that water is dropping astern just as fast as you are rushing ahead.

And now for another phase of the physics of surf-riding. All rules have their exceptions. It is true that the water in a wave does not travel forward. But there is what may be called the send of the sea. The water in the overtoppling crest does move forward, as you will speedily realise if you are slapped in the face by it, or if you are caught under it and are pounded by one mighty blow down under the surface, panting and gasping for half a minute. The water in the top of a wave rests upon the water in the bottom of the wave. But when the bottom of the wave strikes the land, it stops, while the top goes on. It no longer has the bottom of the wave to hold it up. Where was solid water beneath it is now air, and for the first time it feels the grip of gravity, and down it falls, at the same time being torn asunder from the lagging bottom of the wave and flung forward. And it is because of this that riding a surfboard is something more than a mere placid sliding down a hill. In truth, one is caught up and hurled shoreward as by some Titan's hand.

I deserted the cool shade, put on a swimming suit and got hold of a surfboard. It was too small a board. But I didn't know, and nobody told me. I joined some little Kanaka boys in shallow water, where the breakers were well spent and small – a regular kindergarten school. I watched the little Kanaka boys. When a likely-looking breaker came along, they flopped upon their stomachs on their boards, kicked like mad with their feet and rode the breaker in to the beach. I tried to emulate them. I watched them, tried to do everything that they did and failed utterly. The breaker swept past, and I was not on it. I tried again and again. I kicked twice as madly as they did, and failed. Half a dozen would be around. We would all leap on our boards in front of a good breaker. Away our feet would churn like the stern-wheels of river steamboats, and away the little rascals would scoot while I remained in disgrace behind.

I tried for a solid hour, and not one wave could I persuade to boost me shoreward. And then arrived a friend, Alexander Hume Ford, a globetrotter by profession, bent ever on the pursuit of sensation. And he had found it at Waikiki. Heading for Australia, he had stopped off for a week to find out if there were any thrills in surf-riding, and he had become wedded to it. He had been at it every day for a month and could not yet see any symptoms of the fascination lessening on him. He spoke with authority.

'Get off that board,' he said. 'Chuck it away at once. Look at the way you're trying to ride it. If ever the nose of that board hits bottom, you'll be disembowelled. Here, take my board. It's a man's size.'

I am always humble when confronted by knowledge. Ford knew. He showed me how properly to mount his board. Then he waited for a good breaker, gave me a shove at the right moment and started me in. Ah, delicious moment when I felt that breaker grip and fling me.

On I dashed, a hundred and fifty feet, and subsided with the breaker on the sand. From that moment I was lost. I waded back to Ford with his board. It was a large one, several inches thick, and weighed all of seventy-five pounds. He gave me advice, much of it. He had had no one to teach him, and all that he had laboriously learned in several weeks he communicated to me in half an hour. I really learned by proxy. And inside of half an hour I was able to start myself and ride in. I did it time after time, and Ford applauded and advised. For instance, he told me to get just so far forward on the board and no farther. But I must have got some farther, for as I came charging in to land, that miserable board poked its nose down to bottom, stopped abruptly and turned a somersault, at the same time violently severing our relations. I was tossed through the air like a chip and buried ignominiously under the downfalling breaker. And I realised that if it hadn't been for Ford, I'd have been disembowelled. That particular risk is part of the sport, Ford says. Maybe he'll have it happen to him before he leaves Waikiki, and then, I feel confident, his yearning for sensation will be satisfied for a time.

When all is said and done, it is my steadfast belief that homicide is worse than suicide, especially if, in the former case, it is a woman. Ford saved me from being a homicide. 'Imagine your legs are a rudder,' he said. 'Hold them close together, and steer with them.' A few minutes later I came charging in on a comber. As I neared the beach, there in the water, up to her waist, dead in front of me, appeared a woman. How was I to stop that comber on whose back I was? It looked like a dead woman. The board weighed seventy-five pounds, I weighed a hundred and sixty-five. The added weight had a velocity of fifteen miles per hour. The board and I constituted a projectile. I leave it to the physicists to figure out the force of the impact upon that poor, tender woman. And then I remembered my guardian angel, Ford. 'Steer with your legs!' rang through my brain. I steered with my legs, I steered sharply, abruptly, with all my legs and with all my might. The board sheered around broadside on the crest. Many things happened simultaneously. The wave gave me a passing buffet, a light tap as the taps of waves go, but a tap sufficient to knock me off the board and smash me down through the rushing water to bottom, with which I came in violent collision and upon which I was rolled over and over. I got my head out for a breath of air and then gained my feet. There stood the woman before me. I felt like a hero. I had saved her life. And she laughed at me. It was not hysteria. She had never dreamed of her danger. Anyway, I solaced myself, it was not I but Ford that saved her, and I didn't have to feel like a hero. And besides, that leg-steering was great. In a few minutes more of practice I was able to thread my way in and out past several bathers and to remain on top my breaker instead of going under it.

'Tomorrow,' Ford said, 'I am going to take you out into the blue water.'

I looked seaward where he pointed, and saw the great smoking combers that made the breakers I had been riding look like ripples. I don't know what I might have said had I not recollected just then that I was one of a kingly species. So all that I did say was, 'All right, I'll tackle them tomorrow.'

The water that rolls in on Waikiki Beach is just the same as the water that laves the shores of all the Hawaiian Islands; and in ways, especially from the swimmer's standpoint, it is wonderful water. It is cool enough to be comfortable while it is warm enough to permit a swimmer to stay in all day without experiencing a chill. Under the sun or the stars, at high noon or at midnight, in midwinter or in midsummer, it does not matter when it is always the same temperature – not too warm, not too cold, just right. It is wonderful water, salt as old ocean itself, pure and crystal clear. When the nature of the water is considered, it is not so remarkable after all that the Kanakas are one of the most expert of swimming races.

So it was, next morning, when Ford came along, that I plunged into the wonderful water for a swim of indeterminate length. Astride of our surfboards, or, rather, flat down upon them on our stomachs, we paddled out through the kindergarten where the little Kanaka boys were at play. Soon we were out in deep water where the big smokers came roaring in. The mere struggle with them, facing them and paddling seaward over them and through them, was sport enough in itself. One had to have his wits about him, for it was a battle in which mighty blows were struck on one side, and in which cunning was used on the other side – a struggle between insensate force and intelligence. I soon learned a bit. When a breaker curled over my head, for a swift instant I could see the light of day through its emerald body; then down would go my head, and I would clutch the board with all my strength. Then would come the blow, and to the onlooker on shore I would be blotted out. In reality the board and I have passed through the crest and emerged in the respite of the other side. I should not recommend those smashing blows to an invalid or delicate person. There is weight behind them, and the impact of the driven water is like a sandblast. Sometimes one passes through half a dozen combers in quick succession, and it is just about that time that he is liable to discover new merits in the stable land and new reasons for being on shore.

Out there in the midst of such a succession of big smoky ones, a third man was added to our party, one Freeth. Shaking the water from my eyes as I emerged from one wave and peered ahead to see what the next one looked like, I saw him tearing in on the back of it, standing upright on his board, carelessly poised, a young god bronzed with sunburn. We went through the wave on the back of which he rode. Ford called to him. He turned an airspring from his wave, rescued his board from its maw, paddled over to us and joined Ford in showing me things. One thing in particular I learned from Freeth, namely, how to encounter the occasional breaker of exceptional size that rolled in. Such breakers were really ferocious, and it was unsafe to meet them on top of the board. But Freeth showed me, so that whenever I saw one of that calibre rolling down on me, I slid off the rear end of the board and dropped down beneath the surface, my arms over my head and holding the board. Thus, if the wave ripped the board out of my hands and tried to strike me with it (a common trick of such waves), there would be a cushion of water a foot or more in depth between my head and the blow. When the wave passed, I climbed upon the board and paddled on. Many men have been terribly injured, I learn, by being struck by their boards.

The whole method of surf-riding and surf-fighting, learned, is one of non-resistance. Dodge the blow that is struck at you. Dive through the wave that is trying to slap you in the face. Sink down, feet first, deep under the surface, and let the big smoker that is trying to smash you go by far overhead. Never be rigid. Relax. Yield yourself to the waters that are ripping and tearing at you. When the undertow catches you and drags you seaward along the bottom, don't struggle against it. If you do, you are liable to be drowned, for it is stronger than you. Yield yourself to that undertow. Swim with it, not against it, and you will find the pressure removed. And, swimming with it, fooling it so that it does not hold you, swim upward at the same time. It will be no trouble at all to reach the surface.

The man who wants to learn surf-riding must be a strong swimmer, and he must be used to going under the water. After that, fair strength and common sense are all that is required. The force of the big comber is rather unexpected. There are mix-ups in which board and rider are torn apart and separated by several hundred feet. The surf-rider must take care of himself. No matter how many riders swim out with him, he cannot depend upon any of them for aid. The fancied security I had in the presence of Ford and Freeth made me forget that it was my first swim out in deep water among the big ones. I recollected, however, and rather suddenly, for a big wave came in, and away went the two men on its back all the way to shore. I could have been drowned a dozen different ways before they got back to me.

One slides down the face of a breaker on his surfboard, but he has to get started to sliding. Board and rider must be moving shoreward at a good rate before the wave overtakes them. When you see the wave coming that you want to ride in, you turn tail to it and paddle shoreward with all your strength, using what is called the windmill stroke. This is a sort of spurt performed immediately in front of the wave. If the board is going fast enough, the wave accelerates it, and the board begins its quarter-of-a-mile slide.

I shall never forget the first big wave I caught out there in the deep water. I saw it coming, turned my back on it and paddled for dear life. Faster and faster my board went, till it seemed my arms would drop off. What was happening behind me I could not tell. One cannot look behind and paddle the windmill stroke. I heard the crest of the wave hissing and churning, and then my board was lifted and flung forward. I scarcely knew what happened the first half-minute. Though I kept my eyes open, I could not see anything, for I was buried in the rushing white of the crest. But I did not mind. I was chiefly conscious of ecstatic bliss at having caught the wave. At the end of the half-minute, however, I began to see things, and to breathe. I saw that three feet of the nose of my board was clear out of water and riding on the air. I shifted my weight forward and made the nose come down. Then I lay, quite at rest in the midst of the wild movement, and watched the shore and the bathers on the beach grow distinct. I didn't cover quite a quarter of a mile on that wave because, to prevent the board from diving, I shifted my weight back, but shifted it too far and fell down the rear slope of the wave. It was my second day at surf-riding, and I was quite proud of myself. I stayed out there four hours, and when it was over, I was resolved that on the morrow I'd come in standing up. Upon one thing I am resolved: the *Snark* shall not sail from Honolulu until I too wing my heels with the swiftness of the sea, and become a sunburnt, skin-peeling Mercury.

LADY MARY WORTLEY MONTAGU
INTRODUCTION

Lady Mary Wortley Montagu was well connected even as a child. In 1696, aged just seven, she was selected as a mascot for the Kit-Kat Club, an influential London gentlemen's club comprising politicians, writers and thinkers committed to a Protestant line of succession. (And who spent most of their time drinking toasts to mascots.)

She made her name as a writer thanks to the publication of her personal correspondence. Written to 'persons of distinction and men of letters', these were mostly fellow bluebloods, literary figures and senior churchmen. One regular correspondent was the satirist Alexander Pope. Their epistolary relationship was notable for its blend of gossip and high-minded meditations, Montagu engaging Pope as a sounding board for her various enquiries on the classics, on art and sculpture but also on the nature of love. It was the last of these that led Pope to suspect he held a place in her affections. In England, however, and in person, Lady Montagu rejected his advances. An embittered Pope dedicated a significant part of his literary output thereafter to casting slights on her character.

The most well known of her collections is *Letters from Turkey* (1725), a title that marks the first study of the East focusing on society rather than religion; the fact it was published by a woman, given the prevailing attitudes of the time, makes it all the more impressive.

Lady Montagu travelled to Istanbul with her husband, Edward Wortley Montagu, following his appointment in 1716 as British Ambassador to Turkey. They travelled overland, through Austria, Hungary and the Balkans, time that allowed Lady Montagu to indulge her passion for people-watching. In Turkey, and later the wider Ottoman Empire, she chronicled local customs exhaustively, and those of wealthy women in particular. This was thanks to the access she was granted to zenanas – intimate, private spaces from which men were banned, such as women-only Turkish baths.

One custom in particular, children's inoculations against smallpox, provided the most important legacy of her travels. The disease accounted for the deaths of 10% of the British population, and it had marred Lady Montagu's life. One of her brothers, aged 20, died of smallpox, leaving behind a wife and two children. Lady Montagu herself contracted smallpox in 1715, and though she survived, feared the scarring to her face had damaged her looks. (Lady Montagu was regarded as something of a society beauty.)

It was her fears for her own children that led Lady Montagu to promote smallpox inoculation, known as variolation, on her return to England in 1718. She was prepared to stand by what she believed in after having witnessed a child being inoculated against the disease. Shortly before her family's homecoming, Lady Montagu's four-year-old son, Edward, had been vaccinated in Istanbul by the embassy surgeon, Charles Maitland. The procedure was repeated on Montagu's daughter, also Mary, three years later, in 1721.

Western physicians were dismissive of variolation, considering the practice little more than Eastern superstition. An important ally was the Princess of Wales, later Queen Caroline, whose own daughters were inoculated the following year, in 1722. The princess and Lady Montagu exchanged frequent letters during the Montagus' travels in the Ottoman Empire; as the extract here shows, Lady Montagu considered herself something of a special rapporteur for the royal household.

A safer form of smallpox inoculation was later invented by the physician Edward Jenner, and went into widespread use around 1840. Lady Montagu would have been thrilled.

THE LETTERS OF
LADY MARY WORTLEY MONTAGU

LETTER XXV

To Her R. H. The Princess of Wales
Adrianople, 1 April, 1717

I have now, Madam, finished a journey that has not been undertaken by any Christian since the time of the Greek emperors: and I shall not regret all the fatigues I have suffered in it if it gives me an opportunity of amusing Your R. H. by an account of places utterly unknown amongst us; the emperor's ambassadors, and those few English that have come hither, always going on the Danube to Nicopolis. But the river was now frozen, and Mr W—— [Wortley Montagu] was so zealous for the service of His Majesty that he would not defer his journey to wait for the convenience of that passage. We crossed the deserts of Servia, almost quite overgrown with wood, through a country naturally fertile. The inhabitants are industrious; but the oppression of the peasants is so great, they are forced to abandon their houses, and neglect their tillage, all they have being a prey to the janizaries whenever they please to seize upon it. We had a guard of five hundred of them, and I was almost in tears every day to see their insolencies in the poor villages through which we passed. After seven days travelling through thick woods, we came to Nissa, once the capital of Servia, situated in a fine plain on the River

Nissava, in a very good air, and so fruitful a soil, that the great plenty is hardly credible. I was certainly assured that the quantity of wine last vintage was so prodigious that they were forced to dig holes in the earth to put it in, not having vessels enough in the town to hold it. The happiness of this plenty is scarce perceived by the oppressed people. I saw here a new occasion for my compassion. The wretches that had provided twenty wagons for our baggage from Belgrade hither for a certain hire, being all sent back without payment, some of their horses lamed, and others killed, without any satisfaction made for them. The poor fellows came round the house weeping and tearing their hair and beards in a most pitiful manner without getting anything but drubs from the insolent soldiers. I cannot express to Your R. H. how much I was moved at this scene. I would have paid them the money out of my own pocket with all my heart; but it would only have been giving so much to the aga, who would have taken it from them without any remorse. After four days' journey from this place over the mountains, we came to Sophia, situated in a large beautiful plain on the River Isca, and surrounded with distant mountains. 'Tis hardly possible to see a more agreeable landscape. The city itself is very large, and extremely populous. Here are hot baths, very famous for their medicinal virtues.

Four days journey from hence we arrived at Philippopolis, after having passed the ridges between the mountains of Haemus and Rhodope, which are always covered with snow. This town is situated on a rising ground near the river Hebrus, and is almost wholly inhabited by Greeks; here are still some ancient Christian churches. They have a bishop; and several of the richest Greeks live here; but they are forced to conceal their wealth with great care, the appearance of poverty (which includes part of its inconveniences) being all their security against feeling it in earnest. The country from hence to Adrianople is the finest in the world. Vines grow wild on all the hills; and the perpetual spring they enjoy makes everything gay and flourishing. But this climate, happy as it seems, can never be preferred to England, with all its frosts and snows, while we are blessed with an easy government, under a king who makes his own happiness consist in the liberty of his people, and chooses rather to be looked upon as their father than their master. This theme would carry me very far, and I am sensible; I have already tired out Your R. H.'s patience. But my letter is in your hands, and you may make it as short as you please by throwing it into the fire when weary of reading it.

LETTER XXX

To Mr Pope
Adrianople, 1 April, 1717

I dare say you expect, at least, something very new in this letter after I have gone a journey not undertaken by any Christian for some hundred years. The most remarkable accident that happened to me was my being very near overturned into the Hebrus; and, if I had much regard for the glories that one's name enjoys after death, I should certainly be sorry for having missed the romantic conclusion of swimming down the same river in which the musical head of Orpheus repeated verses so many ages since.

I am at this present moment writing in a house situated on the banks of the Hebrus, which runs under my chamber window. My garden is full of all cypress trees, upon the branches of which several couple of true turtles are saying soft things to one another from morning till night. How naturally do boughs and vows come into my mind at this minute? and must not you confess, to my praise, that 'tis more than an ordinary discretion that can resist the wicked suggestions of poetry in a place where truth, for once, furnishes all the ideas of pastoral. The summer is already far advanced in this part of the world; and, for some miles round

Adrianople, the whole ground is laid out in gardens, and the banks of the rivers are set with rows of fruit trees under which all the most considerable Turks divert themselves every evening, not with walking; that is not one of their pleasures; but a set party of them choose out a green spot where the shade is very thick, and there they spread a carpet on which they sit drinking their coffee, and are generally attended by some slave with a fine voice, or that plays on some instrument. Every twenty paces you may see one of these little companies listening to the dashing of the river; and this taste is so universal, that the very gardeners are not without it. I have often seen them and their children sitting on the banks of the river, and playing on a rural instrument, perfectly answering the description of the ancient fistula, being composed of unequal reeds, with a simple but agreeable softness in the sound.

Mr. Addison might here make the experiment he speaks of in his travels; there not being one instrument of music among the Greek or Roman statues that is not to be found in the hands of the people of this country. The young lads generally divert themselves with making garlands for their favourite lambs, which I have often seen painted and adorned with flowers, lying at their feet while they sung or played. It is not that they ever read romances, but these are the ancient amusements here, and as natural to them as cudgel-playing and football to our British swains; the softness and warmth of the climate forbidding all rough exercises, which were never so much as heard of amongst them, and naturally inspiring a laziness and aversion to labour, which the great plenty indulges. These gardeners are the only happy race of country people in Turkey. They furnish all the city with fruits and herbs, and seem to live very easily. They are most of them Greeks, and have little houses in the midst of their gardens, where their wives and daughters take a liberty not permitted in the town, I mean, to go unveiled. These wenches are very neat and handsome, and pass their time at their looms under the shade of the trees.

I no longer look upon Theocritus as a romantic writer; he has only given a plain image of the way of life amongst the peasants of his country, who, before oppression had reduced them to want, were, I suppose, all employed as the better sort of them are now. I don't doubt, had he been born a Briton, but his Idyliums had been filled with descriptions of threshing and churning, both which are unknown here, the corn being all trod out by oxen; and butter (I speak it with sorrow) unheard of.

I read over your Homer here with an infinite pleasure, and find several little passages explained that I did not before entirely comprehend the beauty of; many of the customs, and much of the dress then in fashion, being yet retained. I don't wonder to find more remains here of an age so distant than is to be found in any other country, the Turks not taking that pains to introduce their own manners, as has been generally practised by other nations, that imagine themselves more polite. It would be too tedious to you to point out all the passages that relate to present customs. But I can assure you that the princesses and great ladies pass their time at their looms embroidering veils and robes, surrounded by their maids, which are always very numerous, in the same manner as we find Andromache and Helen described. The description of the belt of Menelaus exactly resembles those that are now worn by the great men, fastened before with broad golden clasps, and embroidered round with rich work. The snowy veil that Helen throws over her face is still fashionable; and I never see half a dozen of old bashaws (as I do very often) with their reverend beards sitting basking in the sun, but I recollect good King Priam and his counsellors. Their manner of dancing is certainly the same that Diana is said to have danced on the banks of Eurotas. The great lady still leads the dance, and is followed by a troop of young girls who imitate her steps and, if she sings, make up the chorus. The tunes are extremely gay and lively, yet with something in them wonderfully soft. The steps are varied according to the pleasure of her that leads the dance, but always in exact time, and infinitely more agreeable than any of our dances, at least in my opinion. I sometimes make one in the train, but am not skilful enough to lead; these are the Grecian dances, the Turkish being very different.

I should have told you in the first place that the Eastern manners give a great light into many scripture passages that appear odd to us, their phrases being commonly what we should call scripture language. The vulgar Turk is very different from what is spoke at court, or amongst the people of figure, who always mix so much Arabic and Persian in their discourse that it may very well be called another language. And 'tis as ridiculous to make use of the expressions commonly used in speaking to a great man or lady, as it would be to speak accents of broad Yorkshire or Somersetshire in the drawing room. Besides this distinction, they have what they call the sublime, that is, a style proper for poetry, and which is the exact scripture style. I believe you will be pleased to see a genuine example of this; and I am very glad I have it in my power to satisfy your curiosity by sending you a faithful copy of the verses that Ibrahim Bassa, the reigning favourite, has made for the young princess, his contracted wife, whom he is not yet permitted to visit without witnesses, though she is gone home to his house. He is a man of wit and learning; and whether or no he is capable of writing good verse, you may be sure that, on such an occasion, he would not want the assistance of the best poets in the empire. Thus the verses may be looked upon as a sample of their finest poetry; and I don't doubt you'll be of my mind that it is most wonderfully resembling The Song of Solomon, which was also addressed to a royal bride.

JOHN MUIR
INTRODUCTION

John Muir's work changed the way Americans thought about nature. The son of a Presbyterian minister, Muir was born in 1838 in Dunbar, in south-east Scotland. The family immigrated to the state of Wisconsin in the US in 1849. It was during his time at the University of Wisconsin–Madison that Muir first took an interest in botany. An incurable restlessness meant he failed to graduate, so Muir instead decided upon a tour of North America: Michigan, Indiana, Ontario and New York. In 1868 he visited Cuba, sailing for San Francisco on his return. Muir's first visit to Yosemite that same year was the start of a lifelong love affair that would help drive his founding of the Sierra Club, one of America's leading conservation organisations. *My First Summer in the Sierra* is a memoir of his time employed to shepherd a flock from the lowlands of the San Joaquin Valley to the relative cool of the California uplands in Yosemite's Tuolumne Meadows. What the book became, however, was a timeless hymn to the breathtaking majesty of the area and the delicate beauty of its flora and fauna. In the book, Muir's duties as a shepherd remain unclear. Narrative steps aside for the most part to be replaced by a kind of lyrical poetry.

Muir was a man of science who believed in God. An early adopter of the theory that mountains were shaped by glaciation, he held also that there was little need to build cathedrals when Nature herself had created such amphitheatres of wonder. 'We are now in the mountains,' he wrote upon reaching the Sierra Nevadas, 'and they are in us, kindling enthusiasm, making every nerve quiver, filling every pore and cell of us. Our flesh-and-bone tabernacle seems transparent as glass to the beauty about us, as if truly an inseparable part of it...a part of all nature, neither old nor young, sick nor well, but immortal.'

His writing inspired millions of American to visit the area, among them President Theodore Roosevelt, who arrived in Yosemite in 1903, famously slipped his escort and went camping with Muir. Roosevelt subsequently established America's first national monuments, eighteen in total, and, through the continual lobbying of Congress, five national parks: in addition to Yosemite and Sequoia in California, the Grand Canyon and Petrified Forest in Arizona and Mt. Rainier in Washington.

The documentary-maker Ken Burns believes Muir should be considered one of the foremost Americans, inducted into 'the pantheon of the highest individuals in our country' and ranked among the likes of Abraham Lincoln, Thomas Jefferson and Jackie Robinson. Muir is, rightly, acknowledged as the father of American conservation, and believed the only way to truly experience nature was to walk through it. 'How fresh the woods are and calm after the last films of clouds have been wiped from the sky,' he wrote. 'A few minutes ago every tree was excited, bowing to the roaring storm, waving, swirling, tossing their branches in glorious enthusiasm like worship. But though to the outer ear these trees are now silent, their songs never cease. Every hidden cell is throbbing with music and life, every fibre thrilling like harp strings, while incense is ever flowing from the balsam bells and leaves.'

The 211-mile (340 km) John Muir Trail, which runs from Yosemite to the summit of Mount Whitney, was inaugurated in 1938, exactly 100 years after Muir's death. In the 1950s, Muir's Sierra Club was also responsible for the creation of the Yosemite Decimal Rating System, which grades the difficulty of walks and climbs in the US from easy strolls to technical ascents.

In the ongoing debates around climate change, not least the issue of water in his adopted California, Muir is quoted at length and often, and has proved an inspiration to the likes of Ansel Adams and Barack Obama. Regularly dubbed a 'prophet' of the wilderness, Muir believed in the interconnectedness of the natural world, and his travels were always an attempt to reach closer into its heart.

MY FIRST SUMMER IN THE SIERRA
BY JOHN MUIR

July 16. My enjoyments yesterday afternoon, especially at the head of the fall, were too great for good sleep. Kept starting up last night in a nervous tremor, half awake, fancying that the foundation of the mountain we were camped on had given way and was falling into Yosemite Valley. In vain I roused myself to make a new beginning for sound sleep. The nerve strain had been too great, and again and again I dreamed I was rushing through the air above a glorious avalanche of water and rocks. One time, springing to my feet, I said, 'This time it is real all must die, and where could a mountaineer find a more glorious death!'

Left camp soon after sunrise for an all-day ramble eastward. Crossed the head of Indian Basin, forested with Abies magnifica, underbrush mostly Ceanothus cordulatus and manzanita, a mixture not easily trampled over or penetrated, for the ceanothus is thorny and grows in dense snow-pressed masses, and the manzanita has exceedingly crooked, stubborn branches. From the head of the cañon continued on past North Dome into the basin of Dome or Porcupine Creek. Here are many fine meadows imbedded in the woods, gay with Lilium parvum and its companions; the elevation, about eight thousand feet, seems to be best suited for it – saw specimens that were a foot or two higher than my head. Had more magnificent views of the upper mountains, and of the great South Dome, said to be the grandest rock in the world. Well it may be, since it is of such noble dimensions and sculpture. A wonderfully impressive monument, its lines exquisite in fineness, and though sublime in size, is finished like the finest work of art, and seems to be alive.

July 17. A new camp was made today in a magnificent silver fir grove at the head of a small stream that flows into Yosemite by way of Indian Cañon. Here we intend to stay several weeks, – a fine location from which to make excursions about the great valley and its fountains. Glorious days I'll have sketching, pressing plants, studying the wonderful topography and the wild animals, our happy fellow mortals and neighbours. But the vast mountains in the distance, shall I ever know them, shall I be allowed to enter into their midst and dwell with them?

We were pelted about noon by a short, heavy rainstorm, sublime thunder reverberating among the mountains and cañons, some strokes near, crashing, ringing in the tense crisp air with startling keenness, while the distant peaks loomed gloriously through the cloud fringes and sheets of rain. Now the storm is past, and the fresh washed air is full of the essences of the flower gardens and groves. Winter storms in Yosemite must be glorious. May I see them!

Have got my bed made in our new camp, – plushy, sumptuous and deliciously fragrant, most of it magnifica fir plumes, of course, with a variety of sweet flowers in the pillow. Hope to sleep tonight without tottering nerve-dreams. Watched a deer eating ceanothus leaves and twigs.

July 18. Slept pretty well; the valley walls did not seem to fall, though I still fancied myself at the brink, alongside the white, plunging flood, especially when half asleep. Strange the danger of that adventure should be more troublesome now that I am in the bosom of the peaceful woods, a mile or more from the fall, than it was while I was on the brink of it.

Bears seem to be common here, judging by their tracks. About noon we had another rainstorm with keen startling thunder, the metallic, ringing, clashing, clanging notes gradually fading into low bass rolling and muttering in the distance. For a few minutes the rain came in a grand torrent like a waterfall, then hail; some of the hailstones an inch in diameter, hard, icy and irregular in form, like those oftentimes seen in Wisconsin. Carlo watched them with intelligent astonishment as they came pelting and thrashing through the quivering branches of the trees. The cloud scenery sublime. Afternoon calm, sunful and clear, with delicious freshness and fragrance from the firs and flowers and steaming ground.

July 19. Watching the daybreak and sunrise. The pale rose and purple sky changing softly to daffodil yellow and white, sunbeams pouring through the passes between the peaks and over the Yosemite domes, making their edges burn; the silver firs in the middle ground catching the glow on their spiry tops, and our camp grove fills and thrills with the glorious light. Everything awakening alert and joyful; the birds begin to stir and innumerable insect people. Deer quietly withdraw into leafy hiding places in the chaparral; the dew vanishes, flowers spread their petals, every pulse beats high, every life cell rejoices, the very rocks seem to thrill with life. The whole landscape glows like a human face in a glory of enthusiasm, and the blue sky, pale around the horizon, bends peacefully down over all like one vast flower.

About noon, as usual, big bossy cumuli began to grow above the forest, and the rainstorm pouring from them is the most imposing I have yet seen. The silvery zigzag lightning lances are longer than usual, and the thunder gloriously impressive, keen, crashing, intensely concentrated, speaking with such tremendous energy it would seem that an entire mountain is being shattered at every stroke, but probably only a few trees are being shattered, many of which I have seen on my walks hereabouts strewing the ground. At last the clear ringing strokes are succeeded by deep low tones that grow gradually fainter as they roll afar into the recesses of the echoing mountains, where they seem to be welcomed home. Then another and another peal, or rather crashing, splintering stroke, follows in quick succession, perchance splitting some giant pine or fir from top to bottom into long rails and slivers, and scattering them to all points of the compass. Now comes the rain, with corresponding extravagant grandeur, covering the ground high and low with a sheet of flowing water, a transparent film fitted like a skin upon the rugged anatomy of the landscape, making the rocks glitter and glow, gathering in the ravines, flooding the streams and making them shout and boom in reply to the thunder.

How interesting to trace the history of a single raindrop! It is not long, geologically speaking, as we have seen, since the first raindrops fell on the newborn leafless Sierra landscapes. How different the lot of these falling now! Happy the showers that fall on so fair a wilderness, – scarce a single drop can fail to find a beautiful spot, – on the tops of the peaks, on the shining glacier pavements, on the great smooth domes, on forests and gardens and brushy moraines, plashing, glinting, pattering, laving. Some go to the high snowy fountains to swell their well-saved stores; some into the lakes, washing the mountain windows, patting their smooth glassy levels, making dimples and bubbles and spray; some into the waterfalls and cascades, as if eager to join in their dance and song and beat their foam yet finer; good luck and good work for the happy mountain raindrops, each one of them a high waterfall in itself, descending from the cliffs and hollows of the clouds to the cliffs and hollows of the rocks, out of the sky-thunder into the thunder of the falling rivers. Some, falling on meadows and bogs, creep silently out of sight to the grass roots, hiding softly as in a nest, slipping, oozing hither, thither, seeking and finding their appointed work. Some, descending through the spires of the woods, sift spray through the shining needles, whispering peace and good cheer to each one of them. Some drops with happy aim glint on the sides of crystals, – quartz, hornblende, garnet, zircon, tourmaline, feldspar, – patter on grains of gold and heavy way-worn nuggets; some, with blunt plap-plap and low bass drumming, fall on the broad leaves of veratrum, saxifrage, cypripedium. Some happy drops fall straight into the cups of flowers, kissing the lips of lilies. How far they have to go, how many cups to fill, great and small, cells too small to be seen, cups holding half a drop as well as lake basins between the hills, each replenished with equal care, every drop in all the blessed throng a silvery newborn star with lake and river, garden and grove, valley and mountain, all that the landscape holds reflected in its crystal depths, God's messenger, angel of love sent on its way with majesty and pomp and display of power that make man's greatest shows ridiculous.

Now the storm is over, the sky is clear, the last rolling thunder wave is spent on the peaks, and where are the raindrops now – what has become of all the shining throng? In winged vapour rising some are already hastening back to the sky, some have gone into the plants, creeping through invisible doors into the round rooms of cells, some are locked in crystals of ice, some in rock crystals, some in porous moraines to keep their small springs flowing, some have gone journeying on in the rivers to join the larger raindrop of the ocean. From form to form, beauty to beauty, ever changing, never resting, all are speeding on with love's enthusiasm, singing with the stars the eternal song of creation.

July 20. Fine calm morning; air tense and clear; not the slightest breeze astir; everything shining, the rocks with wet crystals, the plants with dew, each receiving its portion of irised dewdrops and sunshine like living creatures getting their breakfast, their dew manna coming down from the starry sky like swarms of smaller stars. How wondrous fine are the particles in showers of dew, thousands required for a single drop, growing in the dark as silently as the grass! What pains are taken to keep this wilderness in health, – showers of snow, showers of rain, showers of dew, floods of light, floods of invisible vapour, clouds, winds, all sorts of weather, interaction of plant on plant, animal on animal, etc., beyond thought! How fine Nature's methods! How deeply with beauty is beauty overlaid! The ground covered with crystals, the crystals with mosses and lichens and low-spreading grasses and flowers, these with larger plants leaf over leaf with ever-changing colour and form, the broad palms of the firs outspread over these, the azure dome over all like a bell-flower, and star above star.

Yonder stands the South Dome, its crown high above our camp, though its base is four thousand feet below us; a most noble rock, it seems full of thought, clothed with living light, no sense of dead stone about it, all spiritualized, neither heavy looking nor light, steadfast in serene strength like a god.

Our shepherd is a queer character and hard to place in this wilderness. His bed is a hollow made in red dry-rot punky dust beside a log which forms a portion of the south wall of the corral. Here he lies with his wonderful everlasting clothing on, wrapped in a red blanket, breathing not only the dust of the decayed wood but also that of the corral, as if determined to take ammoniacal snuff all night after chewing tobacco all day. Following the sheep, he carries a heavy six-shooter swung from his belt on one side and his luncheon on the other. The ancient cloth in which the meat, fresh from the frying pan, is tied serves as a filter through which the clear fat and gravy juices drip down on his right hip and leg in clustering stalactites. This oleaginous formation is soon broken up, however, and diffused and rubbed evenly into his scanty apparel by sitting down, rolling over, crossing his legs while resting on logs, etc., making shirt and trousers watertight and shiny. His trousers, in particular, have become so adhesive with the mixed fat and resin that pine needles, thin flakes and fibres of bark, hair, mica scales and minute grains of quartz, hornblende, etc., feathers, seed wings, moth and butterfly wings, legs and antennae of innumerable insects, or even whole insects such as the small beetles, moths and mosquitoes, with flower petals, pollen dust and indeed bits of all plants, animals and minerals of the region adhere to them and are safely imbedded, so that though far from being a naturalist he collects fragmentary specimens of everything and becomes richer than he knows. His specimens are kept passably fresh too by the purity of the air and the resiny bituminous beds into which they are pressed. Man is a microcosm, at least our shepherd is, or rather his trousers. These precious overalls are never taken off, and nobody knows how old they are, though one may guess by their thickness and concentric structure. Instead of wearing thin they wear thick, and in their stratification have no small geological significance.

Besides herding the sheep, Billy is the butcher, while I have agreed to wash the few iron and tin utensils and make the bread. Then, these small duties done, by the time the sun is fairly above the mountaintops I am beyond the flock, free to rove and revel in the wilderness all the big immortal days.

Sketching on the North Dome. It commands views of nearly all the valley besides a few of the high mountains. I would fain draw everything in sight – rock, tree and leaf. But little can I do beyond mere outlines, marks with meanings like words, readable only to myself, yet I sharpen my pencils and work on as if others might possibly be benefited. Whether these picture-sheets are to vanish like fallen leaves or go to friends like letters, matters not much; for little can they tell to those who have not themselves seen similar wildness, and like a language have learned it. No pain here, no dull empty hours, no fear of the past, no fear of the future. These blessed mountains are so compactly filled with God's beauty, no petty personal hope or experience has room to be. Drinking this champagne water is pure pleasure; so is breathing the living air, and every movement of limbs is pleasure, while the whole body seems to feel beauty when exposed to it as it feels the campfire or sunshine, entering not by the eyes alone, but equally through all one's flesh like radiant heat, making a passionate ecstatic pleasure glow not explainable. One's body then seems homogeneous throughout, sound as a crystal.

Perched like a fly on this Yosemite dome, I gaze and sketch and bask, oftentimes settling down into dumb admiration without definite hope of ever learning much, yet with the longing, unresting effort that lies at the door of hope, humbly prostrate before the vast display of God's power, and eager to offer self-denial and renunciation with eternal toil to learn any lesson in the divine manuscript.

It is easier to feel than to realize, or in any way explain, Yosemite grandeur. The magnitudes of the rocks and trees and streams are so delicately harmonized they are mostly hidden. Sheer precipices three thousand feet high are fringed with tall trees growing close like grass on the brow of a lowland hill, and extending along the feet of these precipices a ribbon of meadow a mile wide and seven or eight long that seems like a strip a farmer might mow in less than a day. Waterfalls, five hundred to one or two thousand feet high, are so subordinated to the mighty cliffs over which they pour that they seem like wisps of smoke, gentle as floating clouds, though their voices fill the valley and make the rocks tremble. The mountains too along the eastern sky, and the domes in front of them, and the succession of smooth rounded waves between, swelling higher, higher, with dark woods in their hollows, serene in massive exuberant bulk and beauty, tend yet more to hide the grandeur of the Yosemite temple and make it appear as a subdued subordinate feature of the vast harmonious landscape. Thus every attempt to appreciate any one feature is beaten down by the overwhelming influence of all the others. And, as if this were not enough, lo! in the sky arises another mountain range with topography as rugged and substantial-looking as the one beneath it – snowy peaks and domes and shadowy Yosemite valleys – another version of the snowy Sierra, a new creation heralded by a thunderstorm. How fiercely, devoutly wild is Nature in the midst of her beauty-loving tenderness! – painting lilies, watering them, caressing them with gentle hand, going from flower to flower like a gardener while building rock mountains and cloud mountains full of lightning and rain. Gladly we run for shelter beneath an overhanging cliff and examine the reassuring ferns and mosses, gentle love tokens growing in cracks and chinks. Daisies too and ivesias, confiding wild children of light, too small to fear. To these one's heart goes home, and the voices of the storm become gentle. Now the sun breaks forth and fragrant steam arises. The birds are out singing on the edges of the groves. The west is flaming in gold and purple, ready for the ceremony of the sunset, and back I go to camp with my notes and pictures, the best of them printed in my mind as dreams. A fruitful day, without measured beginning or ending.

FRIDTJOF NANSEN
INTRODUCTION

In the pioneering era of polar exploration, Norway's Fridtjof
Nansen was the go-to guy. When Roald Amundsen beat Robert
Falcon Scott to the South Pole in 1911, it was Nansen's ingenious
ship, the *Fram*, he used in the Southern Ocean. Scott himself was
an admirer; so too Ernest Shackleton. Nansen's renown stemmed
from his own attempt in 1893 to be first to the North Pole. 'To
penetrate,' as he wrote in *Farthest North*, his widely read account
of the expedition, 'the secrets of the domain of ice.'

Nansen put his faith in a theory, having studied meticulously
voyages in the northern oceans, specifically through the Bering
Strait. The first recorded attempt was by Captain James Cook in
1776, the last by a ship called the *Jeannette* in 1879. Under its
American captain, George De Long, the *Jeannette* had been
sailing north when it became stuck in pack ice. Two years later, in
1881, the ship was finally crushed and sank off the New Siberian
Islands, some 3000 miles west. The *Jeanette*'s drift seemed to
confirm an east-west current that ran across the entire polar basin,
perhaps as far north as the pole itself. Nansen's plan was to
recreate the *Jeanette*'s fate. Rather than navigate through the ice,
he proposed to use it as a slingshot, deliberately taking a ship into
the floes, which would then transport him to the pole.

The plan was controversial. Fellow explorers doubted a ship
could be built strong enough to withstand the near-tectonic forces.
Adolphus Greely, the American explorer whose polar expedition
of 1881 had set a then-furthest north latitude of 83°24', dubbed it
'an illogical scheme of self-destruction'. *The New York Times* ran
the headline: 'Will Nansen come back?' Nansen's first move was
to engage an innovative Norwegian shipbuilder, Colin Archer. It
was Archer's idea to give the ship a round hull, thereby allowing
the ice minimal purchase. 'For this reason too,' Nansen wrote, 'the

keel was sunk in the planking, so that barely three inches protruded, and its edges were rounded. The object was that the whole craft should be able to slip like an eel out of the embraces of the ice.'

They set sail from Kristiania (now Oslo) to great fanfare on 24 June 1893, opting to avoid the Bering Strait and instead take a north-easterly passage. 'Behind me lay all I held dear in life,' Nansen wrote as he watched his wife, Eva, and daughter, Liv, receding. On 20 September, close to the New Siberian Islands at 76° north, they found what they were looking for. Eight days later they were stuck fast. Drifting proved inconsistent; in the first few days of October alone, they drifted 16 minutes south. 'This is too much,' Nansen wrote in frustration, 'we must get north.' The months ticked by, the *Fram*, on occasion, covering as little as a mile a day. (There were positives – the *Fram*'s design worked just as Archer had hoped.) Nansen calculated that, assuming the current was favourable, it might take five years to reach the North Pole. An overland route was necessary.

They had loaded huskies along the Siberian coast. Nansen considered dogs 'an excellent method of locomotion'. With the *Fram* still marooned, Nansen began experimenting with different combinations of land transport. His conclusion that cross-country skiing alongside dog sleds offered the optimum balance between provisions and speed is a technique polar explorers have used ever since. (And one that Scott, to his detriment, ignored.) On 17 February 1895, Nansen, in company with the ship's stoker, Hjalmar Johansen, struck out for the North Pole accompanied by 28 dogs.

Nansen was an accomplished winter sportsman. In 1888, with countryman Otto Sverdrup, the *Fram*'s captain, he had skied across Greenland. The polar ice was different; vast, rearing blocks rendering any form of locomotion impossible. Three weeks after setting out, with more than half the 410-mile journey still to complete, Nansen and Johansen were forced to turn back. They had reached a record northern latitude, 86° 14', but an equally arduous return lay ahead. It took them 15 months, eight of which they spent camped in the inhospitable Franz Josef Land. Nansen returned to civilisation on 17 June 1896 when, by chance, he and Johansen met the English explorer, Frederick Jackson, at Cape Flora. The *Fram* was eventually released two months later, near Spitsbergen, on 13 August. Nansen's theory of an east-west current was proved correct.

Farthest North was published in 1897 to much acclaim. Nansen's subsequent achievements were equally notable. His research at the University of Bergen helped identify the existence and function of nerve cells, or neurons. He went on to become a political agitator and staunch advocate of Norwegian independence, his homeland having shared a union with Sweden for the best part of a century. His fame brought him influential friends. One of them, Prince Carl of Denmark, Nansen persuaded to become the first king of the newly independent Norway in 1905. His skills as a diplomat saw him appointed High Commissioner for Refugees at the League of Nations in 1921. He worked tirelessly on behalf of nationals displaced by the first world war, and created the Nansen Passport, a system of identity documents for stateless refugees. In 1922, Fridtjof Nansen was awarded the Nobel Peace Prize.

FARTHEST NORTH
BY FRIDTJOF NANSEN

Saturday, October 7th. Still cold, with the same northerly wind we have had all these last days. I am afraid we are drifting far south now. A few days ago, we were, according to the observations, in 78° 47' north latitude. That was 16' south in less than a week. This is too much; but we must make it up again; we must get north. It means going away from home now, but soon it will mean going nearer home. What depth of beauty, with an undercurrent of endless sadness, there is in these dreamily glowing evenings! The vanished sun has left its track of melancholy flame. Nature's music, which fills all space, is instinct with sorrow that all this beauty should be spread out day after day, week after week, year after year, over a dead world. Why? Sunsets are always sad at home too. This thought makes the sight seem doubly precious here and doubly sad. There is red burning blood in the west against the cold snow – and to think that this is the sea, stiffened in chains, in death, and that the sun will soon leave us and we shall be in the dark alone! 'And the earth was without form and void'; is this the sea that is to come?

Sunday, October 8th. Beautiful weather. Made a snowshoe expedition westward, all the dogs following. The running was a little spoiled by the brine, which soaks up through the snow from the surface of the ice – flat, newly frozen ice, with older, uneven blocks breaking through it. I seated myself on a snow hummock far away out; the dogs crowded round to be patted. My eye wandered over the great snow plain, endless and solitary – nothing but snow, snow everywhere.

The observations today gave us an unpleasant surprise; we are now down in 78° 35' north latitude; but there is a simple enough explanation of this when one thinks of all the northerly and northwesterly wind we have had lately, with open water not far to the south of us. As soon as everything is frozen we must go north again; there can be no question of that; but nonetheless this state of matters is unpleasant. I find some comfort in the fact that we have also drifted a little east, so that at all events we have kept with the wind and are not drifting down westward.

Monday, October 9th. I was feverish both during last night and today. Goodness knows what is the meaning of such nonsense. When I was taking water samples in the morning I discovered that the water-lifter suddenly stopped at the depth of a little less than 80 fathoms. It was really the bottom. So we have drifted south again to the shallow water. We let the weight lie at the bottom for a little, and saw by the line that for the moment we were drifting north. This was some small comfort, anyhow.

All at once in the afternoon, as we were sitting idly chattering, a deafening noise began, and the whole ship shook. This was the first ice pressure. Everyone rushed on deck to look. The *Fram* behaved beautifully, as I had expected she would. On pushed the ice with steady pressure, but down under us it had to go, and we were slowly lifted up. These 'squeezings' continued off and on all the afternoon, and were sometimes so strong that the *Fram* was lifted several feet; but then the ice could no longer bear her, and she broke it below her. Towards evening the whole slackened again, till we lay in a good-sized piece of open water, and had hurriedly to moor her to our old floe, or we should have drifted off. There seems to be a good deal of movement in the ice here. Peter has just been telling us that he hears the dull booming of strong pressures not far off.

Tuesday, October 10th. The ice continues disturbed.

Wednesday, October 11th. The bad news was brought this afternoon that 'Job' is dead, torn in pieces by the other dogs. He was found a good way from the ship, 'Old Suggen' lying watching the corpse, so that no other dog could get to it. They are wretches, these dogs; no day passes without a fight. In the daytime one of us is generally at hand to stop it, but at night they seldom fail to tear and bite one of their comrades. Poor 'Barabbas' is almost frightened out of his wits. He stays on board now, and dares not venture on the ice, because he knows the other monsters would set on him. There is not a trace of chivalry about these curs. When there is a fight, the whole pack rush like wild beasts on the loser. But is it not, perhaps, the law of nature that the strong, and not the weak, should be protected? Have not we human beings, perhaps, been trying to turn nature topsy-turvy by protecting and doing our best to keep life in all the weak?

The ice is restless, and has pressed a good deal today again. It begins with a gentle crack and moan along the side of the ship, which gradually sounds louder in every key. Now it is a high, plaintive tone, now it is a grumble, now it is a snarl, and the ship gives a start up. The noise steadily grows till it is like all the pipes of an organ; the ship trembles and shakes, and rises by fits and starts or is sometimes gently lifted. There is a pleasant, comfortable feeling in sitting listening to all this uproar and knowing the strength of our ship. Many a one would have been crushed long ago. But outside the ice is ground against our ship's sides, the piles of broken-up floe are forced under her heavy, invulnerable hull, and we lie as if in a bed. Soon the noise begins to die down; the ship sinks into its old position again, and presently all is silent as before. In several places round us the ice is piled up, at one spot to a considerable height. Towards evening there was a slackening, and we lay again in a large, open pool.

Thursday, October 12th. In the morning we and our floe were drifting on blue water in the middle of a large, open lane, which stretched far to the north, and in the north the atmosphere at the horizon was dark and blue. As far as we could see from the crow's nest with the small field glass, there was no end to the open water, with only single pieces of ice sticking up in it here and there. These are extraordinary changes. I wondered if we should prepare to go ahead. But they had long ago taken the machinery to pieces for the winter, so that it would be a matter of time to get it ready for use again. Perhaps it would be best to wait a little. Clear weather, with sunshine – a beautiful, inspiriting winter day – but the same northerly wind. Took soundings, and found 50 fathoms of water (90 metres). We are drifting slowly southward. Towards evening the ice packed together again with much force; but the *Fram* can hold her own. In the afternoon I fished in a depth of about 27 fathoms (50 metres) with Murray's silk net, and had a good take, especially of small crustaceans (Copepoda, Ostracoda, Amphipoda, etc.) and of a little Arctic worm (Spadella) that swims about in the sea. It is horribly difficult to manage a little fishing here. No sooner have you found an opening to slip your tackle through than it begins to close again, and you have to haul up as hard as you can, so as not to get the line nipped and lose everything. It is a pity, for there are interesting hauls to be made. One sees phosphorescence in the water here whenever there is the smallest opening in the ice. There is by no means such a scarcity of animal life as one might expect.

Friday, October 13th. Now we are in the very midst of what the prophets would have had us dread so much. The ice is pressing and packing round us with a noise like thunder. It is piling itself up into long walls, and heaps high enough to reach a good way up the *Fram*'s rigging; in fact, it is trying its very utmost to grind the *Fram* into powder. But here we sit quite tranquil, not even going up to look at all the hurly-burly, but just chatting and laughing as usual. Last night there was tremendous pressure round our old dog-floe. The ice had towered up higher than the highest point of the floe and hustled down upon it. It had quite spoiled a well, where we till now had found good drinking water, filling it with brine. Furthermore, it had cast itself over our stern ice anchor and part of the steel cable which held it, burying them so effectually that we had afterwards to cut the cable. Then it covered our planks and sledges, which stood on the ice. Before long the dogs were in danger, and the watch had to turn out all hands to save them. At last the floe split in two. This morning the ice was one scene of melancholy confusion, gleaming in the most glorious sunshine. Piled up all round us were high, steep ice walls. Strangely enough, we had lain on the very verge of the worst confusion, and had escaped with the loss of an ice anchor, a piece of steel cable, a few planks and other bits of wood and half of a Samoyede sledge, all of which might have been saved if we had looked after them in time. But the men have grown so indifferent to the pressure now that they do not even go up to look, let it thunder ever so hard. They feel that the ship can stand it, and so long as that is the case there is nothing to hurt except the ice itself.

In the morning the pressure slackened again, and we were soon lying in a large piece of open water, as we did yesterday. Today, again, this stretched far away towards the northern horizon, where the same dark atmosphere indicated some extent of open water. I now gave the order to put the engine together again; they told me it could be done in a day and a half or at most two days. We must go north and see what there is up there. I think it possible that it may be the boundary between the ice drift the *Jeannette* was in and the pack we are now drifting south with – or can it be land?

We had kept company quite long enough with the old, now broken-up floe, so worked ourselves a little way astern after dinner, as the ice was beginning to draw together. Towards evening the pressure began again in earnest, and was especially bad round the remains of our old floe, so that I believe we may congratulate ourselves on having left it. It is evident that the pressure here stands in connection with – is perhaps caused by – the tidal wave. It occurs with the greatest regularity. The ice slackens twice and packs twice in 24 hours. The pressure has happened about 4, 5 and 6 o'clock in the morning, and almost at exactly the same hour in the afternoon, and in between we have always lain for some part of the time in open water. The very great pressure just now is probably due to the spring tide; we had new moon on the 9th, which was the first day of the pressure. Then it was just after midday when we noticed it, but it has been later every day, and now it is at 8 p.m.

The theory of the ice pressure being caused to a considerable extent by the tidal wave has been advanced repeatedly by Arctic explorers. During the *Fram*'s drifting we had better opportunity than most of them to study this phenomenon, and our experience seems to leave no doubt that over a wide region the tide produces movement and pressure of the ice. It occurs especially at the time of the spring tides, and more at new moon than at full moon. During the intervening periods there was, as a rule, little or no trace of pressure. But these tidal pressures did not occur during the whole time of our drifting. We noticed them especially the first autumn, while we were in the neighbourhood of the open sea north of Siberia, and the last year, when the *Fram* was drawing near the open Atlantic Ocean; they were less noticeable while we were in the polar basin. Pressure occurs here more irregularly, and is mainly caused by the wind driving the ice. When one pictures to one's self these enormous ice masses drifting in a certain direction, suddenly meeting hindrances – for example, ice masses drifting from the opposite direction, owing to a change of wind in some more or less distant quarter – it is easy to understand the tremendous pressure that must result.

Such an ice conflict is undeniably a stupendous spectacle. One feels one's self to be in the presence of titanic forces, and it is easy to understand how timid souls may be overawed and feel as if nothing could stand before it. For when the packing begins in earnest it seems as though there could be no spot on the earth's surface left unshaken. First you hear a sound like the thundering rumbling of an earthquake far away on the great waste; then you hear it in several places, always coming nearer and nearer. The silent ice world re-echoes with thunders; nature's giants are awakening to the battle. The ice cracks on every side of you, and begins to pile itself up; and all of a sudden you too find yourself in the midst of the struggle. There are howlings and thunderings round you; you feel the ice trembling, and hear it rumbling under your feet; there is no peace anywhere. In the semi-darkness, you can see it piling and tossing itself up into high ridges nearer and nearer you – floes 10, 12, 15 feet thick, broken and flung on the top of each other as if they were featherweights. They are quite near you now, and you jump away to save your life. But the ice splits in front of you, a black gulf opens and water streams up. You turn in another direction, but there through the dark you can just see a new ridge of moving ice blocks coming towards you. You try another direction, but there it is the same. All round there is thundering and roaring, as of some enormous waterfall, with explosions like cannon salvoes. Still nearer you it comes. The floe you are standing on gets smaller and smaller; water pours over it; there can be no escape except by scrambling over the rolling ice blocks to get to the other side of the pack. But now the disturbance begins to calm down. The noise passes on, and is lost by degrees in the distance.

This is what goes on away there in the north month after month and year after year. The ice is split and piled up into mounds, which extend in every direction. If one could get a bird's-eye view of the ice fields, they would seem to be cut up into squares or meshes by a network of these packed ridges, or pressure dikes, as we called them, because they reminded us so much of snow-covered stone dikes at home, such as, in many parts of the country, are used to enclose fields. At first sight these pressure ridges appeared to be scattered about in all possible directions, but on closer inspection I was sure that I discovered certain directions which they tended to take, and especially that they were apt to run at right angles to the course of the pressure which produced them. In the accounts of Arctic expeditions one often reads descriptions of pressure ridges or pressure hummocks as high as 50 feet. These are fairy tales. The authors of such fantastic descriptions cannot have taken the trouble to measure. During the whole period of our drifting and of our travels over the ice fields in the far north I only once saw a hummock of a greater height than 23 feet. Unfortunately, I had not the opportunity of measuring this one, but I believe I may say with certainty that it was very nearly 30 feet high. All the highest blocks I measured – and they were many – had a height of 18 to 23 feet; and I can maintain with certainty that the packing of sea ice to a height of over 25 feet is a very rare exception.

Saturday, October 14th. Today we have got on the rudder; the engine is pretty well in order, and we are clear to start north when the ice opens tomorrow morning. It is still slackening and packing quite regularly twice a day, so that we can calculate on it beforehand. Today we had the same open channel to the north, and beyond it open sea as far as our view extended. What can this mean? This evening the pressure has been pretty violent. The floes were packed up against the *Fram* on the port side, and were once or twice on the point of toppling over the rail. The ice, however, broke below; they tumbled back again, and had to go under us after all. It is not thick ice, and cannot do much damage; but the force is something enormous. On the masses come incessantly without a pause; they look irresistible; but slowly and surely they are crushed against the *Fram*'s sides. Now (8.30 p.m.) the pressure has at last stopped. Clear evening, sparkling stars and flaming northern lights.

MUNGO PARK
INTRODUCTION

'They sing extempore songs in honour of their chief men,' wrote the 18th-century explorer Mungo Park of the praise singers of West Africa. 'In war, they accompany the soldiers to the field, in order, by reciting the great actions of their ancestors to awaken in them a spirit of glorious emulation.' It was a familiar theme – contemporary European depictions of Africa featured noble savages as a matter of course. And yet, in Park's account of his journeys in the region during the 1790s, he offers much more than the usual cliches. While his mission to find the source of the Niger River was part of a larger project of European colonisation, what sets the book apart is his acknowledgement of the complexity of tribal societies.

Born near Selkirk in Scotland in 1771, Park studied medicine at the University of Edinburgh. He was well connected. His brother-in-law, James Dickson, was a founder of the Linnean Society, and Park had served with the East India Company (as a surgeon in Sumatra), thanks to a recommendation from Sir Joseph Banks, the leading naturalist. In 1794, Banks recommended him again, this time to the African Association (later the Royal Geographical Society), as leader of an expedition to locate the Niger's headwaters.

Park sailed from Portsmouth aboard the *Endeavour*, an ivory-trading ship, on 22 May 1795. He reached the Gambia River a month later. Tracing it 100 miles inland, he arrived at Pisania, a British trading station. Africa's interior was to 18th-century explorers what the North and South Poles became to their 20th-century counterparts. The region was known to be hostile. Park's predecessor, Major Daniel Houghton, had disappeared and was eventually found dead. Banks called Park's expedition 'the most dangerous a man can undertake'.

Park took a more enlightened view, spending six months learning the language, Mandingo, to better understand what he saw. 'I had a passionate desire to examine into the productions of a country so little known,' he wrote, 'and to become experimentally acquainted with the modes of life and character.' On 2 December, accompanied by an interpreter and armed with his trusty volume of Robbie Burns' poetry, Park set out for Ludamar, a Moorish stronghold some 560 miles to the east. His route took him along the Senegal River basin and across Kaarta, a desert kingdom of the Bambara people, in what is today western Mali.

Park reached Ludamar in late February 1796, only to be taken captive by a local chief. He was unable to make his escape for four months, securing his freedom, along with that of his horse, on 1 July. He eventually reached the Niger, the first European to do so, at the bustling city of Sego (now Segou). His description of the area, featured here, is typical of his style, especially his observations on social protocols.

Park followed the river downstream for 80 miles. By now he was running a high fever, and the weather was against him. 'The rain falls in torrents,' he noted, 'suffocating heats oppress by day and the night is spent...listening to the croaking of frogs (of which the numbers are beyond imagination).' Eight days after embarking he turned back. Retracing his steps, from Segou he plotted an alternative course, gaining 220 miles before illness overtook him. That he survived at all was thanks to months of care and hospitality in the home of a local fisherman. He made it home to Scotland, only to die on another expedition in Africa years later.

Among those Park inspired was a young Joseph Conrad. Since 1930, the Royal Scottish Geographical Society has annually awarded the Mungo Park Medal for outstanding contributions to geographical knowledge. In the modern era, with the motives and accomplishments of Victorian explorers under scrutiny, Park's sensitive and informed approach feels relevant, though still a cautionary tale.

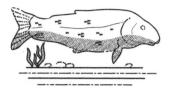

TRAVELS IN THE INTERIOR OF AFRICA
BY MUNGO PARK

July 18 We continued our journey, but, owing to a light supper the preceding night we felt ourselves rather hungry this morning, and endeavoured to procure some corn at a village, but without success.

My horse becoming weaker and weaker every day, was now of very little service to me; I was obliged to drive him before me for the greater part of the day, and did not reach Geosorro until eight o'clock in the evening. I found my companions wrangling with the dooty, who had absolutely refused to give or sell them any provisions; and as none of us had tasted victuals for the last twenty-four hours, we were by no means disposed to fast another day if we could help it. But finding our entreaties without effect, and being very much fatigued, I fell asleep, from which I was awakened about midnight with the joyful information Kinne nata! ('The victuals are come!') This made the remainder of the night pass away pleasantly, and at daybreak, July 19th, we resumed our journey, proposing to stop at a village called Doolinkeaboo for the night following. My fellow travellers, having better horses than myself, soon left me, and I was walking barefoot, driving my horse, when I was met by a coffle of slaves, about seventy in number, coming from Sego. They were tied together by their necks with thongs of a bullock's hide, twisted like a rope – seven slaves upon a thong, and a man with a musket between every seven. Many of the slaves were ill conditioned, and a great number of them women. In the rear came Sidi Mahomed's servant, whom I remembered to have seen at the camp of Benowm. He presently knew me, and told me that these slaves were going to Morocco by the way of Ludamar and the Great Desert.

In the afternoon, as I approached Doolinkeaboo, I met about twenty Moors on horseback, the owners of the slaves I had seen in the morning. They were well armed with muskets, and were very inquisitive concerning me, but not so rude as their countrymen generally are. From them I learned that Sidi Mahomed was not at Sego, but had gone to Kancaba for gold dust.

When I arrived at Doolinkeaboo I was informed that my fellow travellers had gone on, but my horse was so much fatigued that I could not possibly proceed after them. The dooty of the town at my request gave me a draught of water, which is generally looked upon as an earnest of greater hospitality, and I had no doubt of making up for the toils of the day by a good supper and a sound sleep; unfortunately, I had neither the one nor the other. The night was rainy and tempestuous, and the dooty limited his hospitality to the draught of water.

July 20 In the morning I endeavoured, both by entreaties and threats, to procure some victuals from the dooty, but in vain. I even begged some corn from one of his female slaves, as she was washing it at the well, and had the mortification to be refused. However, when the dooty was gone to the fields, his wife sent me a handful of meal, which I mixed with water and drank for breakfast. About eight o'clock I departed from Doolinkeaboo, and at noon stopped a few minutes at a large korree, where I had some milk given me by the Foulahs, and hearing that two [men] were going from thence to Sega, I was happy to have their company, and we set out immediately.

About four o'clock we stopped at a small village, where one of the [men] met with an acquaintance, who invited us to a sort of public entertainment which was conducted with more than common propriety. A dish made of sour milk and meal called sinkatoo, and beer made from their corn, was distributed with great liberality, and the women were admitted into the society, a circumstance I had never before observed in Africa. There was no compulsion – everyone was at liberty to drink as he pleased – they nodded to each other when about to drink, and on setting down the calabash commonly said Berka ('Thank you'). Both men and women appeared to be somewhat intoxicated, but they were far from being quarrelsome.

Departing from thence, we passed several large villages where I was constantly taken for a Moor and became the subject of much merriment to the Bambarrans, who, seeing me drive my horse before me, laughed heartily at my appearance. 'He has been at Mecca,' says one, 'you may see that by his clothes'; another asked me if my horse was sick; a third wished to purchase it, so that, I believe, the very slaves were ashamed to be seen in my company. Just before it was dark we took up our lodging for the night at a small village, where I procured some victuals for myself and some corn for my horse, at the moderate price of a button; and was told that I should see the Niger (which the locals call Joliba, or the Great Water) early the next day. The lions are here very numerous; the gates are shut a little after sunset, and nobody allowed to go out. The thoughts of seeing the Niger in the morning, and the troublesome buzzing of mosquitoes, prevented me from shutting my eyes during the night; and I had saddled my horse, and was in readiness before daylight, but, on account of the wild beasts, we were obliged to wait until the people were stirring and the gates opened. This happened to be a market day at Sego, and the roads were everywhere filled with people carrying different articles to sell. We passed four large villages, and at eight o'clock saw the smoke over Sego.

As we approached the town I was fortunate enough to overtake the fugitive Kaartans, to whose kindness I had been so much indebted in my journey through Bambarra. They readily agreed to introduce me to the king; and we rode together through some marshy ground, where, as I was anxiously looking around for the river, one of them called out, Geo affili! ('See the water!') and, looking forwards, I saw with infinite pleasure the great object of my mission – the long-sought-for majestic Niger, glittering in the morning sun, as broad as the Thames at Westminster, and flowing slowly to the eastward. I hastened to the brink, and having drunk of the water, lifted up my fervent thanks in prayer to the Great Ruler of all things for having thus far crowned my endeavours with success.

The circumstance of the Niger's flowing towards the east, and its collateral points, did not, however, excite my surprise, for, although I had left Europe in great hesitation on this subject, and rather believed that it ran in the contrary direction, I had made such frequent inquiries during my progress concerning this river, and received from the men of different nations such clear and decisive assurances that its general course was towards the rising sun, as scarce left any doubt on my mind, and more especially as I knew that Major Houghton had collected similar information in the same manner.

Sego, the capital of Bambarra, at which I had now arrived, consists, properly speaking, of four distinct towns – two on the northern bank of the Niger, called Sego Korro and Sego Boo; and two on the southern bank, called Sego Soo Korro and Sego See Korro. They are all surrounded with high mud walls. The houses are built of clay, of a square form with flat roofs – some of them have two storeys, and many of them are whitewashed. Besides these buildings, Moorish mosques are seen in every quarter; and the streets, though narrow, are broad enough for every useful purpose, in a country where wheel carriages are entirely unknown. From the best inquiries I could make, I have reason to believe that Sego contains altogether about thirty thousand inhabitants. The King of Bambarra constantly resides at Sego See Korro. He employs a great many slaves in conveying people over the river, and the money they receive (though the fare is only ten cowrie shells for each individual) furnishes a considerable revenue to the king in the course of a year. The canoes are of a singular construction, each of them being formed of the trunks of two large trees rendered concave, and joined together, not side by side, but endways – the junction being exactly across the middle of the canoe: they are therefore very long, and disproportionably narrow, and have neither decks nor masts: they are, however, very roomy, for I observed in one of them four horses and several people crossing over the river. When we arrived at this ferry, with a view to pass over to that part of the town in which the king resides, we found a great number waiting for a passage: they looked at me with silent wonder, and I distinguished with concern many Moors among them. There were three different places of embarkation, and the ferrymen were very diligent and expeditious; but from the crowd of people I could not immediately obtain a passage, and sat down upon the bank of the river to wait for a more favourable opportunity. The view of this extensive city – the numerous canoes upon the river – the crowded population, and the cultivated state of the surrounding country – formed altogether a prospect of civilisation and magnificence which I little expected to find in the bosom of Africa.

I waited more than two hours without having an opportunity of crossing the river, during which time the people who had crossed carried information to Mansong, the king, that a white man was waiting for a passage, and was coming to see him. He immediately sent over one of his chief men, who informed me that the king could not possibly see me until he knew what had brought me into his country; and that I must not presume to cross the river without the king's permission. He therefore advised me to lodge at a distant village, to which he pointed, for the night, and said that in the morning he would give me further instructions how to conduct myself. This was very discouraging. However, as there was no remedy, I set off for the village, where I found, to my great mortification, that no person would admit me into his house. I was regarded with astonishment and fear, and was obliged to sit all day without victuals in the shade of a tree; and the night threatened to be very uncomfortable – for the wind rose, and there was great appearance of a heavy rain – and the wild beasts are so very numerous in the neighbourhood that I should have been under the necessity of climbing up a tree and resting amongst the branches. About sunset, however, as I was preparing to pass the night in this manner, and had turned my horse loose that he might graze at liberty, a woman returning from the labours of the field stopped to observe me, and perceiving that I was weary and dejected, inquired into my situation, which I briefly explained to her; whereupon, with looks of great compassion, she took up my saddle and bridle, and told me to follow her. Having conducted me into her hut, she lighted up a lamp, spread a mat on the floor and told me I might remain there for the night. Finding that I was very hungry, she said she would procure me something to eat. She accordingly went out, and returned in a short time with a very fine fish, which, having caused to be half broiled upon some embers, she gave me for supper. The rites of hospitality being thus performed towards a stranger in distress, my worthy benefactress (pointing to the mat, and telling me I might sleep there without apprehension) called to the female part of her family, who had stood gazing on me all the while in fixed astonishment, to resume their task of spinning cotton, in which they continued to employ themselves the great part of the night. They lightened their labour by songs, one of which was composed extempore, for I was myself the subject of it. It was sung by one of the young women, the rest joining in a sort of chorus. The air was sweet and plaintive, and the words, literally translated, were these: 'The winds roared, and the rains fell. The poor white man, faint and weary, came and sat under our tree. He has no mother to bring him milk, no wife to grind his corn.' Chorus: 'Let us pity the white man, no mother has he.' Trifling as this recital may appear to the reader, to a person in my situation the circumstance was affecting in the highest degree. I was oppressed by such unexpected kindness, and sleep fled from my eyes. In the morning, I presented my compassionate landlady with two of the four brass buttons which remained on my waistcoat – the only recompense I could make her.

WILLIAM EDWARD PARRY
INTRODUCTION

The quest for a north-west passage, a sea route connecting the Atlantic with the Pacific via the North American coast, dates back to the 16th century. What started as a desire among European traders for a simpler, westbound voyage to Asia became, for more than 400 years, one of the greatest challenges of exploration. The first attempt to navigate the Canadian Arctic Archipelago was made in 1497 by John Cabot at the behest of Henry VIII. The intervening dramatis personae includes such luminaries as James Cook, Robert McClure and John Rae. The search for the north-west passage led to the discovery of the Hudson River by Henry Hudson in 1609, and the loss of John Franklin's expedition in 1847. The ghoulish reports that followed, of cannibalism among Franklin's crew, shocked Britain.

All of which helps credit the voyage made by William Edward Parry in 1819 as one of the most successful. Parry was Royal Navy through and through; he joined at the age of 13 as a ship's boy, and rose to the rank of Rear-Admiral. On 11 May 1819, Parry set sail aboard the *Hecla*, a 'bomb-ship' for the transport of guns and munitions, whose conversion to an icebreaker saw it clad with 3-inch oak panels and reinforced with iron plates. Parry's expedition was also notable for its pioneering provisions; tinned food, albeit in the era before can openers and blissfully unaware of the toxic lead contained in the cans themselves.

Parry was a man with a point to prove, having been part of a failed expedition the previous year under the leadership of Sir John Ross. The British expedition of 1818 had discovered a navigable route around Baffin Bay and into Lancaster Sound that would later prove to be the passage's entrance. Having reached 110 degrees, the furthest position west recorded thus far, Ross gave the order to turn back. A range sighted at some distance, later named the Croker Mountains, appeared to close off the channel. Despite the protests of Parry and others that a closer inspection might reveal a way through, Ross was unmoved. (When it later transpired Parry was right, Ross' reputation was ruined.)

Given his own command, Parry bypassed Baffin Bay altogether and sailed instead directly for Lancaster Sound, more certain than ever the Croker range was not an obstacle. On 28 July, after they had battled heavy ice, a route of clear water opened before them. The Navy's participation demonstrated the passage's strategic importance; when Parry passed Ross' 'furthest west' position, on 4 September, he and his crew claimed a £5,000 reward offered by the British Parliament. (Among the beneficiaries was James Clark Ross, Sir John's nephew, and a member of Parry's crew.)

The arrival of winter meant a 10-month layover at Melville Island. By August 1820, the expedition prepared to set off once more, as Parry recalls in the extract here. This time the ice forced them south, as much as 100 miles before they could head west again. The *Hecla* reached a new furthest west, 113°46', before Parry decided there was no way through. At the point at which he turned back, Parry had navigated three-quarters of the way across the Arctic Archipelago.

The first clear navigation by ship would not be made until 1906, and by another man: Roald Amundsen. Amundsen's success saw him follow John Franklin's fateful route of 1847 to King William Island. Amundsen spent two winters in the region conducting experiments; one of his discoveries was that the magnetic North Pole moved. Amundsen left King William Island in August 1905, making for the Bering Strait. A US whaling ship coming in the opposite direction confirmed he would make it through. Parry's caution had been well advised; Amundsen's boat was small, just 47 tonnes. In places the channel he encountered was so shallow, as low as one metre, it would have grounded the vast tonnage of the *Hecla*, perhaps fatally. (The creation of a deeper channel, a result of global warming, means it is now possible for larger vessels to pass.) Parry made two more attempts, in 1821 and 1824, though neither expedition was as successful as his first.

THE JOURNAL OF A VOYAGE FOR THE DISCOVERY OF A NORTH-WEST PASSAGE

BY WILLIAM EDWARD PARRY

August 1820 It now became evident, from the combined experience of this and the preceding year, that there was something peculiar about the south-west extremity of Melville Island, which made the icy sea there extremely unfavourable to navigation, and which seemed likely to bid defiance to all our efforts to proceed much farther to the westward in this parallel of latitude.

We had arrived off it on the 17th of September 1819, after long and heavy gales from the north-westward, by which alone the ice is ever opened on this coast, and found it, in unusually heavy and extensive fields, completely closing in the land a mile or two to the eastward of where we were now lying. We again arrived here in the early part of August, and though the rest of the navigation had been remarkably clear for the fifty miles between this and Winter Harbour, seeming to afford a presumptive proof that the season was rather a favourable one than otherwise, the same obstruction presented itself as before; nor did there appear, from our late experience, a reasonable ground of hope that any fortuitous circumstance, such as an alteration in winds or currents, was likely to remove the formidable impediments which we had now to encounter. The increased dimensions of the ice hereabouts would not alone have created an insurmountable difficulty in the navigation, but that it was very naturally accompanied by a degree of closeness which seldom or never admitted an open space of clear water of sufficient size for a ship, or even a boat, to sail in.

We had been lying near our present station with an easterly wind blowing fresh for thirty-six hours together; and although this was considerably off the land, beyond the western point of the island now in sight, the ice had not, during the whole of that time, moved a single yard from the shore; affording a proof that there was no space in which the ice was at liberty to move to the westward, and offering a single and a striking exception to our former experience.

Under these circumstances, I began to consider whether it would not be advisable, whenever the ice would allow us to move, to sacrifice a few miles of the westing we had already made, and to run along the margin of the floes in order to endeavour to find an opening leading to the southward, by taking advantage of which we might be enabled to prosecute the voyage to the westward in a lower latitude. I was the more inclined to make this attempt, from its having long become evident to us that the navigation of this part of the Polar Sea is only to be performed by watching the occasional openings between the ice and the shore; and that, therefore, a continuity of land is essential, if not absolutely necessary, for this purpose.

Such a continuity of land, which was here about to fail us, must necessarily be furnished by the northern coast of America in whatsoever latitude it may be found; and, as a large portion of our short season had already been occupied in fruitless attempts to penetrate further to the westward in our present parallel under circumstances of more than ordinary risk to the ships, I determined whenever the ice should open sufficiently to put into execution the plan I had proposed.

The westerly wind cleared us by slow degrees of the loose masses of ice about the ship, and in the afternoon the main body went off about three hundred yards, drifting also a little to the eastward. It may always be expected in icy seas that a breeze of wind, however light, will set the ice in motion, if there be any room for it to move; such cases, the smaller pieces of course begin to drift first, and the heavier ones soon follow, though at a slower rate; among loose ice, therefore, almost every separate piece is seen to move with a different velocity, proportioned to its depth underwater.

Having gone on shore in the evening to make some observations for the variation, I afterwards ascended the hill in order to take a view of the state of the ice in the offing. The breeze had now begun to open several holes, particularly in the west and south-east quarters; it was most loose in the latter direction, except close along the land to the eastward, where a ship might possibly have been got, had this been our immediate object. The ice, however, looked just as promising to the westward as in any other quarter, and I found before I returned on board that it continued to drift to the eastward, and to leave more and more space of clear water in the required direction. I, therefore, communicated to Lieutenant Liddon my intention of pushing on to the westward the instant the sea became clear enough for the ships to make any progress with a beating wind; but, in the event of failing to do so, that I should next try what could be done by attempting a passage considerably to the southward of our present parallel.

At seven P.M., we shipped the rudder, and crossed the top-gallant yards in readiness for moving; and I then again ascended the hill, and walked a mile to the westward along the brow of it, that not a moment might be lost after the ice to the westward should give us the slightest hope of making any progress by getting underway. Although the holes had certainly increased in size and extent, there was still not sufficient room even for one of our boats to have worked to windward; and the impossibility of the ship's doing so was rendered more apparent, on account of the current which, as I have before had occasion to remark, is always produced in these seas, soon after the springing up of a breeze, and which was now running to the eastward, at the rate of at least one mile per hour. It was evident that any attempt to get the ships to the westward must, under circumstances so unfavourable, be attended with the certain consequence of their being drifted the contrary way; and nothing could, therefore, be done but still to watch, which we did most anxiously, every alteration in the state of the ice.

The wind, however, decreasing as the night came on, served to diminish the hopes which we had flattered ourselves of being speedily extricated from our present confined and dangerous situation. At half past ten P.M., Lieutenant Beechey, at my request, ascended the hill; and, on his return at eleven o'clock, reported that the ice was slack but that without a leading wind, it did not appear that a ship could make any way among it.

At one A.M. on the llth, I despatched Mr. Ross to the top of the hill, from whence he observed that the ice had slackened considerably but was still too close for a ship to work among it. At this time the wind was dying away gradually; and, at four A.M., when Mr. Ross again ascended the hill, it had fallen quite calm. The ice immediately ceased to drift to the eastward, and at half past five, a light breeze springing up from the south-east caused it at once to return in the opposite direction. Being desirous, if possible, to take advantage of this breeze, Lieutenant Beechey and myself again went on shore in order to form a judgment whether there was room for the ships to sail among the ice, should it appear otherwise expedient to get them underway. We agreed that it was by no means practicable with the present light wind, which would scarcely have given them steerage-way, even in a clear and unencumbered sea, and much less, therefore, could have enabled them to force their way through the numberless heavy masses which lay in our way to the westward. So close, indeed, did the ice about us still continue that it was necessary to shift the *Hecla* once more round to the westward of the point of land, to secure her from that which the change of wind was once more bringing back in great abundance, and at the rate of nearly a mile per hour. In an hour after we had effected this, I had reason to be satisfied with the determination to which I had come of not getting the ships underway, for there was literally not a single hole of open water visible from the masthead in which a boat would have floated, except immediately under the lee of the point where we were lying, and within one hundred yards of the ship.

There was nothing in the appearance or productions of this part of the island different from those which had been found elsewhere, except that the ravines were more strikingly grand and picturesque, in consequence of the greater height of the land upon this part of the coast; this, as I have before remarked, was found, in one instance, to exceed eight hundred feet above the level of the sea; and the hills, immediately at the back of this, at the distance of nine or ten miles, appeared to be at least one or two hundred feet higher; so that the extreme height of Melville Island, as far as we had an opportunity of seeing it, may, perhaps, be fairly estimated at about one thousand feet. The rocks consisted entirely of sandstone in horizontal strata, and the soil of sand, intermixed occasionally with decayed plants, forming here and there a sort of vegetable mould on which the other plants, and a few tufts of very luxuriant moss, were growing: we remarked that almost the whole of the plants had a part of their flowers cropped by the hares, and other animals which are fond of feeding in the sheltered and warm situations afforded by the banks next the sea.

The weather was foggy for some hours in the morning, but cleared up in the afternoon as the sun acquired power. The wind increased to a fresh gale from the eastward, at nine P.M., being the second time that it had done so while we had been lying at this station; a circumstance which we were the more inclined to notice, as the easterly winds had hitherto been more faint and less frequent than those from the westward. In this respect, therefore, we considered ourselves unfortunate, as experience had already shown us that none but a westerly wind ever produced upon this coast, or, indeed, on the southern coast of any of the North Georgian Islands, the desired effect of clearing the shores of ice.

At nine P.M., Lieutenant Beechey could discover from the top of the hill no clear water in any direction. After ten o'clock the wind blew much harder, which obliged us to strike the top-gallant yards, and to brace the yards to the wind; the ice had by this time ceased moving to the westward. The electrometer was tried in the course of the evening in the usual manner, the sky being full of hard dense clouds, and the wind blowing strong; but no sensible effect was produced upon the gold leaf.

The gale continued strong during the night, and the ice quite stationary. Not a pool of clear water could be seen in any direction, except just under the lee of our point, where there was a space large enough to contain half a dozen sail of ships, till about noon, when the whole closed in upon us without any apparent cause, except that the wind blew in irregular puffs about that time, and at one P.M. it was alongside. The ship was placed in the most advantageous manner for taking the beach, or rather the shelf of submarine ice, and the rudder again unshipped and hung across the stem. The ice which came in contact with the ship's side consisted of very heavy loose pieces, drawing twelve or fourteen feet water, which, however, we considered as good fenders, comparatively with the enormous fields which covered the sea just without them. So much, indeed, do we judge at all times by comparison that this kind of ice, which in Davis Strait we should not like to have had so near us, was now considered of infinite service when interposed between the ship and the heavier floes. Everything remained quiet for the rest of the day without producing any pressure of consequence; the wind came round to at night, but without moving the ice off the land.

MARCO POLO
INTRODUCTION

Marco Polo's account of the Mongol empire of Kublai Khan gave 13th-century Europeans their first glimpse of the East. It introduced the concept of global trade, and challenged the authority of the Catholic Church. That parts of Polo's account are considered fiction is due, in part, to the manner of its creation. Among Marco's fellow inmates was one Rustichello of Pisa, a professional writer with a thing for King Arthur and the Round Table, and to whom Polo recounted his adventures. In taking down the story, it is likely Rustichello made embellishments. Though in part a work of fabulism, for centuries it served as a touchstone text for explorers and travellers.

The Silk Road trading routes with which Marco Polo has become synonymous had criss-crossed Asia since the Han dynasty in 200 BC. The region was rich in resources and wise to their application: gold and silver jewellery, gems, ceramics and silks. Kublai Khan was a monarch of legend even at the time of Polo's journey into his realm, grandson of Genghis and commemorated (as 'Kubla Khan' nearly 500 years later) in the poem by Samuel Taylor Coleridge. Until the rise of Genghis, the countries of the Silk Road had seen numerous conflicts. Genghis brought order but at a cost. The siege of Nishapur (1221), just a few decades before the Polo family's first foray to Asia, resulted in the slaughter of every living creature in the city.

If Kublai Khan's court was not quite one of stately pleasure domes, sacred rivers and sunless seas, there was much else to discover. Marco and Kublai got on famously, such that the Venetian became a de facto emissary in his travels across Khan's empire and was rewarded for his trouble. The extract here features his observations on the Tartars of Central Asia.

The finished book, *Il Milione* ('The Million'), proved an instant hit, and soon began to circulate throughout Europe. In France, it became *The Book of Marvels*, in Britain *The Travels*. As the book predated the printing press by nearly 150 years, copies were made by hand. The paid scribes who created them sought to further improve the story as a matter of principle. So, across the pages of some editions trots the occasional unicorn; across others, men with tails.

Omissions, meanwhile, are notable. For example, there is no mention of China's Great Wall, despite Polo visiting the region, or everyday cultural references, such as chopsticks or tea, which Polo would have encountered in all parts of Kublai's empire. Some scholars believe he simply exaggerated his own importance. (Polo claimed to have been the governor of Yangzhou for three years, although records suggest otherwise.) It is also likely he had enemies in high places. The map of the known world was, in the 13th century, smaller than it is today, thanks to a Catholic Church whose cartographic vision insisted there was, among other things, no human habitation south of the equator.

Beyond Rustichello's original, a definitive version of *The Travels* has likely never existed. At one stage, no fewer than 140 surviving manuscripts staked a claim. The contentious elements of Polo's *Travels* are, given the doctorates devoted to subject, too many to list here, yet his legacy, regardless of veracity, is undeniable. *The Travels* inspired Columbus to strike out for the new world, and the Italian cartographer Fra Mauro also drew on Polo's writings. And unicorns or no, readers can still find much to admire.

THE TRAVELS OF MARCO POLO
BY MARCO POLO AND RUSTICHELLO OF PISA

TRANSLATED BY SIR HENRY YULE

The Tartar custom is to spend the winter in warm plains, where they find good pasture for their cattle, whilst in summer they betake themselves to a cool climate among the mountains and valleys, where water is to be found, as well as woods and pastures.

Their houses are circular, and are made of wands covered with felts. These are carried along with them whithersoever they go; for the wands are so strongly bound together, and likewise so well combined, that the frame can be made very light. Whenever they erect these huts the door is always to the south. They also have wagons covered with black felt so efficaciously that no rain can get in. These are drawn by oxen and camels, and the women and children travel in them. The women do the buying and selling, and whatever is necessary to provide for the husband and household; for the men all lead the life of gentlemen, troubling themselves about nothing but hunting and hawking, and looking after their goshawks and falcons, unless it be the practice of warlike exercises.

They live on the milk and meat which their herds supply, and on the produce of the chase; and they eat all kinds of flesh, including that of horses and dogs, and Pharaoh's rats, of which last there are great numbers in burrows on those plains. Their drink is mare's milk.

They are very careful not to meddle with each other's wives, and will not do so on any account, holding that to be an evil and abominable thing. The women too are very good and loyal to their husbands, and notable housewives withal. Ten or twenty of them will dwell together in charming peace and unity, nor shall you ever hear an ill word among them.

The marriage customs of Tartars are as follows. Any man may take a hundred wives if he so please, and if he be able to keep them. But the first wife is ever held most in honour, and as the most legitimate and the same applies to the sons whom she may bear. The husband gives a marriage payment to his wife's mother, and the wife brings nothing to her husband. They have more children than other people, because they have so many wives. They may marry their cousins, and if a father dies, his son may take any of the wives, his own mother always excepted; that is to say the eldest son may do this, but no other. A man may also take the wife of his own brother after the latter's death. Their weddings are celebrated with great ado.

CONCERNING THE GOD OF THE TARTARS

This is the fashion of their religion. They say there is a Most High God of Heaven, whom they worship daily with thurible and incense, but they pray to Him only for health of mind and body. But they have also a certain other god of theirs called Natigay, and they say he is the god of the Earth, who watches over their children, cattle and crops. They show him great worship and honour, and every man hath a figure of him in his house, made of felt and cloth; and they also make in the same manner images of his wife and children. The wife they put on the left hand, and the children in front. And when they eat, they take the fat of the meat and grease the god's mouth withal, as well as the mouths of his wife and children. Then they take of the broth and sprinkle it before the door of the house; and that done, they deem that their god and his family have had their share of the dinner.

Their drink is mare's milk, prepared in such a way that you would take it for white wine; and a right good drink it is, called by them Kemiz.

The clothes of the wealthy Tartars are for the most part of gold and silk stuffs, lined with costly furs such as sable and ermine, vair and fox skin, in the richest fashion.

CONCERNING THE TARTAR CUSTOMS OF WAR

All their harness of war is excellent and costly. Their arms are bows and arrows, sword and mace; but above all the bow, for they are capital archers, indeed the best that are known. On their backs they wear armour of cuirbouly, prepared from buffalo and other hides, which is very strong. They are excellent soldiers, and passing valiant in battle. They are also more capable of hardships than other nations; for many a time, if need be, they will go for a month without any supply of food, living only on the milk of their mares and on such game as their bows may win them. Their horses also will subsist entirely on the grass of the plains, so that there is no need to carry store of barley or straw or oats; and they are very docile to their riders. These, in case of need, will abide on horseback the livelong night, armed at all points, while the horse will be continually grazing.

Of all troops in the world these are they which endure the greatest hardship and fatigue, and which cost the least; and they are the best of all for making wide conquests of country. And this you will perceive from what you have heard and shall hear in this book; and (as a fact) there can be no manner of doubt that now they are the masters of the biggest half of the world. Their troops are admirably ordered in the manner that I shall now relate.

You see, when a Tartar prince goes forth to war, he takes with him, say, 100,000 horses. Well, he appoints an officer to every ten men, one to every hundred, one to every thousand, and one to every ten thousand, so that his own orders have to be given to ten persons only, and each of these ten persons has to pass the orders only to another ten, and so on; no one having to give orders to more than ten. And every one in turn is responsible only to the officer immediately over him; and the discipline and order that comes of this method is marvellous, for they are a people very obedient to their chiefs. Further, they call the corps of 100,000 men a Tuc; that of 10,000 they call a Toman; the hundred Guz. And when the army is on the march they have always 200 horsemen, very well mounted, who are sent a distance of two marches in advance to reconnoitre, and these always keep ahead. They have a similar party detached in the rear, and on either flank, so that there is a good lookout kept on all sides against a surprise. When they are going on a distant expedition they take no gear with them except two leather bottles for milk, a little earthenware pot to cook their meat in and a little tent to shelter them from rain. And in case of great urgency they will ride ten days on end without lighting a fire or taking a meal. On such an occasion, they will sustain themselves on the blood of their horses, opening a vein and letting the blood jet into their mouths, drinking till they have had enough, and then staunching it.

They also have milk dried into a kind of paste to carry with them; and when they need food they put this in water, and beat it up till it dissolves and then drink it. It is prepared in this way; they boil the milk, and when the rich part floats on the top they skim it into another vessel, and of that they make butter; for the milk will not become solid till this is removed. Then they put the milk in the sun to dry. And when they go on an expedition, every man takes some ten pounds of this dried milk with him. And of a morning he will take a half pound of it and put it in his leather bottle, with as much water as he pleases. So, as he rides along, the milk paste and the water in the bottle get well churned together into a kind of pap, and that makes his dinner.

When they come to an engagement with the enemy, they will gain the victory in this fashion. They never let themselves get into a regular medley, but keep perpetually riding round and shooting into the enemy. And as they do not count it any shame to run away in battle, they will sometimes pretend to do so, and in running away they turn in the saddle and shoot hard and strong at the foe, and in this way make great havoc. Their horses are trained so perfectly that they will double hither and thither, just like a dog, in a way that is quite astonishing. Thus, they fight to as good purpose in running away as if they stood and faced the enemy, because of the vast volleys of arrows that they shoot in this way, turning round upon their pursuers, who are fancying that they have won the battle. But when the Tartars see that they have killed and wounded a good many horses and men, they wheel round bodily, and return to the charge in perfect order and with loud cries; and in a very short time the enemy are routed. In truth, they are stout and valiant soldiers, and inured to war. And you perceive that it is just when the enemy sees them run, and imagines that he has gained the battle, that he has in reality lost it; for the Tartars wheel round in a moment when they judge the right time has come. And after this fashion they have won many a fight.

All this that I have been telling you is true of the manners and customs of the genuine Tartars. But I must add also that in these days they are greatly degenerated; for those who are settled in Cathay have taken up the practices of the Idolaters of the country, and have abandoned their own institutions; whilst those who have settled in the Levant have adopted the customs of the Saracens.

CONCERNING THE ADMINISTERING OF JUSTICE AMONG THE TARTARS

The way they administer justice is this. When any one has committed a petty theft, they give him, under the orders of authority, seven blows of a stick, or seventeen, or twenty-seven, or thirty-seven, or forty-seven and so forth, always increasing by tens in proportion to the injury done, and running up to one hundred and seven. Of these beatings sometimes they die. But if the offence be horse-stealing, or some other great matter, they cut the thief in two with a sword. Howbeit, if he be able to ransom himself by paying nine times the value of the thing stolen, he is let off. Every Lord or other person who possesses beasts has them marked with his peculiar brand, be they horses, mares, camels, oxen, cows or other great cattle, and then they are sent abroad to graze over the plains without any keeper. They get all mixt together, but eventually every beast is recovered by means of its owner's brand, which is known. For their sheep and goats they have shepherds. All their cattle are remarkably fine, big and in good condition.

They have another notable custom, which is this. If any man have a daughter who dies before marriage, and another man have had a son also die before marriage, the parents of the two arrange a grand wedding between the dead lad and lass. And marry them they do, making a regular contract! And when the contract papers are made out, they put them in the fire, in order (as they will have it) that the parties in the other world may know the fact, and so look on each other as man and wife. And the parents thenceforward consider themselves sib to each other, just as if their children had lived and married. Whatever may be agreed on between the parties as dowry, those who have to pay it cause to be painted on pieces of paper and then put these in the fire, saying that in that way the dead person will get all the real articles in the other world.

Now I have told you all about the manners and customs of the Tartars; but you have heard nothing yet of the great state of the Grand Khan, who is the Lord of all the Tartars and of the Supreme Imperial Court. All that I will tell you in this book in proper time and place, but meanwhile I must return to my story which I left off in that great plain when we began to speak of the Tartars.

SUSANNA CARSON RIJNHART
INTRODUCTION

The idea of missionary work is, in the modern secular world, one freighted with baggage. In times past, however, it was a convenient way for those with faith, but not funds, to travel the world. In the case of Susanna Carson Rijnhart, she might have wished it otherwise.

The book Carson Rijnhart wrote of her time in the East, *With the Tibetans in Tent and Temple* (1902), is a broad survey of the region's cultures and customs. Written to promote 'the evangelization of Tibet', Carson Rijnhart's conclusion that 'the work does not aim at literary finish, for it has been written under the stress of many public engagements', is harsh; she writes well. What distinguishes the book, and what made those engagements so vexatious, was the story an intrigued public wanted to hear first-hand.

Born in Canada in 1868, 'Susie' Carson qualified as a physician. In 1894, she met a charismatic Dutch preacher, Petrus Rijnhart, who was raising funds for the China Inland Mission (CIM), an organisation dedicated to spreading the gospel in the East. Susie and Petrus married that same year and departed for China.

By June 1895, they had reached Lusar, a satellite village of the Kumbum monastery, located in what is now China's Qinghai province. One of the most important shrines in Tibetan Buddhism, Kumbum remains second only to the Drepung monastery in Lhasa. The latter was, in fact, the Rijnharts' ultimate destination. Sealed off from the west since 1846, entry into Tibet was only possible by way of secret – and very high – mountain passes. (And with the right guide for the right price.)

The following year, 1896, Lusar experienced what Susie describes as 'a Mohammedan revolt', one of the frequent clashes between warring Muslim sects, themselves victims of a heavy-handed Chinese army. The Rijnharts took sanctuary inside the monastery's fortifications. Petrus was already a good friend of the abbot, having first visited

Kumbum in 1892, when he had earned the epithet 'white lama'. Susie spent her time tending to the wounded, many of whom 'arrived more dead than alive', and whose increasing numbers soon led to outbreaks of smallpox and diphtheria. In June 1897, Susie gave birth to a son, Charles. In May 1898, with Charles less than a year old, they set off for Lhasa, a journey of 800 miles and countless Himalayan passes, some as high as 16,000ft. Their supplies included 200 Bibles.

When trouble arrived, it did so in earnest. In July, their guides deserted them, and the Rijnharts' supplies were stolen. In August, in the town of Nagqu, just 100 miles north of Lhasa and at an altitude of nearly 15,000ft, Charles died unexpectedly. Petrus conducted the burial service personally, Susie recounts, 'and the cold earth of Tibet, the great forbidden land, closed over the body of the first Christian child committed to its bosom'.

Despite their grief, they were determined to reach Lhasa, but Tibetan officials refused them permission to travel further. With little option, the Rijnharts made for Kangding, a missionary outpost in Sichuan province, some 600 miles away.

On the night of 25 September 1898, after constant harassment from bandits, the Rijnharts camped beside the Dang Chu River. The following morning, spotting a Tibetan encampment on the opposite bank and seeking to hire a horse following the death of his own, Petrus left Susie alone. He was never seen again. There followed a terrifying night, and Susie's account is featured here. Travelling many more miles in fear for her life, on 26 November she arrived in Kangding, on the verge of starvation.

During the many lecture tours she gave following her return to Canada, in 1900, Susie spoke well of her husband. Only years later was it revealed that Petrus had a secret. His visit to Canada in 1894 had been made to escape a charge of sexual assault. Keen to avoid any publicity, the China Inland Mission had already expelled him – in 1893. There is no record of Petrus' whereabouts to this day.

WITH THE TIBETANS
IN TENT AND TEMPLE
BY SUSANNA CARSON RIJNHART

We rose on the morning of September 26th, had breakfast and my husband prepared for departure. Cutting our rubber sheeting in two, he used part of it to wrap about his dry underwear, jacket, trousers, a piece of silver, five ounces in weight, some katas and my light revolver. Binding the whole tightly, he strapped it on his back and, taking the staff in his hand to deal with the dogs when he reached the tents, started away cheerfully, telling me not to be afraid, but to use his big revolver, which he had given me in place of my small one, if anyone went to harm me.

He said he would return before dark, if possible; but if not, he would call out when near me, so that I would not be frightened. When a few steps away he turned to wave his hand, and said 'ta-ta'. Reaching the river's edge, he threw off on the bank his heavy wadded Chinese jacket of dark blue cloth, and entered the river. Wading half across, he put out his arms to make the first stroke, but suddenly turned around and walked back again to the bank where he had first entered the water.

Shouting something up to me which I did not hear on account of the rushing river, he walked upstream in the opposite direction to the tents he had set out for. Then he followed a little path around the rocks that had obstructed our way the day before until out of sight, and I never saw him again. To swim across a river along both banks of which are numerous overhanging cliffs, and which pursues a serpentine course, is by no means easy, for the current carries a swimmer down sometimes to a place where he cannot land.

When Mr Rijnhart turned and waded back to the place at which he had entered, I hastily concluded that he intended to make another trial higher up, where the landing was level and good; for opposite us there were rocks that were in places almost a complete barrier to his getting a footing on shore. I watched for him to enter the water again beyond the large rock behind which he had disappeared; but not seeing him at once I took the telescope and walked a distance down the hill, so that my range of vision should command the bank.

To my great surprise, I saw flocks of sheep and numbers of cattle just beyond the rocks, on the same side of the river that I was on, and only a short distance away, almost near enough for me to have thrown a stone at them. I knew then that Mr Rijnhart, when he turned about in the water so suddenly, had caught a glimpse of these tents in our vicinity, and had hailed the sight with gladness, feeling that going to them he would need to be away from me only a short time, in comparison with that which he would necessarily occupy in crossing the river, and making his way down to the tents he had first proposed to visit. I also was much pleased at our discovery, for I expected him back perhaps in an hour or so with some of the natives, and at least felt sure that he would not be away until dark.

Varied were the thoughts that passed through my mind, for in my imagination I saw him in his clothing wet from wading in the water, as he had not waited a moment to divest himself of the wet garments, nor to pick up and throw about him his warm jacket which he had left on the bank; but accompanying that came a scene beside the fires of the tent where he was probably drinking steaming tea, while he explained his mission to the owners of those sheep and cattle, and bargained with them for animals.

A thought of his meeting with trouble did not enter my mind until the hours sped on and he came not; but even then, I did not fear, for we had always been treated with the greatest kindness and hospitality whenever we had met the people at their homes, although it is understood by all that the natives are robbers when away from home. He himself had not thought of difficulty, for he did not wait to remove from his bundle the revolver that might have had a moral effect over the tent people; but went around the rock buoyantly and sure that I would no longer have to walk, and that his heavy burden would be carried by strong yak, and doubtless entertaining the hope of being able to get aid from the abbot of Tashi Gomba in tracing our lost horses, resulting perhaps in their recovery.

Soon the sun went down over the top of the hill on which I sat, and the shadows grew longer and longer. Four bears gambolled about on the hillside until the shade fell on them and they shuffled away. I prayed for strength to be quiet, for God to give me freedom from anxiety as the time passed on and there was no appearance of him for whom I had watched all day. The cattle and the sheep across the river were rounded up and driven home to be tethered near the tents, but, besides the bears and my horse, there was not a sign of any living creature on the same bank where I was, for the flocks and herds towards which my husband had gone had long since disappeared. Knowing that the Tibetans are sometimes dilatory and hard to manage, I tried to think that the tents were some distance away, that the natives refused to help us unless my husband would remain until morning, and so I consoled myself with the thought that daylight would bring him to me. Reason told me he had fallen prey to wicked men, but I would not, because I had no desire to, listen to it, and my heart hoped against hope.

Dusk settled into darkness, and a desolate solitude reigned over hill and valley, almost chilling me to the heart as I sat alone in the stillness of that oriental night, broken by no sound of human voice, with no sympathy of friends to fall back upon, not even the companionship of the faithful Topsy. I thought of the possible strain both physical and mental of him who had gone so cheerfully around the rock that day.

What he must have suffered; did he have time to think of his wife alone and in danger! I knew that, unless he had hopes of helping me himself, every thought was a prayer that his loving Father would tenderly care for the one alone on the hillside. I tied my horse among the bushes and lay down, more for protection from the cold than from any desire to sleep, and spent a quiet, peaceful, though slumberless night, in a mood not to be surprised if the sound of that precious voice rang out my name through the deathly stillness, remembering what he had said about calling to me if he should return after dark – but in vain.

Morning came, and with it I rose to use the telescope once more, and wait for the hoped and longed-for return of my husband. The cattle and sheep spread out over the hills across the river, and all nature basked in the sunshine, but as the hours of the second day sped on and no trace of him was seen, my heart almost ceased beating. Well it was that we had learned to trust God in hard and difficult places. What else supported me through the leaden hours of that day but the thought that I was in God's hands? But I must admit it was a faith amidst a darkness thick and black that I could not enjoy the sunshine.

Evening found me still alone with God, just as I had been the night before. My undefined fear had shaped itself into almost a certainty, leaving me with scarcely any hope of ever seeing my husband again, and with just as little, probably, of my getting away from the same people who had seemingly murdered him, and indeed, I must confess I had no desire to leave that hill.

The conviction that the tents beyond those rocks belonged to the robbers who had stolen our horses was forced upon me, and I concluded also that when Mr. Rijnhart suddenly came into their presence they thought he had come for his horses, and would accuse them to their chief, thus causing the loss of the goods they had; and so, to avoid trouble, they had shot him and thrown his body into the river. Some days' journey from there the celebrated traveller Dutreuil de Khins had been killed in 1894, and the Tibetans had thrown his body into the river, but were compelled to pay dearly for it in silver, and a lama had been beheaded for the crime.

This was all well known to the men near us, and if I am correct in my surmise that these were the robbers, my brave and fearless husband had fallen a prey to their distrust and fear.

M. Grenard, who was Dutreuil's compagnon-de-voyage on the expedition on which the former was killed, as soon as he heard of Mr. Rijnhart's disappearance, wrote that the tribes in the locality where we had met our trouble were the most hostile they had seen, refusing to sell them anything even for large sums of money – and Miss Annie Taylor just avoided being stoned as a witch by the people of Tashi Gomba.

These circumstances add weight to what I myself had thought at the time. The second night I lay awake watching the stars that twinkled joyously, meditating and praying for some light as to my future, and asking God not to permit me to be rash and make mistakes. Oh! if I could only have helped Mr. Rijnhart. Morning came, and with it no solution of the impenetrable difficulty, and it seemed to me that I must stay on and wait for someone to come. About ten o'clock I stood scanning the landscape with the telescope, when suddenly I heard a shout from behind me on the hill.

My heart bounded with delight under the impulse of the moment, for I concluded it was the voice I so longed to hear, and that the yak I saw were some he had hired to help us. Therefore, I was only the more disappointed to see that they belonged to two lamas and several armed Tibetans coming from the opposite direction. I shouted to them, and as the lamas came down the hill I went up towards them, and we sat down to converse while their comrades went on with their yak. After the usual civilities had been exchanged they asked me where my husband was, and I replied that he had gone to some tents and had yet not returned. They inquired if I were not afraid to stay alone; and for answer I showed them my revolver, explaining that I could easily fire six shots from it before a native could fire one from his gun, and that each bullet could go through three men; whereupon they remarked to each other that no one had better try to harm me, as I could wound eighteen men before I could be touched.

They were travelling, they said, to a place three days' journey away, and as they were apparently friendly, I at first thought of journeying with them in the hope of enlisting their help, but gave that up as impossible. Then I asked them to take me across the river on their yak, and in answer they inquired if I had money. I said yes, I would pay them well for it. They jumped up, and, saying they would go for the yak, ran up the hill and out of sight in the direction of the tents to which my husband had gone. I waited in the same place all that day, but there was no sign of Mr. Rijnhart, nor did the men return when the sun had gone down.

I felt that my life would not be worth anything if I remained there all night, and that I must get away from that place; but whither I was to go I did not know. I tried to cross the river on my horse, but he would not venture into the water. Then I dragged him up the hill, sat down once more and reviewed the situation when the thought came: 'Why! I can never get away from here safely anyway. I will never be able to get out of the country, I am so far from the border; I may as well be killed first as last, and so I will go where my precious husband has gone.'

And once more I pulled my horse down the hill intending to go around the rock. But I was not to go. The impression grew upon me that it was rash to rush into almost certain death, and thus neither be any help to my husband nor leave any trace of the three of us who had left Tankar in such good spirits, thereby bringing untold sorrow and suspense to our home friends. Then there was the thought of future work. Had we not both consecrated ourselves to the evangelization of Tibet, and now that my dear husband had fallen, was the work and its responsibility any the less mine?

THEODORE ROOSEVELT
INTRODUCTION

When Theodore Roosevelt was invited to explore the rainforests of Brazil in 1913, it led to an unlikely pairing. He was joined by Cândido Mariano da Silva Rondon, the country's foremost adventurer. Rondon's father was Portuguese, but his maternal grandparents were from two indigenous tribes, the Terena and Bororo. A lifelong advocate for Indian rights, Rondon had made first contact with numerous 'lost' peoples, including the fearsome Nambikwara.

Roosevelt's conservation record was mixed. On the one hand, following a visit to Yosemite in 1903, he helped establish America's national parks. On the other, his appetite for hunting left destruction in his wake. A lifetime member of the National Rifle Association (NRA), on one 1904 trip he made to southern Africa in the company of his son, Kermit, he accounted for 11,000 slaughtered animals, of which 500 were big game. His attitude towards other cultures was likewise less than admirable from a modern perspective, as can be seen in his opinion that the locals needed 'raising up' by more 'civilised' outsiders.

Roosevelt had long planned a lecture tour of South America, including an Amazon cruise. Engagements were scheduled for Uruguay, Argentina and Chile, as well as Brazil. Meanwhile, during an expedition Rondon made in 1909 to map the many waterways Brazil's indigenous people called home, he stumbled upon the headwaters of a 1000-mile-long channel he named the Rio da Dúvida, the River of Doubt. Rondon was keen to ascertain whether it was a significant tributary of the Amazon. It was the suggestion of General Lauro Muller, Brazil's Secretary of State for Foreign Affairs, that the two men join forces.

Roosevelt fitted himself out as he had for Africa: khaki clothing, hobnail shoes and a small arsenal with which he armed the rest of the party; one Springfield rifle, two Winchesters, a selection of shotguns and revolvers courtesy of Messrs Colt, Smith and Wesson. The group of 20 included Kermit, the polar explorer Anthony Fiala, naturalist George Cherrie and Father John Zahm, clerical adviser during Roosevelt's time in office.

The Roosevelt-Rondon Scientific Expedition set out in early December 1913, travelling up the Paraguay River (Roosevelt took the opportunity to hunt tapirs) before traversing Brazil's western highlands. The jungle proved challenging. 'In these forests,' Roosevelt wrote, 'the multitude of insects that bite, sting, devour and prey upon other creatures, often with accompaniments of atrocious suffering, passes belief. The very myth of beneficent nature could not deceive even the least wise being if he once saw for himself the iron cruelty of life in the tropics.'

They reached the River of Doubt on 27 February 1914. Their problems began almost immediately. The frequency and size of the rapids forced them to regularly carry their canoes; when they did run the river, the supply dugouts they had purchased from local tribes were turned over or smashed against the rocks. Progress was slow. After three weeks, they had travelled just 87 of the total 660 miles they would cover in 60 days. The group was followed for much of the journey by the Cinta Larga, a tribe known to practise cannibalism; Rondon's dogs were killed by jaguars. Even calm water offered little respite: cayman and, of course, the infamous piranha. On one occasion, Roosevelt observed how 'the skinned carcass of a good-sized monkey was at once seized, pulled under the water and completely devoured by the blood-crazy fish'.

All but Rondon succumbed to malaria. Teddy Roosevelt contracted a flesh-eating bacterial infection so serious that, at one point, he urged Kermit to leave him behind to die. Back in Rio, the publicity machine told a different story. The River of Doubt was renamed the Roosevelt River (Rio Teodoro) while the expedition was still in progress, although its importance was not established. (It is several tributaries removed from the Amazon.)

Through the Brazilian Wilderness was published in 1914. Critics accused its author of employing artistic licence, specifically in his observations around flora and fauna. Roosevelt was outraged, convening a public forum in Washington at which he berated his doubters. Future expeditions would confirm many of his findings, but the toll on his long-term health was severe enough that he walked with a cane thereafter; he lost so much weight, *The New York Times* ran a before-and-after picture story. In subsequent decades Roosevelt was accused of showboating, of presenting himself, and not Rondon, as the Indians' champion. Rondon returned whence he came, a leading rights campaigner against the threat facing Brazil's rainforest peoples. In 1957, the Explorers' Club of New York nominated Rondon for the Nobel Peace Prize.

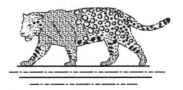

THROUGH THE BRAZILIAN WILDERNESS
BY THEODORE ROOSEVELT

Our northward trail led along the high ground a league or two
to the east of the northward-flowing Rio Sacre. Each night we
camped on one of the small tributary brooks that fed it. Fiala,
Kermit and I occupied one tent. In the daytime, the pium flies,
vicious little sandflies, became bad enough to make us finally
use gloves and head nets. There were many heavy rains, which
made the travelling hard for the mules. The soil was more
often clay than sand, and it was slippery when wet. The
weather was overcast, and there was usually no oppressive
heat even at noon. At intervals along the trail we came on the
staring skull and bleached skeleton of a mule or ox. Day after
day we rode forward across endless flats of grass and of low
open scrubby forest, the trees standing far apart and in most
places being but little higher than the head of a horseman.
Some of them carried blossoms, white, orange, yellow, pink;
and there were many flowers, the most beautiful being the
morning glories. Among the trees were bastard rubber trees,
and dwarf palmetto; if the latter grew more than a few feet
high, their tops were torn and dishevelled by the wind. There
was very little bird or mammal life; there were few long vistas,
for in most places it was not possible to see far among the
grey, gnarled trunks of the wind-beaten little trees. Yet the
desolate landscape had a certain charm of its own, although

not a charm that would be felt by any man who does not take pleasure in mere space, and freedom and wildness, and in plains standing empty to the sun, the wind and the rain. The country bore some resemblance to the country west of Redjaf on the White Nile, the home of the giant eland; only here there was no big game, no chance of seeing the towering form of the giraffe, the black bulk of elephant or buffalo, the herds of straw-coloured hartebeests or the ghostly shimmer of the sun glinting on the coats of roan and eland as they vanished silently in the grey sea of withered scrub.

One feature in common with the African landscape was the abundance of anthills, some as high as a man. They were red in the clay country, grey where it was sandy; and the dirt houses were also in trees, while their raised tunnels traversed trees and ground alike. At some of the camping places we had to be on our watch against the swarms of leaf-carrying ants. These are so called in the books – the Brazilians call them carregadores, or porters – because they are always carrying bits of leaves and blades of grass to their underground homes. They are inveterate burden bearers, and they industriously cut into pieces and carry off any garment they can get at; and we had to guard our shoes and clothes from them, just as we had often had to guard all our belongings against the termites. These ants did not bite us; but we encountered huge black ants, an inch and a quarter long, which were very vicious, and their bite was not only painful but quite poisonous. Praying mantis were common, and one evening at supper one had a comical encounter with a young dog, a jovial near-puppy, of Colonel Rondon's, named Cartucho. He had been christened the jolly-cum-pup, from a character in one of Frank Stockton's stories, which I suppose are now remembered only by elderly people, and by them only if they are natives of the United States. Cartucho was lying with his head on the oxhide that served as table, waiting with poorly dissembled impatience for his share of the banquet. The mantis flew down on the oxhide and proceeded to crawl over it, taking little flights from one corner to another; and whenever it thought itself menaced it assumed an attitude of seeming devotion and real defiance. Soon it lit in front of Cartucho's nose. Cartucho cocked his big ears forward, stretched his neck and cautiously sniffed at the new arrival, not with any hostile design, but merely to find out whether it would prove to be a playmate. The mantis promptly assumed an attitude of prayer. This struck Cartucho as both novel and interesting, and he thrust his sniffing black nose still nearer. The mantis dexterously thrust forward first one and then the other armed foreleg, touching the intrusive nose, which was instantly jerked back and again slowly and inquiringly brought forward. Then the mantis suddenly flew in Cartucho's face, whereupon Cartucho, with a smothered yelp of dismay, almost turned a back somersault; and the triumphant mantis flew back to the middle of the oxhide, among the plates, where it reared erect and defied the laughing and applauding company.

On the morning of the 29th we were rather late in starting, because the rain had continued through the night into the morning, drenching everything. After nightfall there had been some mosquitoes, and the piums were a pest during daylight; where one bites it leaves a tiny black spot on the skin which lasts for several weeks. In the slippery mud one of the pack mules fell and injured itself so that it had to be abandoned. Soon after starting we came on the telegraph line, which runs from Cuyaba. This was the first time we had seen it. Two Parecis Indians joined us, leading a pack bullock. They were dressed in hat, shirt, trousers and sandals, precisely like the ordinary Brazilian caboclos, as the poor backwoods peasants, usually with little white blood in them, are colloquially and half-derisively styled – caboclo being originally a Guarany word meaning 'naked savage'. These two Indians were in the employ of the Telegraphic Commission, and had been patrolling the telegraph line. The bullock carried their personal belongings and the tools with which they could repair a break. The commission pays the ordinary Indian worker 66 cents a day; a very good worker gets $1, and the chief $1.66. No man gets anything unless he works. Colonel Rondon, by just, kindly and understanding treatment of these Indians, who previously had often been exploited and maltreated by rubber gatherers, has made them the loyal friends of the government. He has gathered them at the telegraph stations, where they cultivate fields of mandioc, beans, potatoes, maize and other vegetables, and where he is introducing them to stock-raising; and the entire work of guarding and patrolling the line is theirs.

After six hours' march we came to the crossing of the Rio Sacre at the beautiful waterfall appropriately called the Salto Bello. This is the end of the automobile road. Here there is a small Parecis village. The men of the village work the ferry by which everything is taken across the deep and rapid river. The ferry boat is made of planking placed on three dugout canoes, and runs on a trolley. Before crossing we enjoyed a good swim in the swift, clear, cool water. The Indian village where we camped is placed on a jutting tongue of land round which the river sweeps just before it leaps from the overhanging precipice. The falls themselves are very lovely. Just above them is a wooded island, but the river joins again before it races forward for the final plunge. There is a sheer drop of forty or fifty yards, with a breadth two or three times as great; and the volume of water is large. On the left or hither bank a cliff extends for several hundred yards below the falls. Green vines have flung themselves down over its face, and they are met by other vines thrusting upward from the mass of vegetation at its foot, glistening in the perpetual mist from the cataract, and clothing even the rock surfaces in vivid green. The river, after throwing itself over the rock wall, rushes off in long curves at the bottom of a thickly wooded ravine, the white water churning among the black boulders. There is a perpetual rainbow at the foot of the falls. The masses of green water that are hurling themselves over the brink dissolve into shifting, foaming columns of snowy lace.

On the edge of the cliff below the falls Colonel Rondon had placed benches, giving a curious touch of rather conventional tourist civilisation to this cataract far out in the lonely wilderness. It is well worth visiting for its beauty. It is also of extreme interest because of the promise it holds for the future. Lieutenant Lyra informed me that they had calculated that this fall would furnish thirty-six thousand horsepower. Eight miles off we were to see another fall of much greater height and power. There are many rivers in this region which would furnish almost unlimited motive force to populous manufacturing communities. The country round about is healthy. It is an upland region of good climate; we were visiting it in the rainy season, the season when the nights are far less cool than in the dry season, and yet we found it delightful. There is much fertile soil in the neighbourhood of the streams, and the teeming lowlands of the Amazon and the Paraguay could readily – and with immense advantage to both sides – be made tributary to an industrial civilisation seated on these highlands. A telegraph line has been built to and across them. A railroad should follow. Such a line could be easily built, for there are no serious natural obstacles. In advance of its construction a trolley line could be run from Cuyaba to the falls, using the power furnished by the latter. Once this is done the land will offer extraordinary opportunities to settlers of the right kind: to homemakers and to enterprising business men of foresight, coolness and sagacity who are willing to work with the settlers, the immigrants, the homemakers, for an advantage which shall be mutual.

The Parecis Indians whom we met here were exceedingly

interesting. They were to all appearance an unusually cheerful, good-humoured, pleasant-natured people. Their teeth were bad; otherwise they appeared strong and vigorous, and there were plenty of children. The colonel was received as a valued friend and as a leader who was to be followed and obeyed. He is raising them by degrees – the only way by which to make the rise permanent. In this village he has got them to substitute for the flimsy Indian cabins houses of the type usual among the poorer field labourers and backcountry dwellers in Brazil. These houses have roofs of palm thatch, steeply pitched. They are usually open at the sides, consisting merely of a framework of timbers, with a wall at the back; but some have the ordinary four walls, of erect palm logs. The hammocks are slung in the houses, and the cooking is also done in them, with pots placed on small open fires, or occasionally in a kind of clay oven. The big gourds for water and the wicker baskets are placed on the ground, or hung on the poles.

The men had adopted, and were wearing, shirts and trousers, but the women had made little change in their clothing. A few wore print dresses, but obviously only for ornament. Most of them, especially the girls and young married women, wore nothing but a loincloth in addition to bead necklaces and bracelets. The nursing mothers – and almost all the mothers were nursing – sometimes carried the child slung against their side of hip, seated in a cloth belt, or sling, which went over the opposite shoulder of the mother. The women seemed to be well treated, although polygamy is practised. The children were loved by everyone; they were petted by both men and women, and they behaved well to one another, the boys not seeming to bully the girls or the smaller boys. Most of the children were naked, but the girls early wore the loincloth; and some, both of the little boys and the little girls, wore coloured print garments, to the evident pride of themselves and their parents. In each house there were several families, and life went on with no privacy but with good humour, consideration and fundamentally good manners. The man or woman who had nothing to do lay in a hammock or squatted on the ground, leaning against a post or wall. The children played together, or lay in little hammocks or tagged round after their mothers; and when called they came trustfully up to us to be petted or given some small trinket; they were friendly little souls, and accustomed to good treatment. One woman was weaving a cloth, another was making a hammock; others made ready melons and other vegetables and cooked them over tiny fires. The men, who had come in from work at the ferry or along the telegraph lines, did some work themselves or played with the children; one cut a small boy's hair, and then had his own hair cut by a friend. But the absorbing amusement of the men was an extraordinary game of ball.

Well, these Parecis Indians enthusiastically play football with their heads. The game is not only native to them, but I have never heard or read of its being played by any other tribe or people. They use a light hollow rubber ball, of their own manufacture. It is circular and about eight inches in diameter. The players are divided into two sides, and stationed much as in association football, and the ball is placed on the ground to be put in play as in football. Then a player runs forward, throws himself flat on the ground and butts the ball toward the opposite side. This first butt, when the ball is on the ground, never lifts it much and it rolls and bounds toward the opponents. One or two of the latter run toward it; one throws himself flat on his face and butts the ball back. Usually this butt lifts it, and it flies back in a curve well up in the air; and an opposite player, rushing toward it, catches it on his head with such a swing of his brawny neck, and such precision and address that the ball bounds back through the air as a football soars after a drop kick. If the ball flies off to one side or the other, it is brought back, and again put in play. Often it will be sent to and fro a dozen times, from head to head, until finally it rises with such a sweep that it passes far over the heads of the opposite players and descends behind them. Then shrill, rolling cries of good-humoured triumph arise from the victors; and the game instantly begins again with fresh zest. There are, of course, no such rules as in a specialised ball game of civilisation; and I saw no disputes. There may be eight or ten, or many more, players on each side. The ball is never touched with the hands or feet, or with anything except the top of the head. It is hard to decide whether to wonder most at the dexterity and strength with which it is hit or butted with the head, as it comes down through the air, or at the reckless speed and skill with which the players throw themselves headlong on the ground to return the ball if it comes low down. Why they do not grind off their noses I cannot imagine. Some of the players hardly ever failed to catch and return the ball if it came in their neighbourhood, and with such a vigorous toss of the head that it often flew in a great curve for a really astonishing distance.

ERNEST SHACKLETON
INTRODUCTION

Sir Ernest Shackleton considered himself a modern explorer. Born in County Kildare, the charismatic Irishman sought to dispense with the stuffy officer protocol of his forebears, notably Robert Falcon Scott. During Shackleton's Imperial Trans-Antarctic Expedition (1914–17), he joined in jokes and songs aboard his ship, the *Endurance*. Shackleton blurred class boundaries further by apportioning mundane chores among his men regardless of rank. A well-known photograph shows a trio scrubbing the deck: not able seamen but rather the expedition's geologist, surgeon and third officer.

It is the doomed *Endurance*, a symbol of forbearance captured so hauntingly by the photographer Frank Hurley, that gives lustre to the Shackleton legend. In truth, she was barely up to the job. Hurley, who dubbed the ship a 'bride of the sea', deployed clever camera angles to transform what was a standard, sail-assisted steamboat into a square-rigged and redoubtable frigate. Under Hurley's gaze, notes the critic Jonathan Raban, she resembled 'a revenant ghost from England's nautical past'.

Shackleton began raising funds in 1913. To achieve his aim of making the first 1800-mile crossing of Antarctica, Shackleton planned to use two vessels. The *Endurance* would carry the main party into the Weddell Sea and to Vahsel Bay, from where Shackleton's six-strong team would commence an overland trek. A second ship, the *Aurora*, would ferry a supporting party to McMurdo Sound, on the opposite side of the continent. This group would then lay supply depots to the Beardmore Glacier, for the additional provisions Shackleton's party would require.

The timing of the expedition was controversial. The *Endurance* set sail from London on 1 August 1914. Britain declared war on Germany three days later. Offering the Admiralty his services, Shackleton was hugely relieved when it declined, not least because he had laid considerable groundwork for what he hoped would be his glorious homecoming.

Shackleton had registered a film company, the Imperial Trans-Antarctic Film Syndicate, believing moving images crucial for commercial success – a way to pack lecture theatres on his return. The *Daily Chronicle* bought advance newspaper rights, while Heinemann purchased his book, subsequently titled *South*, which it published in 1919. Hurley's appointment proved a masterstroke. The Australian's images of the spectral *Endurance*, but also of dramatic ice caves and yawning chasms, seared the expedition into the national consciousness, as well as for generations to come; chronicling not just Shackleton's exploits, but making a key contribution to the canon of photographic art.

At South Georgia, the expedition left Grytviken on 5 December, bound for Antarctica. Over the following weeks, as ice grew more prevalent, Shackleton's primary concern was for 'growlers', sharp fragments of ice floating on the surface. These eventually gave way to great floes of pack ice, and by 19 January 1915, the *Endurance* was held fast. Shackleton planned to wait until spring, but the ice had other ideas, squeezing the hull of the ship until, on 24 October, she began to let in water. Shackleton gave the order to abandon ship. Four weeks later, on 21 November, the *Endurance* sank. (In the extract here, Shackleton acknowledges the inevitable as ice 'annihilates' the vessel.)

For the next five months, the men camped on the floes. On 9 April 1916, the approach of spring caused the ice to break up, forcing the team into their lifeboats. They made land at Elephant Island a week later – nearly 350 miles from the *Endurance*'s last position. With little chance of rescue, Shackleton instructed Henry McNish, the carpenter, to bolster one lifeboat, the *James Caird*, for a long sea voyage. With a makeshift deck, a five-man crew launched the vessel on 24 April. Shackleton took provisions enough for one month, believing if they had not reached land by then, all would be lost. On 20 May 1916, having covered 700 miles, Shackleton's party arrived at Stromness, a South Georgia whaling station. The remaining 22 men were recovered from Elephant Island the following September.

'Not a life lost' became a rallying cry, a cause for national celebration – Shackleton had survived where Scott had not. At the same time, it seemed to trivialise uncomfortable truths. The battles at Ypres, Verdun and the Somme had seen unprecedented deaths. (Shackleton's first question, upon his arrival at Stromness, was when the war had finished.) Aware of public sentiment – that he should have been fighting in France rather than gadding about on the ice – Shackleton dedicated *South* thus: 'To My Comrades who Fell in the White Warfare of the South and on the Red fields of France and Flanders.'

SOUTH
BY ERNEST SHACKLETON

After long months of ceaseless anxiety and strain, after times
when hope beat high and times when the outlook was black
indeed, the end of the *Endurance* has come. But though we
have been compelled to abandon the ship, which is crushed
beyond all hope of ever being righted, we are alive and well,
and we have stores and equipment for the task that lies before
us. The task is to reach land with all the members of the
Expedition. It is hard to write what I feel. To a sailor his ship
is more than a floating home, and in the *Endurance* I had
centred ambitions, hopes and desires. Now, straining and
groaning, her timbers cracking and her wounds gaping, she
is slowly giving up her sentient life at the very outset of her
career. She is crushed and abandoned after drifting more than
570 miles in a northwesterly direction during the 281 days
since she became locked in the ice. The distance from the
point where she became beset to the place where she now
rests mortally hurt in the grip of the floes is 573 miles, but the
total drift through all observed positions has been 1186 miles,
and probably we actually covered more than 1500 miles. We
are now 346 miles from Paulet Island, the nearest point where
there is any possibility of finding food and shelter. A small hut
built there by the Swedish expedition in 1902 is filled with
stores left by the Argentine relief ship. I know all about those

stores, for I purchased them in London on behalf of the
Argentine government when they asked me to equip the relief
expedition. The distance to the nearest barrier west of us is
about 180 miles, but a party going there would still be about 360
miles from Paulet Island, and there would be no means of
sustaining life on the barrier. We could not take from here food
enough for the whole journey; the weight would be too great.

This morning, our last on the ship, the weather was clear,
with a gentle south-southeasterly to south-southwesterly
breeze. From the crow's nest, there was no sign of land of any
sort. The pressure was increasing steadily, and the passing
hours brought no relief or respite for the ship. The attack of
the ice reached its climax at 4 p.m. The ship was hove stern up
by the pressure, and the driving floe, moving laterally across
the stern, split the rudder and tore out the rudder post and
stern post. Then, while we watched, the ice loosened and the
Endurance sank a little. The decks were breaking upwards,
and the water was pouring in below. Again the pressure began,
and at 5 p.m. I ordered all hands on to the ice. The twisting,
grinding floes were working their will at last on the ship. It
was a sickening sensation to feel the decks breaking up under
one's feet, the great beams bending and then snapping with a
noise like heavy gunfire. The water was overmastering the
pumps, and to avoid an explosion when it reached the boilers I
had to give orders for the fires to be drawn and the steam let
down. The plans for abandoning the ship in case of emergency
had been made well in advance, and men and dogs descended
to the floe and made their way to the comparative safety of an
unbroken portion of the floe without a hitch. Just before
leaving, I looked down the engine-room skylight as I stood on
the quivering deck, and saw the engines dropping sideways as
the stays and bedplates gave way. I cannot describe the
impression of relentless destruction that was forced upon me
as I looked down and around. The floes, with the force of

millions of tonnes of moving ice behind them, were simply annihilating the ship.

Essential supplies had been placed on the floe about 100 yds. from the ship, and there we set about making a camp for the night. But about 7 p.m., after the tents were up, the ice we were occupying became involved in the pressure and started to split and smash beneath our feet. I had the camp moved to a bigger floe about 200 yds. away, just beyond the bow of the ship. Boats, stores and camp equipment had to be conveyed across a working pressure ridge. The movement of the ice was so slow that it did not interfere much with our short trek, but the weight of the ridge had caused the floes to sink on either side, and there were pools of water there. A pioneer party with picks and shovels had to build a snow causeway before we could get all our possessions across. By 8 p.m. the camp had been pitched again. We had two pole-tents and three hoop-tents. I took charge of the small pole-tent, No. 1, with Hudson, Hurley and James as companions; Wild had the small hoop-tent, No. 2, with Wordie, McNeish and McIlroy. These hoop-tents are very easily shifted and set up. The eight forward hands had the large hoop-tent, No. 3; Crean had charge of No. 4 hoop-tent with Hussey, Marston and Cheetham; and Worsley had the other pole-tent, No. 5, with Greenstreet, Lees, Clark, Kerr, Rickenson, Macklin and Blackborrow, the last named being the youngest of the forward hands.

Tonight the temperature has dropped to –16° Fahr., and most of the men are cold and uncomfortable. After the tents had been pitched I mustered all hands and explained the position to them briefly and, I hope, clearly. I have told them the distance to the Barrier and the distance to Paulet Island, and have stated that I propose to try to march with equipment across the ice in the direction of Paulet Island. I thanked the men for the steadiness and good morale they have shown in these trying circumstances, and told them I had no doubt that, provided they continued to work their utmost and to trust me, we will all reach safety in the end. Then we had supper, which the cook had prepared at the big blubber stove, and after a watch had been set, all hands except the watch turned in. For myself, I could not sleep. The destruction and abandonment of the ship was no sudden shock. The disaster had been looming ahead for many months, and I had studied my plans for all contingencies a hundred times. But the thoughts that came to me as I walked up and down in the darkness were not particularly cheerful. The task now was to secure the safety of the party, and to that I must bend my energies and mental power and apply every bit of knowledge that experience of the Antarctic had given me. The task was likely to be long and strenuous, and an ordered mind and a clear programme were essential if we were to come through without loss of life. A man must shape himself to a new mark directly the old one goes to ground.

At midnight I was pacing the ice, listening to the grinding floe and to the groans and crashes that told of the death agony of the *Endurance*, when I noticed suddenly a crack running across our floe right through the camp. The alarm whistle brought all hands tumbling out, and we moved the tents and stores lying on what was now the smaller portion of the floe to the larger portion. Nothing more could be done at that moment, and the men turned in again; but there was little sleep. Each time I came to the end of my beat on the floe I could just see in the darkness the uprearing piles of pressure ice, which toppled over and narrowed still further the little floating island we occupied. I did not notice at the time that my tent, which had been on the wrong side of the crack, had not been erected again. Hudson and James had managed to squeeze themselves into other tents, and Hurley had wrapped himself in the canvas of No. 1 tent. I discovered this about 5 a.m. All night long the electric light gleamed from the stern of the dying *Endurance*. Hussey had left this light switched on when he took a last observation, and, like a lamp in a cottage window, it braved the night until in the early morning the *Endurance* received a particularly violent squeeze. There was a sound of rending beams, and the light disappeared. The connexion had been cut.

Morning came in chill and cheerless. All hands were stiff and weary after their first disturbed night on the floe. Just at daybreak I went over to the *Endurance* with Wild and Hurley in order to retrieve some tins of petrol that could be used to boil up milk for the rest of the men. The ship presented a painful spectacle of chaos and wreck. The jib-boom and bowsprit had snapped off during the night and now lay at right angles to the ship, with the chains, martingale and bobstay dragging them as the vessel quivered and moved in the grinding pack. The ice had driven over the forecastle, and she was well down by the head. We secured two tins of petrol with some difficulty, and postponed the further examination of the ship until after breakfast. Jumping across cracks with the tins, we soon reached camp, and built a fireplace out of the triangular watertight tanks we had ripped from the lifeboat. This we had done in order to make more room. Then we pierced a petrol tin in half a dozen places with an ice axe and set fire to it. The petrol blazed fiercely under the five-gallon drum we used as a cooker, and the hot milk was ready in quick time. Then we three ministering angels went round the tents with the life-giving drink, and were surprised and a trifle chagrined at the matter-of-fact manner in which some of the men accepted this contribution to their comfort. They did not quite understand what work we had done for them in the early dawn, and I heard Wild say, 'If any of you gentlemen would like your boots cleaned, just put them outside'. This was his gentle way of reminding them that a little thanks will go a long way on such occasions.

The cook prepared breakfast, which consisted of biscuit and hoosh, at 8 a.m., and I then went over to the *Endurance* again and made a fuller examination of the wreck. Only six of the cabins had not been pierced by floes and blocks of ice. Every one of the starboard cabins had been crushed. The whole of the after part of the ship had been crushed concertina fashion. The forecastle and the Ritz were submerged, and the wardroom was three-quarters full of ice. The starboard side of the wardroom had come away. The motor-engine forward had been driven through the galley. Petrol cases that had been stacked on the foredeck had been driven by the floe through the wall into the wardroom and had carried before them a large picture. Curiously enough, the glass of this picture had not been cracked, whereas in the immediate neighbourhood I saw heavy iron davits that had been twisted and bent like the ironwork of a wrecked train. The ship was being crushed remorselessly.

Under a dull, overcast sky I returned to camp and examined our situation. The floe occupied by the camp was still subject to pressure, and I thought it wise to move to a larger and apparently stronger floe about 200 yds. away, off the starboard bow of the ship. This camp was to become known as Dump Camp, owing to the amount of stuff that was thrown away there. We could not afford to carry unnecessary gear, and a drastic sorting of equipment took place. I decided to issue a complete new set of Burberrys and underclothing to each man, and also a supply of new socks. The camp was transferred to the larger floe quickly, and I began there to direct the preparations for the long journey across the floes to Paulet Island or Snow Hill.

Hurley meanwhile had rigged his kinematograph-camera and was getting pictures of the *Endurance* in her death throes. While he was engaged thus, the ice, driving against the standing rigging and the fore-, main- and mizzen-masts, snapped the shrouds. The foretop and topgallant mast came down with a run and hung in wreckage on the foremast, with the foreyard vertical. The main mast followed immediately, snapping off about 10 ft. above the main deck. The crow's nest fell within 10 ft. of where Hurley stood turning the handle of his camera, but he did not stop the machine, and so secured a unique, though sad, picture.

The issue of clothing was quickly accomplished. Sleeping bags were required also. We had eighteen fur bags, and it was necessary, therefore, to issue ten of the Jaeger woollen bags in order to provide for the twenty-eight men of the party. The woollen bags were lighter and less warm than the reindeer bags, and so each man who received one of them was allowed also a reindeer skin to lie upon. It seemed fair to distribute the fur bags by lot, but some of us older hands did not join in the lottery. We thought we could do quite as well with the Jaegers as with the furs. With quick dispatch the clothing was apportioned, and then we turned one of the boats on its side and supported it with two broken oars to make a lee for the galley. The cook got the blubber stove going, and a little later, when I was sitting round the corner of the stove, I heard one man say, 'Cook, I like my tea strong'. Another joined in, 'Cook, I like mine weak.' It was pleasant to know that their minds were untroubled, but I thought the time opportune to mention that the tea would be the same for all hands and that we would be fortunate if two months later we had any tea at all. It occurred to me at the time that the incident had psychological interest. Here were men, their home crushed, the camp pitched on the unstable floes and their chance of reaching safety apparently remote, calmly attending to the details of existence and giving their attention to such trifles as the strength of a brew of tea.

During the afternoon the work continued. Every now and then we heard a noise like heavy guns or distant thunder, caused by the floes grinding together.

The pressure caused by the congestion in this area of the

pack is producing a scene of absolute chaos. The floes grind stupendously, throw up great ridges and shatter one another mercilessly. The ridges, or hedgerows, marking the pressure lines that border the fast-diminishing pieces of smooth floe ice, are enormous. The ice moves majestically, irresistibly. Human effort is not futile, but man fights against the giant forces of Nature in a spirit of humility.

ROBERT LOUIS STEVENSON
INTRODUCTION

Robert Louis Stevenson's travel writing predates his most celebrated fiction by the best part of a decade. *Strange Case of Dr Jekyll and Mr Hyde* and *Kidnapped* were both published in 1886. *Travels with a Donkey in the Cévennes*, Stevenson's tale of his fortnight as a 'muleteer' and widely hailed as a masterpiece, was published in 1879 as the successor to 1878's *An Inland Voyage*. Among the many admirers of his travel works was Robert Byron, whose *Road to Oxiana* has tacit nods to Stevenson with its blend of conversational asides and soaring prose.

In *Travels with a Donkey*, Stevenson contemplates the restorative nature of simple tasks dutifully executed. In 1876, he met Fanny Van de Grift Osbourne, a married American who later became his lover (and even later his wife), whose return to San Francisco in the summer of 1878 left the author at a loss. Convinced physical activity would allay his lassitude, Stevenson chose to visit the Cévennes, part of the Massif Central in southern France. And a donkey was part of the picture. 'To hold a pack upon a packsaddle...is no high industry,' he wrote, 'but it is one that serves to occupy and compose the mind. And when the present is so exacting, who can annoy himself about the future?'

Stevenson set out from Le Monastier. It was here he purchased, from a Father Adam, his companion for the trip. The donkey of the title is Modestine, 'not much bigger than a dog, the colour of a mouse, with a kindly eye and a determined under-jaw'. Rather than simply a beast of burden, Stevenson conferred upon her the status of friend. His anthropomorphism was rewarded not by keen service but a pace so slow 'it kept me hanging on each foot for an incredible length of time; in five minutes it exhausted the spirit and set up a fever in all the muscles of the leg'.

An encounter with 'the green donkey driver', a redoubtable

expert, remedied the problem.

'"Your donkey,' says he, 'is very old?"

I told him, I believed not.

Then, he supposed, we had come far.

I told him, we had but newly left Monastier.

"Et vous marchez comme ça!" cried he, and...began to lace Modestine about the stern-works, uttering a cry. The rogue pricked up her ears and broke into a good round pace, which she kept up...without exhibiting the least symptom of distress.'

Stevenson and Modestine went on to cover 120 miles, crossing 'several respectable ridges'. Their route took them to St Jean du Gard, by way of Gévaudan, Cheylard, Luc and Goulet. There is also a lengthy, lively passage on Stevenson's night in Our Lady of the Snows, a Trappist monastery in Vivarais, and featured in the extract here.

Travels with a Donkey is, more often than not, a comedy. Stevenson 'spent about a month of fine days' in the region, half of those walking with Modestine and registering the beauty in small details, of which he was a master.

He and Modestine even became friends. 'Although sometimes I was hurt and distant in manner,' he wrote when the time came for parting, 'I still kept my patience; and as for her, poor soul, she had come to regard me as a god. She loved to eat out of my hand. She was patient, elegant in form...and inimitably small. Her faults were those of her race and sex; her virtues were her own.'

TRAVELS WITH A
DONKEY IN THE CÉVENNES
BY ROBERT LOUIS STEVENSON

The inn was again singularly unpretentious. The whole
furniture of a not ill-to-do family was in the kitchen: the beds,
the cradle, the clothes, the plate rack, the meal chest and the
photograph of the parish priest. There were five children, one
of whom was set to its morning prayers at the stair-foot soon
after my arrival, and a sixth would ere long be forthcoming. I
was kindly received by these good folk. They were much
interested in my misadventure. The wood in which I had slept
belonged to them; the man of Fouzilhac they thought a
monster of iniquity, and counselled me warmly to summon
him at law – 'because I might have died'. The good wife was
horror-stricken to see me drink over a pint of uncreamed milk.

'You will do yourself an evil,' she said. 'Permit me to boil it
for you.'

After I had begun the morning on this delightful liquor, she
having an infinity of things to arrange, I was permitted, nay
requested, to make a bowl of chocolate for myself. My boots
and gaiters were hung up to dry, and, seeing me trying to write
my journal on my knee, the eldest daughter let down a hinged
table in the chimney corner for my convenience. Here I wrote,
drank my chocolate and finally ate an omelette before I left.

The table was thick with dust; for, as they explained, it was not used except in winter weather. I had a clear look up the vent, through brown agglomerations of soot and blue vapour, to the sky; and whenever a handful of twigs was thrown on to the fire, my legs were scorched by the blaze.

The husband had begun life as a muleteer, and when I came to charge Modestine showed himself full of the prudence of his art. 'You will have to change this package,' said he; 'it ought to be in two parts, and then you might have double the weight.'

I explained that I wanted no more weight; and for no donkey hitherto created would I cut my sleeping bag in two.

'It fatigues her, however,' said the innkeeper; 'it fatigues her greatly on the march. Look.'

Alas, there were her two forelegs no better than raw beef on the inside, and blood was running from under her tail. They told me when I started, and I was ready to believe it, that before a few days I should come to love Modestine like a dog. Three days had passed, we had shared some misadventures, and my heart was still as cold as a potato towards my beast of burden. She was pretty enough to look at; but then she had given proof of dead stupidity, redeemed indeed by patience, but aggravated by flashes of sorry and ill-judged light-heartedness. And I own this new discovery seemed another point against her. What the devil was the good of a she-ass if she could not carry a sleeping bag and a few necessaries? I saw the end of the fable rapidly approaching, when I should have to carry Modestine. Aesop was the man to know the world! I assure you I set out with heavy thoughts upon my short day's march.

It was not only heavy thoughts about Modestine that weighted me upon the way; it was a leaden business altogether. For first, the wind blew so rudely that I had to hold on to the pack with one hand from Cheylard to Luc; and second, my road lay through one of the most beggarly countries in the world. It was like the worst of the Scottish

Highlands, only worse; cold, naked and ignoble, scant of wood, scant of heather, scant of life. A road and some fences broke the unvarying waste, and the line of the road was marked by upright pillars, to serve in time of snow.

Why anyone should desire to visit either Luc or Cheylard is more than my much-inventing spirit can suppose. For my part, I travel not to go anywhere, but to go. I travel for travel's sake. The great affair is to move; to feel the needs and hitches of our life more nearly; to come down off this feather bed of civilisation, and find the globe granite underfoot and strewn with cutting flints. Alas, as we get up in life, and are more preoccupied with our affairs, even a holiday is a thing that must be worked for. To hold a pack upon a packsaddle against a gale out of the freezing north is no high industry, but it is one that serves to occupy and compose the mind. And when the present is so exacting, who can annoy himself about the future?

I came out at length above the Allier. A more unsightly prospect at this season of the year it would be hard to fancy. Shelving hills rose round it on all sides, here dabbled with wood and fields, there rising to peaks alternately naked and hairy with pines. The colour throughout was black or ashen, and came to a point in the ruins of the castle of Luc, which pricked up impudently from below my feet, carrying on a pinnacle a tall white statue of Our Lady, which, I heard with interest, weighed fifty quintals, and was to be dedicated on the 6th of October. Through this sorry landscape trickled the Allier and a tributary of nearly equal size, which came down to join it through a broad nude valley in Vivarais. The weather had somewhat lightened, and the clouds massed in squadron; but the fierce wind still hunted them through heaven, and cast great ungainly splashes of shadow and sunlight over the scene.

Luc itself was a straggling double file of houses wedged between hill and river. It had no beauty, nor was there any notable feature save the old castle overhead with its fifty quintals of brand-new Madonna. But the inn was clean and large. The kitchen, with its two box-beds hung with clean check curtains, with its wide stone chimney, its chimney shelf four yards long and garnished with lanterns and religious statuettes, its array of chests and pair of ticking clocks, was the very model of what a kitchen ought to be; a melodrama kitchen, suitable for bandits or noblemen in disguise. Nor was the scene disgraced by the landlady, a handsome, silent, dark old woman, clothed and hooded in black like a nun. Even the public bedroom had a character of its own, with the long deal tables and benches, where fifty might have dined, set out as for a harvest home, and the three box-beds along the wall. In one of these, lying on straw and covered with a pair of table napkins, did I do penance all night long in gooseflesh and chattering teeth, and sigh from time to time as I awakened, for my sheepskin sack and the lee of some great wood.

OUR LADY OF THE SNOWS

'I behold
The House, the Brotherhood austere –
And what am I, that I am here?'
MATTHEW ARNOLD.

FATHER APOLLINARIS

Next morning (Thursday, 26 September) I took the road in a new order. The sack was no longer doubled, but hung at full length across the saddle, a green sausage six feet long with a tuft of blue wool hanging out of either end. It was more picturesque, it spared the donkey and, as I began to see, it would ensure stability, blow high, blow low. But it was not without a pang that I had so decided. For although I had purchased a new cord, and made all as fast as I was able, I was yet jealously uneasy lest the flaps should tumble out and scatter my effects along the line of march.

My way lay up the bald valley of the river, along the march of Vivarais and Gévaudan. The hills of Gévaudan on the right were a little more naked, if anything, than those of Vivarais upon the left, and the former had a monopoly of a low dotty underwood that grew thickly in the gorges and died out in solitary burrs upon the shoulders and the summits. Black bricks of fir wood were plastered here and there upon both sides, and here and there were cultivated fields. A railway ran beside the river; the only bit of railway in Gévaudan, although there are many proposals afoot and surveys being made, and even, as they tell me, a station standing ready built in Mende. A year or two hence and this may be another world. The desert is beleaguered. Now may some Languedocian Wordsworth turn the sonnet into patois: 'Mountains and vales and floods, heard ye that whistle?'

At a place called La Bastide I was directed to leave the river, and follow a road that mounted on the left among the hills of Vivarais, the modern Ardèche; for I was now come within a little way of my strange destination, the Trappist monastery of Our Lady of the Snows. The sun came out as I left the shelter of a pine wood, and I beheld suddenly a fine wild landscape to the south. High rocky hills, as blue as sapphire, closed the view, and between these lay ridge upon ridge, heathery, craggy, the sun glittering on veins of rock, the underwood clambering in the hollows, as rude as God made them at the first. There was not a sign of man's hand in all the prospect; and indeed not a trace of his passage, save where generation after generation had walked in twisted footpaths, in and out among the beeches, and up and down upon the channelled slopes. The mists, which had hitherto beset me, were now broken into clouds, and fled swiftly and shone brightly in the sun. I drew a long breath. It was grateful to come, after so long, upon a scene of some attraction for the human heart. I own I like definite form in what my eyes are to rest upon; and if landscapes were sold, like the sheets of characters of my boyhood, one penny plain and twopence coloured, I should go the length of twopence every day of my life.

But if things had grown better to the south, it was still desolate and inclement near at hand. A spidery cross on every hilltop marked the neighbourhood of a religious house; and a quarter of a mile beyond, the outlook southward opening out and growing bolder with every step, a white statue of the Virgin at the corner of a young plantation directed the traveller to Our Lady of the Snows. Here, then, I struck leftward, and pursued my way, driving my secular donkey before me, and creaking in my secular boots and gaiters, towards the asylum of silence.

I had not gone very far ere the wind brought to me the clanging of a bell, and somehow, I can scarce tell why, my heart sank within me at the sound. I have rarely approached anything with more unaffected terror than the monastery of Our Lady of the Snows. This it is to have had a Protestant education. And suddenly, on turning a corner, fear took hold on me from head to foot – slavish, superstitious fear; and though I did not stop in my advance, yet I went on slowly, like a man who should have passed a bourn unnoticed, and strayed into the country of the dead. For there, upon the narrow new-made road, between the stripling pines, was a mediaeval friar, fighting with a barrowful of turfs. Every Sunday of my childhood I used to study the Hermits of Marco Sadeler – enchanting prints, full of wood and field and mediaeval landscapes, as large as a county, for the imagination to go a-travelling in; and here, sure enough, was one of Marco Sadeler's heroes. He was robed in white like any spectre, and the hood falling back, in the instancy of his contention with the barrow, disclosed a pate as bald and yellow as a skull. He might have been buried any time these thousand years, and all the lively parts of him resolved into earth and broken up with the farmer's harrow.

I was troubled besides in my mind as to etiquette. Durst I

address a person who was under a vow of silence? Clearly not. But drawing near, I doffed my cap to him with a faraway superstitious reverence. He nodded back, and cheerfully addressed me. Was I going to the monastery? Who was I? An Englishman? Ah, an Irishman, then?

'No,' I said, 'a Scotsman.'

A Scotsman? Ah, he had never seen a Scotsman before. And he looked me all over, his good, honest, brawny countenance shining with interest, as a boy might look upon a lion or an alligator. From him I learned with disgust that I could not be received at Our Lady of the Snows; I might get a meal, perhaps, but that was all. And then, as our talk ran on, and it turned out that I was not a pedlar, but a literary man, who drew landscapes and was going to write a book, he changed his manner of thinking as to my reception (for I fear they respect persons even in a Trappist monastery), and told me I must be sure to ask for the Father Prior, and state my case to him in full. On second thoughts he determined to go down with me himself; he thought he could manage for me better. Might he say that I was a geographer?

No; I thought, in the interests of truth, he positively might not.

'Very well, then' (with disappointment), 'an author.'

It appeared he had been in a seminary with six young Irishmen, all priests long since, who had received newspapers and kept him informed of the state of ecclesiastical affairs in England. And he asked me eagerly after Dr Pusey, for whose conversion the good man had continued ever since to pray night and morning.

'I thought he was very near the truth,' he said; 'and he will reach it yet; there is so much virtue in prayer.'

He must be a stiff, ungodly Protestant who can take anything but pleasure in this kind and hopeful story. While he was thus near the subject, the good father asked me if I were a

Christian; and when he found I was not, or not after his way, he glossed it over with great goodwill.

The road which we were following, and which this stalwart father had made with his own two hands within the space of a year, came to a corner, and showed us some white buildings a little farther on beyond the wood. At the same time, the bell once more sounded abroad. We were hard upon the monastery. Father Apollinaris (for that was my companion's name) stopped me.

'I must not speak to you down there,' he said. 'Ask for the Brother Porter, and all will be well. But try to see me as you go out again through the wood, where I may speak to you. I am charmed to have made your acquaintance.'

And then suddenly raising his arms, flapping his fingers and crying out twice, 'I must not speak, I must not speak!' he ran away in front of me, and disappeared into the monastery door.

I own this somewhat ghastly eccentricity went a good way to revive my terrors. But where one was so good and simple, why should not all be alike? I took heart of grace, and went forward to the gate as fast as Modestine, who seemed to have a disaffection for monasteries, would permit. It was the first door, in my acquaintance of her, which she had not shown an indecent haste to enter. I summoned the place in form, though with a quaking heart. Father Michael, the Father Hospitaller, and a pair of brown-robed brothers came to the gate and spoke with me a while. I think my sack was the great attraction; it had already beguiled the heart of poor Apollinaris, who had charged me on my life to show it to the Father Prior. But whether it was my address, or the sack or the idea speedily published among that part of the brotherhood who attend on strangers that I was not a pedlar after all, I found no difficulty as to my reception. Modestine was led away by a layman to the stables, and I and my pack were received into Our Lady of the Snows.

MARK TWAIN
INTRODUCTION

Mark Twain's memoir of his brief career as a steamboat pilot from 1857 to 1861 comprises personal reminiscences, history and geography, but it also has a mournful poetry. Filled with the sorts of characters who would later people his fictional masterpieces, the various adventures of Tom Sawyer and Huckleberry Finn, Twain's Mississippi lament contains sentences that capture a landscape and life now lost.

'When I was a boy,' Twain wrote, 'there was but one permanent ambition among my comrades in our village on the west bank of the Mississippi River. That was to be a steamboatman. We had transient ambitions of other sorts, but they were only transient. When a circus came and went, it left us all burning to become clowns... now and then we had a hope that if we lived and were good, God would permit us to be pirates. These ambitions faded out, each in its turn; but the ambition to be a steamboatman always remained.'

The Mississippi gave Twain his nom de plume – 'mark twain' means a measured depth of thirteen-and-a-half feet, sufficient for a steamboat's draft – and America its new superstar. Twain was born Samuel Clemens in Hannibal, Missouri in 1835. It was a frontier town, and steamboats, thanks to a shallow draft that enabled them to carry large quantities of both passengers and cargo, soon became the workhorses connecting urban centres. Twain embarked on the life of a pilot during the steamboats' heyday, in the years just before the Civil War closed off the river. In fact, their death knell had already been sounded by the harsh whistle of the railroad as early as the 1820s, a development Twain considered a scar upon the land. 'The unholy train comes tearing along,' he wrote, 'ripping the sacred solitude to rags and tatters with its devil's war whoop and the roar and thunder of its rushing wheels.' It is a bittersweet coincidence, perhaps, that the deal to secure Missouri's first railroad was overseen by Twain's father, John Clemens.

Twain Junior went on to international celebrity, a regular guest of presidents and premiers, but it was his time on the water that he recalled most fondly. The Mississippi is an imposing beast and flows for 2320 miles, from Lake Itasca in Minnesota to the Gulf of Mexico – its drainage basin covers 40% of the United States. Second in length only to the Missouri River (and then by just 20 or so miles), the Mississippi takes in Louisiana, Wisconsin, Illinois, Kentucky, Tennessee, Iowa, Missouri, of course, and Arkansas. The channel depth changes constantly, and successfully navigating its broad straights and meandering curves was, for the 19th-century steamboat pilot, a sign of manhood accomplished. Twain was 22 years old when he persuaded a veteran captain, the vexatious and foul-mouthed Horace Bixby, to take him on as an apprentice. '[He] threw open a window, thrust his head out and such an irruption followed as I never had heard before,' Twain wrote on the occasion of Bixby's vessel colliding with a scow. 'When he closed the window he was empty. You could have drawn a seine through his system and not caught curses enough to disturb your mother with.'

If his mentor could prove challenging, so too could the work; the 'leadsman' called the depth (often falsely, to keep Twain on his toes), and the pilot steered the course, learning the intricate contours of the river as he went. The region was opening up fast, 'bristling with great towns, projected day before yesterday, so to speak, and built next morning'. By the time Life on the Mississippi was published in 1883, Twain already had two critically acclaimed works of non-fiction to his name. The Innocents Abroad (published in 1869) chronicles a trip through Europe to the Holy Land with a band of outrageously ill-informed countrymen; and Roughing It (1872), sees Twain recall his less than successful attempts to mine for silver in Nevada.

He developed Life... from sketches published eight years previously in 1875, in The Atlantic Monthly, under the title 'Old

Times on the Mississippi'. The result is more than a pragmatic repackaging of previously published work. America's best-known writer is acknowledging, ruefully it seems, the enforced surrender of his beloved Mississippi to the rush and bustle of the modern world. War was the augur of change. With both the Union and the Confederacy realising the Mississippi's strategic importance, it was the fall of Vicksburg in 1863 that gave the Union control of the river and split the Confederacy in two. Twain joined the Confederate militia, albeit for just two weeks before his confidence in the cause deserted him. He headed west to California to begin his new life as a journalist, novelist and performer, with all the obligations those careers entailed. Yet the Mississippi would always call to him. 'I loved the profession far better than any I have followed since,' Twain wrote of his time on the river, 'and I took a measureless pride in it. The reason is plain: a pilot, in those days, was the only unfettered and entirely independent human being that lived on Earth.'

LIFE ON THE MISSISSIPPI
BY MARK TWAIN

At the end of what seemed a tedious while, I had managed to pack my head full of islands, towns, bars, 'points' and bends; and a curiously inanimate mass of lumber it was too. However, inasmuch as I could shut my eyes and reel off a good long string of these names without leaving out more than ten miles of river in every fifty, I began to feel that I could take a boat down to New Orleans if I could make her skip those little gaps. But of course my complacency could hardly get start enough to lift my nose a trifle into the air before Mr Bixby would think of something to fetch it down again. One day he turned on me suddenly with this settler –

'What is the shape of Walnut Bend?'

He might as well have asked me my grandmother's opinion of protoplasm. I reflected respectfully, and then said I didn't know it had any particular shape. My gunpowdery chief went off with a bang, of course, and then went on loading and firing until he was out of adjectives.

I had learned long ago that he only carried just so many rounds of ammunition, and was sure to subside into a very placable and even remorseful old smooth-bore as soon as they were all gone. That word 'old' is merely affectionate; he was not more than thirty-four. I waited. By and by he said –

'My boy, you've got to know the shape of the river perfectly.

It is all there is left to steer by on a very dark night. Everything else is blotted out and gone. But mind you, it hasn't the same shape in the night that it has in the daytime.'

'How on earth am I ever going to learn it, then?'

'How do you follow a hall at home in the dark? Because you know the shape of it. You can't see it.'

'Do you mean to say that I've got to know all the million trifling variations of shape in the banks of this interminable river as well as I know the shape of the front hall at home?'

'On my honour, you've got to know them better than any man ever did know the shapes of the halls in his own house.'

'I wish I was dead!'

'Now I don't want to discourage you, but–'

'Well, pile it on me; I might as well have it now as another time.'

'You see, this has got to be learned; there isn't any getting around it. A clear starlight night throws such heavy shadows that if you didn't know the shape of a shore perfectly you would claw away from every bunch of timber, because you would take the black shadow of it for a solid cape; and you see you would be getting scared to death every fifteen minutes by the watch. You would be fifty yards from shore all the time when you ought to be within fifty feet of it. You can't see a snag in one of those shadows, but you know exactly where it is, and the shape of the river tells you when you are coming to it. Then there's your pitch-dark night; the river is a very different shape on a pitch-dark night from what it is on a starlight night. All shores seem to be straight lines, then, and mighty dim ones too; and you'd run them for straight lines only you know better. You boldly drive your boat right into what seems to be a solid, straight wall (you knowing very well that in reality there is a curve there), and that wall falls back and makes way for you. Then there's your grey mist. You take a night when there's one of these grisly, drizzly grey mists, and then there isn't any particular shape to a shore. A grey mist would tangle the head of the oldest man that ever lived. Well, then, different kinds of moonlight change the shape of the river in different ways. You see–'

'Oh, don't say any more, please! Have I got to learn the shape of the river according to all these five hundred thousand different ways? If I tried to carry all that cargo in my head it would make me stoop-shouldered.'

'No! you only learn the shape of the river, and you learn it with such absolute certainty that you can always steer by the shape that's in your head, and never mind the one that's before your eyes.'

'Very well, I'll try it; but after I have learned it can I depend on it? Will it keep the same form and not go fooling around?'

Before Mr Bixby could answer, Mr W—— came in to take the watch, and he said –

'Bixby, you'll have to look out for President's Island and all that country clear away up above the Old Hen and Chickens. The banks are caving and the shape of the shores changing like everything. Why, you wouldn't know the point above forty. You can go up inside* the old sycamore-snag now.

So that question was answered. Here were leagues of shore changing shape. My spirits were down in the mud again. Two things seemed pretty apparent to me. One was that in order to be a pilot a man had got to learn more than any one man ought to be allowed to know; and the other was that he must learn it all over again in a different way every twenty-four hours.

That night we had the watch until twelve. Now, it was an ancient river custom for the two pilots to chat a bit when the watch changed. While the relieving pilot put on his gloves and lit his cigar, his partner, the retiring pilot, would say

* 1 'inside' means between the snag and the shore.

something like this –'I judge the upper bar is making down a little at Hale's Point; had quarter twain* with the lower lead and mark twain with the other.'

'Yes, I thought it was making down a little, last trip. Meet any boats?'

'Met one abreast the head of twenty-one, but she was away over hugging the bar, and I couldn't make her out entirely. I took her for the "Sunny South" – hadn't any skylights forward of the chimneys.'

And so on. And as the relieving pilot took the wheel his partner* would mention that we were in such-and-such a bend, and say we were abreast of such-and-such a man's wood-yard or plantation. This was courtesy; I supposed it was necessity. But Mr W—— came on watch full twelve minutes late on this particular night, – a tremendous breach of etiquette; in fact, it is the unpardonable sin among pilots. So Mr Bixby gave him no greeting whatever, but simply surrendered the wheel and marched out of the pilot house without a word. I was appalled; it was a villainous night for blackness, we were in a particularly wide and blind part of the river, where there was no shape or substance to anything, and it seemed incredible that Mr Bixby should have left that poor fellow to kill the boat trying to find out where he was. But I resolved that I would stand by him anyway. He should find that he was not wholly friendless. So I stood around, and waited to be asked where we were. But Mr W— – plunged on serenely through the solid firmament of black cats that stood for an atmosphere, and never opened his mouth. Here is a proud devil, thought I; here is a limb of Satan that would rather send us all to destruction than put himself under obligations to me, because I am not yet one of the salt of the earth and privileged to snub captains and lord it over everything dead and alive in a steamboat. I

* 2 Two fathoms. 'Quarter twain' is two-and-a-quarter fathoms, thirteen-and-a-half feet. 'Mark three' is three fathoms. *3 'Partner' is a technical term for 'the other pilot'.

presently climbed up on the bench; I did not think it was safe to go to sleep while this lunatic was on watch.

However, I must have gone to sleep in the course of time, because the next thing I was aware of was the fact that day was breaking, Mr W—— gone and Mr Bixby at the wheel again. So it was four o'clock and all well – but me; I felt like a skinful of dry bones and all of them trying to ache at once.

Mr Bixby asked me what I had stayed up there for. I confessed that it was to do Mr W—— a benevolence, – tell him where he was. It took five minutes for the entire preposterousness of the thing to filter into Mr Bixby's system, and then I judge it filled him nearly up to the chin; because he paid me a compliment – and not much of a one either. He said,

'Well, taking you by and large, you do seem to be more different kinds of an ass than any creature I ever saw before. What did you suppose he wanted to know for?'

I said I thought it might be a convenience to him.

'Convenience D-nation! Didn't I tell you that a man's got to know the river in the night the same as he'd know his own front hall?'

'Well, I can follow the front hall in the dark if I know it is the front hall; but suppose you set me down in the middle of it in the dark and not tell me which hall it is; how am I to know?'

'Well you've got to, on the river!'

'All right. Then I'm glad I never said anything to Mr W——'

'I should say so. Why, he'd have slammed you through the window and utterly ruined a hundred dollars' worth of window sash and stuff.'

I was glad this damage had been saved, for it would have made me unpopular with the owners. They always hated anybody who had the name of being careless, and injuring things.

I went to work now to learn the shape of the river; and of all the eluding and ungraspable objects that ever I tried to get mind or hands on, that was the chief. I would fasten my eyes upon a sharp, wooded point that projected far into the river some miles ahead of me, and go to laboriously photographing its shape upon my brain; and just as I was beginning to succeed to my satisfaction, we would draw up toward it and the exasperating thing would begin to melt away and fold back into the bank! If there had been a conspicuous dead tree standing upon the very point of the cape, I would find that tree inconspicuously merged into the general forest, and occupying the middle of a straight shore, when I got abreast of it! No prominent hill would stick to its shape long enough for me to make up my mind what its form really was, but it was as dissolving and changeful as if it had been a mountain of butter in the hottest corner of the tropics. Nothing ever had the same shape when I was coming downstream that it had borne when I went up. I mentioned these little difficulties to Mr Bixby. He said –

'That's the very main virtue of the thing. If the shapes didn't change every three seconds they wouldn't be of any use. Take this place where we are now, for instance. As long as that hill over yonder is only one hill, I can boom right along the way I'm going; but the moment it splits at the top and forms a V, I know I've got to scratch to starboard in a hurry, or I'll bang this boat's brains out against a rock; and then the moment one of the prongs of the V swings behind the other, I've got to waltz to larboard again, or I'll have a misunderstanding with a snag that would snatch the keelson out of this steamboat as neatly as if it were a sliver in your hand. If that hill didn't change its shape on bad nights there would be an awful steamboat graveyard around here inside of a year.'

It was plain that I had got to learn the shape of the river in all the different ways that could be thought of, – upside down, wrong end first, inside out, fore and aft and 'thortships', – and then know what to do on grey nights when it hadn't any shape at all. So I set about it. In the course of time I began to get the best of this knotty lesson, and my self-complacency moved to the front once more. Mr Bixby was all fixed, and ready to start it to the rear again. He opened on me after this fashion –

'How much water did we have in the middle crossing at Hole-in-the-Wall, trip before last?'

I considered this an outrage. I said –

'Every trip, down and up, the leadsmen are singing through that tangled place for three-quarters of an hour on a stretch. How do you reckon I can remember such a mess as that?'

'My boy, you've got to remember it. You've got to remember the exact spot and the exact marks the boat lay in when we had the shoalest water in every one of the five hundred shoal places between St. Louis and New Orleans; and you mustn't get the shoal soundings and marks of one trip mixed up with the shoal soundings and marks of another either, for they're not often twice alike. You must keep them separate.'

When I came to myself again, I said –

'When I get so that I can do that, I'll be able to raise the dead, and then I won't have to pilot a steamboat to make a living. I want to retire from this business. I want a slush bucket and a brush; I'm only fit for a roustabout. I haven't got brains enough to be a pilot; and if I had I wouldn't have strength enough to carry them around, unless I went on crutches.'

'Now drop that! When I say I'll learn* a man the river, I mean it. And you can depend on it, I'll learn him or kill him.'

* 'Teach' is not in the river vocabulary.

EDITH WHARTON
INTRODUCTION

Before she became a Pulitzer Prize-winning novelist, Edith
Wharton's first love was architecture; specifically, interior design
and landscape gardening. 'Homes and gardens' might seem a
trivial interest for a writer whose circle included her great friend
and mentor Henry James. Yet Wharton's knowledge was more
than opinion. In the 1890s, Wharton and her husband Teddy had
carried out renovations of two homes in the wealthy suburb of
Newport, Rhode Island. Her collaborator was the renowned
architect Ogden Codman. Together, they determined to bring some
European refinement to a New England resort scarred by the
conspicuous tastes of new money, whose vast properties displayed
Gatsby-style excess. A by-product of that relationship was
Wharton's first book, *The Decoration of Houses*, cowritten with
Codman and published in 1897. 'When the rich man demands
good architecture his neighbours will get it too,' Wharton intoned,
a little sniffily. 'The vulgarity of current decoration has its source in
the indifference of the wealthy to architectural fitness.'

In 1902, with the architect Francis Hoppin, Wharton built the
first house of her own: The Mount, a grand French château-style
property in the hills above Lenox, Massachusetts. That her tastes
were refined and expensive, she made no apology for. It was once
said of Wharton: 'She has seen France, Italy and Spain from a
limousine, and the Parthenon from a yacht.' Her other great love
was travel. Wharton was able to combine her two passions when
she convinced *Scribner*'s to let her write about a 1917 trip to
Morocco. Wharton was an exacting traveller, with little time for the
bumbling American abroad, those compatriots who 'mistake the
Baptistery at Parma for the railway station'. Her previous study of
Italian architecture and landscape design, *Italian Villas and Their
Gardens*, was a serious work of garden archaeology. The majority

of properties Wharton visited on that trip were built during the Baroque and Renaissance periods. Subsequent trustees, Wharton reminded readers – and addressed in the extract here on Venetian villas – looked to a different aesthetic, the flower beds and lawns of English country houses and of French châteaux.

Similarly, she looked at Fez through the lens of its rich architectural history. Now recognised as a Unesco site for its well preserved buildings, Wharton gives testimony to the long, rich heritage of Fez and Marrakesh. Her views on the native peoples of Morocco have not stood the test of time as well, and her positive attitudes toward colonialism mar the travelogue in many places. A chronicler of society's elite and its circle of aspirants, her sympathies rested firmly with the upper classes even as her novels critiqued social mores. When it came to appreciating architecture, however, she had a keen eye.

Just as Henry James went into literary exile in London, Wharton chose to settle in Europe; not in Italy but in France, where she lived from 1912 until her death in 1937. It was in France that she wrote *The Age of Innocence*, her 1921 Pulitzer winner. Throughout, Wharton continued to indulge her love of architecture and design. At Le Castel Sainte-Claire, where she restored a grand house in Hyères, near Toulon. (The town has an Avenue Edith Wharton.) And lastly at the Pavillon Colombe, the country house where she ended her days, then in the rural village of Saint-Brice-sous-Fôret, today a suburb on the outskirts of Paris.

IN MOROCCO
BY EDITH WHARTON

The Almohads were mighty builders, and their great monuments are all of stone. The earliest known example of their architecture which has survived is the ruined mosque of Tinmel, in the High Atlas, discovered and photographed by M. Doutté. This mosque was built by the inspired mystic, Ibn-Toumert, who founded the line. Following him came the great palace-making Sultans whose walled cities of splendid mosques and towers have Romanesque qualities of mass and proportion, and, as M. Raymond Koechlin has pointed out, inevitably recall the "robust simplicity of the master builders who at the very same moment were beginning in France the construction of the first Gothic cathedrals and the noblest feudal castles."

In the thirteenth century, with the coming of the Marinids, Moroccan architecture grew more delicate, more luxurious, and perhaps also more peculiarly itself. That interaction of Spanish and Arab art which produced the style known as Moorish reached, on the African side of the Straits, its greatest completeness in Morocco. It was under the Marinids that Moorish art grew into full beauty in Spain, and under the Marinids that Fez rebuilt the mosque Kairouiyin and that of the Andalusians, and created six of its nine Medersas, the most perfect surviving buildings of that unique moment of sober elegance and dignity.

The Cherifian dynasties brought with them a decline in taste. A crude desire for immediate effect, and the tendency toward a more barbaric luxury, resulted in the piling up of frail palaces as impermanent as tents. Yet a last flower grew from the deformed and dying trunk of the old Empire. The Saadian Sultan who invaded the Sudan and came back laden with gold and treasure from the great black city of Timbuctoo covered Marrakech with hasty monuments of which hardly a trace survives. But there, in a nettle-grown corner of a ruinous quarter, lay hidden till yesterday the Chapel of the Tombs: the last emanation of pure beauty of a mysterious, incomplete, forever retrogressive and yet forever forward-straining people. The Marinid tombs of Fez have fallen; but those of their destroyers linger on in precarious grace, like a flower on the edge of a precipice.

Moroccan architecture, then, is easily divided into four groups: the fortress, the mosque, the collegiate building and the private house.

The kernel of the mosque is always the mihrab, or niche facing toward the Kasbah of Mecca, where the iman stands to say the prayer. This arrangement, which enabled as many as possible of the faithful to kneel facing the mihrab, results in a ground-plan necessarily consisting of long aisles parallel with the wall of the mihrab, to which more and more aisles are added as the number of worshippers grows. Where there was not space to increase these lateral aisles they were lengthened at each end. This typical plan is modified in the Moroccan mosques by a wider transverse space, corresponding with the nave of a Christian church, and extending across the mosque from the praying niche to the principal door. To the right of the mihrab is the minbar, the carved pulpit (usually of cedar-wood incrusted with mother-of-pearl and ebony) from which the Koran is read. In some

Algerian and Egyptian mosques (and at Cordova, for
instance) the mihrab is enclosed in a sort of screen called the
maksoura; but in Morocco this modification of the simpler
plan was apparently not adopted.

The interior construction of the mosque was no doubt
usually affected by the nearness of Roman or Byzantine
ruins. M. Saladin points out that there seem to be few
instances of the use of columns made by native builders; but
it does not therefore follow that all the columns used in the
early mosques were taken from Roman temples or Christian
basilicas. The Arab invaders brought their architects and
engineers with them; and it is very possible that some of the
earlier mosques were built by prisoners or fortune-hunters
from Greece or Italy or Spain.

At any rate, the column on which the arcades of the
vaulting rests in the earlier mosques, as at Tunis and
Kairouan, and the mosque El Kairouiyin at Fez, gives way
later to the use of piers, foursquare, or with flanking engaged
pilasters as at Algiers and Tlemcen. The exterior of the
mosques, as a rule, is almost entirely hidden by a mushroom
growth of buildings, lanes and covered bazaars; but where
the outer walls have remained disengaged they show, as at
Kairouan and Cordova, great masses of windowless masonry
pierced at intervals with majestic gateways.

Beyond the mosque, and opening into it by many wide
doors of beaten bronze or carved cedar-wood, lies the Court
of the Ablutions. The openings in the façade were multiplied
in order that, on great days, the faithful who were not able to
enter the mosque might hear the prayers and catch a glimpse
of the mihrab.

In a corner of the courts stands the minaret. It is the
structure on which Muslim art has played the greatest
number of variations, cutting off its angles, building it on a
circular or polygonal plan, and endlessly modifying the

pyramids and pendentives by which the ground-plan of one story passes into that of the next. These problems of transition, always fascinating to the architect, led in Persia, Mesopotamia and Egypt to many different compositions and ways of treatment; but in Morocco the minaret, till modern times, remained steadfastly square, and proved that no other plan is so beautiful as this simplest one of all.

Surrounding the Court of the Ablutions are the school-rooms, libraries and other dependencies, which grew as the Mahometan religion prospered and Arab culture developed.

The medersa was a farther extension of the mosque: it was the academy where the Muslim schoolman prepared his theology and the other branches of strange learning which, to the present day, make up the curriculum of the Mahometan university. The medersa is an adaptation of the private house to religious and educational ends; or, if one prefers another analogy, it is a fondak built above a miniature mosque. The ground-plan is always the same: in the centre an arcaded court with a fountain, on one side the long narrow praying-chapel with the mihrab, on the other a class-room with the same ground-plan; and on the next story a series of cell-like rooms for the students, opening on carved cedar-wood balconies. This cloistered plan, where all the effect is reserved for the interior façades about the court, lends itself to a delicacy of detail that would be inappropriate on a street-front; and the medersas of Fez are endlessly varied in their fanciful but never exuberant decoration.

M. Tranchant de Lunel has pointed out (in "France-Maroc") with what a sure sense of suitability the Marinid architects adapted this decoration to the uses of the buildings. On the lower floor, under the cloister, is a revêtement of marble (often alabaster) or of the almost indestructible ceramic mosaic. On the floor above, massive cedar-wood corbels ending in monsters of almost Gothic inspiration support the fretted balconies; and above rise stucco interlacings, placed too high up to be injured by man, and guarded from the weather by projecting eaves.

The private house, whether merchant's dwelling or chieftain's palace, is laid out on the same lines, with the addition of the reserved quarters for women; and what remains in Spain and Sicily of Moorish secular architecture shows that, in the Marinid period, the play of ornament must have been – as was natural – even greater than in the medersas.

The Arab chroniclers paint pictures of Marinid palaces, such as the House of the Favourite at Cordova, which the soberer modern imagination refused to accept until the medersas of Fez were revealed, and the old decorative tradition was shown in the eighteenth century Moroccan palaces. The descriptions given of the palaces of Fez and of Marrakech in the preceding articles, which make it unnecessary, in so slight a note as this, to go again into the detail of their planning and decoration, will serve to show how gracefully the art of the mosque and the medersa was lightened and domesticated to suit these cool chambers and flower-filled courts.

With regard to the immense fortifications that are the most picturesque and noticeable architectural features of Morocco, the first thing to strike the traveller is the difficulty of discerning any difference in the probable date of their construction until certain structural peculiarities are examined, or the ornamental details of the great gateways are noted. Thus the Almohad portions of the walls of Fez and Rabat are built of stone, while later parts are of rubble; and the touch of European influence in certain gateways of Meknez and Fez at once situate them in the seventeenth century. But the medieval outline of these great piles of masonry, and certain technicalities in their plan, such as the disposition of the towers, alternating in the inner and outer walls, continued unchanged throughout the different dynasties; and this immutability of the Moroccan military architecture enables the imagination to picture, not only what was the aspect of the fortified cities which the Greeks built in Palestine and Syria, and the Crusaders brought back to Europe, but even that of the far-off Assyrio-Chaldean strongholds to which the whole fortified architecture of the Middle Ages in Europe seems to lead back.

MARY WOLLSTONECRAFT
INTRODUCTION

Like her contemporaries, William Blake and Thomas Paine, Mary Wollstonecraft had a penchant for controversy. Her landmark work, *A Vindication of the Rights of Woman* (1792), became a foundational text of feminism. Less well known is her travel writing. The record of a journey to Scandinavia in 1795, *Letters Written during a Short Residence in Denmark Sweden and Norway* is a book that hides a fascinating secret.

Wollstonecraft's was an itinerant life. Avowedly antimarriage, it was following the end of an affair in London with the Swiss painter Henry Fuseli that she fled to Paris in 1792. The French Revolution was in full swing, the city a hotbed of misplaced artistic idealism. 'Bliss it was in that dawn to be alive,' wrote William Wordsworth famously, albeit from the safety of England once Robespierre's reign of terror got going.

On the rebound, Wollstonecraft began another affair, with Gilbert Imlay, a Kentucky speculator acting as a diplomatic representative for the US government. They had a daughter, Fanny. To avoid Robespierre's men, partial to any well-bred Europeans, Wollstonecraft masqueraded as Imlay's wife at the US embassy. But Imlay had a sideline – looting aristocratic properties for silverware and shipping it to Scandinavia. (Registering his ships in Norway enabled them to pass through the blockade imposed by the Royal Navy.)

That was, until one cargo, carrying silver then worth a quarter of a million dollars, went missing, spirited away by Imlay's equally unscrupulous Norwegian captain, Peder Ellefsen. When Ellefsen's subsequent arrest and trial failed to recover the booty, Imlay dispatched Wollstonecraft, a high-profile figure, to continue the search. She travelled first, again as Mrs Imlay and with Fanny in tow, to Sweden. In Denmark, she was received as the guest of

Andreas Bernstorff, the de facto Prime Minister. '[He] is universally celebrated for his abilities and virtue,' Wollstonecraft gushed about her host. 'The happiness of the people is a substantial eulogium.' In Norway, arriving in Tønsberg, she found the climate agreeable. 'In the evening,' she wrote, 'the [winds] die away, the aspen leaves tremble into stillness and reposing nature seems to be warmed by the moon.' She found her Norwegian hosts equally obliging: 'The sympathy I inspired, thus dropping down from the clouds in a strange land, affected me more than it would have done had not my spirits been harassed by various causes.'

The causes in question are at no point addressed directly. Her hosts, wherever she travelled, had some connection to Imlay's missing silver, a fact Wollstonecraft might not have known, and which only came to light as recently as 2005. (Bernstorff, for example, officially Foreign Minister, maintained Danish trade with both Britain and France.) It began to occur to Wollstonecraft that the treasure's recovery was unlikely, a revelation which prompted hostility in Imlay's letters. On discovering he had a new mistress, Wollstonecraft's attitude toward the country began to harden.

By the time she reached Peder Ellefsen's hometown of Risør (Wollstonecraft spells it Rusoer), the game was up, her world seeming to have closed in. 'I pictured the state of man when the earth could no longer support him,' she wrote as the village hove into view. 'The images fastened on me and the world appeared a vast prison. I was soon to be in a smaller one – for no other name can I give to Rusoer. Talk not of Bastilles! To be born here was to be bastilled by nature – shut out from all that opens the understanding, or enlarges the heart.'

Wollstonecraft's plan, ultimately, was to reach America, convinced, not least by Imlay, that it was the brave new world she sought, that the American Revolution had succeeded where the French had failed. 'I could almost fancy myself in Nootka Sound,' she imagined as she drifted through the Norwegian seascape, 'or on some of the islands on the northwest coast of America.' She returned to England to be thoroughly spurned by Imlay, a fact which prompted her second attempt to commit suicide. (The first came after she discovered his infidelity.)

Wollstonecraft eventually found contentment when she married the philosopher Richard Godwin. It was a brief happiness. Wollstonecraft died in 1797, aged just 38, giving birth to her second child – Mary Shelley, who would go on to write *Frankenstein*.

Stricken with grief, Godwin penned a biography, *Memoirs of the Author of the Vindication of the Rights of Woman*. In it, he candidly revealed, against his publisher's advice, the more unconventional elements of his wife's lifestyle. What was intended to be a celebration of Wollstonecraft's complex nature was, inadvertently, to prove the twisting of the knife. By revealing details of her affairs, even her suicide attempts, Godwin provided just the ammunition her detractors, of whom there were many, required. Yet the legacy of Wollstonecraft's work lived past the scandal to inspire generations.

LETTERS WRITTEN DURING A SHORT RESIDENCE IN DENMARK, SWEDEN AND NORWAY

BY MARY WOLLSTONECRAFT

FROM LETTER X

I was informed that we might still advance a mile and a quarter in our cabrioles; afterwards there was no choice but of a single horse and wretched path, or a boat, the usual mode of travelling.

We therefore sent our baggage forward in the boat, and followed rather slowly, for the road was rocky and sandy. We passed, however, through several beech groves, which still delighted me by the freshness of their light green foliage, and the elegance of their assemblage, forming retreats to veil without obscuring the sun.

I was surprised, at approaching the water, to find a little cluster of houses pleasantly situated, and an excellent inn. I could have wished to have remained there all night; but as the wind was fair, and the evening fine, I was afraid to trust to the wind – the uncertain wind of tomorrow. We therefore left Helgeraac immediately with the declining sun.

Though we were in the open sea, we sailed more amongst the rocks and islands than in my passage from Strömstad; and they often forced very picturesque combinations. Few of the high ridges were entirely bare; the seeds of some pines or firs had been wafted by the winds or waves, and they stood to brave the elements.

Sitting, then, in a little boat on the ocean amidst strangers, with sorrow and care pressing hard on me – buffeting me about from clime to clime – I felt

'Like the lone shrub at random cast,
That sighs and trembles at each blast!'

On some of the largest rocks there were actually groves, the retreat of foxes and hares, which, I suppose, had tripped over the ice during the winter, without thinking to regain the main land before the thaw.

Several of the islands were inhabited by pilots; and the Norwegian pilots are allowed to be the best in the world – perfectly acquainted with their coast, and ever at hand to observe the first signal or sail. They pay a small tax to the king and to the regulating officer, and enjoy the fruit of their indefatigable industry.

One of the islands, called Virgin Land, is a flat, with some depth of earth, extending for half a Norwegian mile, with three farms on it, tolerably well cultivated.

On some of the bare rocks I saw straggling houses; they rose above the denomination of huts inhabited by fishermen. My companions assured me that they were very comfortable dwellings, and that they have not only the necessaries, but even what might be reckoned the superfluities of life. It was too late for me to go on shore, if you will allow me to give that name to shivering rocks, to ascertain the fact.

But rain coming on, and the night growing dark, the pilot declared that it would be dangerous for us to attempt to go to the place of our destination – East Risør – a Norwegian mile and a half further; and we determined to stop for the night at a little haven, some half dozen houses scattered under the curve of a rock. Though it became darker and darker, our pilot avoided the blind rocks with great dexterity.

It was about ten o'clock when we arrived, and the old hostess quickly prepared me a comfortable bed – a little too soft or so, but I was weary; and opening the window to admit the sweetest of breezes to fan me to sleep, I sunk into the most luxurious rest: it was more than refreshing. The hospitable sprites of the grots surely hovered round my pillow; and, if I awoke, it was to listen to the melodious whispering of the wind amongst them, or to feel the mild breath of morn. Light slumbers produced dreams where Paradise was before me. My little cherub was again hiding her face in my bosom. I heard her sweet cooing beat on my heart from the cliffs, and saw her tiny footsteps on the sands. New-born hopes seemed, like the rainbow, to appear in the clouds of sorrow, faint, yet sufficient to amuse away despair.

Some refreshing but heavy showers have detained us; and here I am writing quite alone – something more than gay, for which I want a name.

I could almost fancy myself in Nootka Sound, or on some of the islands on the northwest coast of America. We entered by a narrow pass through the rocks, which from this abode appear more romantic than you can well imagine; and sealskins hanging at the door to dry add to the illusion.

It is indeed a corner of the world, but you would be surprised to see the cleanliness and comfort of the dwelling. The shelves are not only shining with pewter and queen's ware, but some articles in silver, more ponderous, it is true, than elegant. The linen is good, as well as white. All the females spin, and there is a loom in the kitchen. A sort of individual taste appeared in the arrangement of the furniture (this is not the place for imitation) and a kindness in their desire to oblige. How superior to the apish politeness of the towns! where the people, affecting to be well bred, fatigue with their endless ceremony.

The mistress is a widow, her daughter is married to a pilot, and has three cows. They have a little patch of land at about the distance of two English miles, where they make hay for the winter, which they bring home in a boat. They live here very cheap, getting money from the vessels, which stress of weather, or other causes, bring into their harbour. I suspect, by their furniture, that they smuggle a little. I can now credit the account of the other houses, which I last night thought exaggerated.

I have been conversing with one of my companions respecting the laws and regulations of Norway. He is a man with great portion of common sense and heart – yes, a warm heart. This is not the first time I have remarked heart without sentiment; they are distinct. The former depends on the rectitude of the feelings, on truth of sympathy; these characters have more tenderness than passion; the latter has a higher source – call it imagination, genius or what you will, it is something very different. I have been laughing with these simple, worthy folk – to give you one of my half-score Danish words – and letting as much of my heart flow out in sympathy as they can take. Adieu! I must trip up the rocks. The rain is ever. Let me catch pleasure on the wing – I may be melancholy tomorrow. Now all my nerves keep time with the melody of nature. Ah! let me be happy whilst I can. The tear starts as I think of it. I must flee from thought, and find refuge from sorrow in a strong imagination – the only solace for a feeling heart. Phantoms of bliss! ideal forms of excellence! again enclose me in your magic circle, and wipe clear from my remembrance the disappointments that render the sympathy painful, which experience rather increases than damps, by giving the indulgence of feeling the sanction of reason.

LETTER XI

I left Portoer, the little haven I mentioned, soon after I finished my last letter. The sea was rough, and I perceived that our pilot was right not to venture farther during a hazy night. We had agreed to pay four dollars for a boat from Helgeraac. I mention the sum because they would demand twice as much from a stranger. I was obliged to pay fifteen for the one I hired at Strömstad. When we were ready to set out, our boatman offered to return a dollar and let us go in one of the boats of the place, the pilot who lived there being better acquainted with the coast. He only demanded a dollar and a half, which was reasonable. I found him a civil and rather intelligent man; he was in the American service several years, during the Revolution.

I soon perceived that an experienced mariner was necessary to guide us, for we were continually obliged to tack about to avoid the rocks, which, scarcely reaching to the surface of the water, could only be discovered by the breaking of the waves over them.

The view of this wild coast, as we sailed along it, afforded me a continual subject for meditation. I anticipated the future improvement of the world, and observed how much man has still to do to obtain of the earth all it could yield. I even carried my speculations so far as to advance a million or two of years to the moment when the earth would perhaps be so perfectly cultivated, and so completely peopled, as to render it necessary to inhabit every spot – yes, these bleak shores. Imagination went still farther, and pictured the state of man when the earth could no longer support him. Whither was he to flee from universal famine? Do not smile; I really became distressed for these fellow creatures yet unborn. The images fastened on me, and the world appeared a vast prison. I was soon to be in a smaller one – for no other name can I give to Risør. It would be difficult to form an idea of the place if you have never seen one of these rocky coasts.

We were a considerable time entering amongst the islands before we saw about two hundred houses crowded together under a very high rock – still higher appearing above. Talk not of Bastilles! To be born here was to be bastilled by nature – shut out from all that opens the understanding, or enlarges the heart. Huddled one behind another, not more than a quarter of the dwellings even had a prospect of the sea. A few planks formed passages from house to house, which you must often scale, mounting steps like a ladder to enter.

The only road across the rocks leads to a habitation sterile enough, you may suppose, when I tell you that the little earth on the adjacent ones was carried there by the late inhabitant. A path, almost impracticable for a horse, goes on to Arendal, still further to the westward.

I inquired for a walk, and, mounting near two hundred steps made round a rock, walked up and down for about a hundred yards viewing the sea, to which I quickly descended by steps that cheated the declivity. The ocean and these tremendous bulwarks enclosed me on every side. I felt the confinement, and wished for wings to reach still loftier cliffs, whose slippery sides no foot was so hardy as to tread. Yet what was it to see? – only a boundless waste of water – not a glimpse of smiling nature – not a patch of lively green to relieve the aching sight, or vary the objects of meditation.

I felt my breath oppressed, though nothing could be clearer than the atmosphere. Wandering there alone, I found the solitude desirable; my mind was stored with ideas, which this new scene associated with astonishing rapidity. But I shuddered at the thought of receiving existence, and remaining here in the solitude of ignorance, till forced to leave a world of which I had seen so little, for the character of the inhabitants is as uncultivated, if not as picturesquely wild, as their abode.

Having no employment but traffic, of which a contraband trade makes the basis of their profit, the coarsest feelings of honesty are quickly blunted. You may suppose that I speak in general terms; and that, with all the disadvantages of nature and circumstances, there are still some respectable exceptions, the more praiseworthy, as tricking is a very contagious mental disease that dries up all the generous juices of the heart. Nothing genial, in fact, appears around this place, or within the circle of its rocks. And, now I recollect, it seems to me that the most genial and humane characters I have met with in life were most alive to the sentiments inspired by tranquil country scenes. What, indeed, is to humanise these beings, who rest shut up (for they seldom even open their windows), smoking, drinking brandy and driving bargains? I have been almost stifled by these smokers. They begin in the morning, and are rarely without their pipe till they go to bed. Nothing can be more disgusting than the rooms and men towards the evening – breath, teeth, clothes and furniture, all are spoilt. It is well that the women are not very delicate, or they would only love their husbands because they were their husbands. Perhaps, you may add, that the remark need not be confined to so small a part of the world; and, entre nous, I am of the same opinion. You must not term this innuendo saucy, for it does not come home.

If I had not determined to write, I should have found my confinement here, even for three or four days, tedious. I have no books; and to pace up and down a small room, looking at tiles overhung by rocks, soon becomes wearisome. I cannot mount two hundred steps to walk a hundred yards many times in the day. Besides, the rocks, retaining the heat of the sun, are intolerably warm. I am, nevertheless, very well; for though there is a shrewdness in the character of these people, depraved by a sordid love of money which repels me, still the comparisons they force me to make keep my heart calm by exercising my understanding.

Everywhere wealth commands too much respect, but here almost exclusively; and it is the only object pursued, not through brake and briar, but over rocks and waves; yet of what use would riches be to me, I have sometimes asked myself, were I confined to live in such in a spot? I could only relieve a few distressed objects, perhaps render them idle, and all the rest of life would be a blank.

My present journey has given fresh force to my opinion that no place is so disagreeable and unimproving as a country town. I should like to divide my time between the town and country; in a lone house, with the business of farming and planting, where my mind would gain strength by solitary musing, and in a metropolis to rub off the rust of thought, and polish the taste which the contemplation of nature had rendered just. Thus do we wish as we float down the stream of life, whilst chance does more to gratify a desire of knowledge than our best-laid plans. A degree of exertion, produced by some want, more or less painful, is probably the price we must all pay for knowledge. How few authors or artists have arrived at eminence who have not lived by their employment?

I was interrupted yesterday by business, and was prevailed upon to dine with the English vice-consul. His house being open to the sea, I was more at large; and the hospitality of the table pleased me, though the bottle was rather too freely pushed about. Their manner of entertaining was such as I have frequently remarked when I have been thrown in the way of people without education, who have more money than wit – that is, than they know what to do with. The women were unaffected, but had not the natural grace which was often conspicuous at Tønsberg. There was even a striking difference in their dress, these having loaded themselves with finery in the style of the sailors' girls of Hull or Portsmouth. Taste has not yet taught them to make any but an ostentatious display of wealth. Yet I could perceive even here the first steps of the improvement which I am persuaded will make a very obvious progress in the course of half a century, and it ought not to be sooner, to keep pace with the cultivation of the earth. Improving manners will introduce finer moral feelings. They begin to read translations of some of the most useful German productions lately published, and one of our party sung a song ridiculing the powers coalesced against France, and the company drank confusion to those who had dismembered Poland.

The evening was extremely calm and beautiful. Not being able to walk, I requested a boat as the only means of enjoying free air.

The view of the town was now extremely fine. A huge rocky mountain stood up behind it, and a vast cliff stretched on each side, forming a semicircle. In a recess of the rocks was a clump of pines, amongst which a steeple rose picturesquely beautiful.

The churchyard is almost the only verdant spot in the place. Here, indeed, friendship extends beyond the grave, and to grant a sod of earth is to accord a favour. I should rather choose, did it admit of a choice, to sleep in some of the caves of the rocks, for I am become better reconciled to them since I climbed their craggy sides last night, listening to the finest echoes I ever heard. We had a French horn with us, and there was an enchanting wildness in the dying away of the reverberation that quickly transported me to Shakespeare's magic island. Spirits unseen seemed to walk abroad, and flit from cliff to cliff to soothe my soul to peace.

I reluctantly returned to supper, to be shut up in a warm room, only to view the vast shadows of the rocks extending on the slumbering waves. I stood at the window some time before a buzz filled the drawing room, and now and then the dashing of a solitary oar rendered the scene still more solemn.

Before I came here I could scarcely have imagined that a simple object (rocks) could have admitted of so many interesting combinations, always grand and often sublime.

INDEX

Afghanistan 26
Algeria 291
Antarctica 5, 38–49, 197, 256–266
architecture 29–37, 115–124, 289–294
Arctic 197–208, 220–226
Argentina 245
Australia 15, 50–58, 60, 146, 165, 171
Austria 178

Barker, Lady Anne 6–14
Bird, Lady Isabella 15–25
Botswana 157
Brazil 4, 245–255
Bulgaria 181
Byron, Robert 4, 26–37

Canada 236, 237
    Arctic Archipeago 219;
    Newfoundland 50; Ontario 186;
    Québec 50
Cape Verde 59
Carson Rijnhart, Susanna 236–244
Cherry-Garrard, Apsley 38–49
Chile 245
China 228–235
    Qinghai 236; Sichuan 237;
    Tibet 15, 236–244
Cook, James 50–58
Cuba 186
Cyprus 26, 108

Darwin, Charles 59–70
Denmark 199, 296
Dickens, Charles 71–85

Easter Island 51
Egypt 28, 104, 106–112, 122, 292
England 96, 297
    Cornwall 146, 152; Hull 305;
    Isle of Wight 86; London 5, 86, 122,
    125–137, 138, 178, 256–258;
    Portsmouth 209, 305
Ethiopia 104
exploration 52–60, 61–70, 220–226,
    229–235, 248–255, 259–266

extreme weather 8–14, 41–49,
    200–208, 220–226, 259–266

Fielding, Henry 86–94
France 5, 146, 149
    Marseilles 28; Massif Central
    267–276; Paris 122, 125, 132, 134,
    288, 295; Toulon 288; Tours 122
Fuller, Margaret 5, 95–103

Galapagos Islands 60–70
Greece 104–105, 149
Greenland 198

Hawaii 4
Herodotus 5, 104–112
Hungary 178

India 15
Indonesia (Sumatra) 209
Iran
    Isfahan 4, 29–34; Yezd 34–37
Ireland (County Kildare) 256
Irving, Washington 4, 113–124
Italy
    Palermo 145; Parma 287;
    Ravenna 26; Rome 96, 131;
    Sardinia 4, 145–156; Sicily 149;
    Venice 26

James, Henry 5, 125–137
Japan 165
Johnson, Samuel 5, 138–144
journeys by foot 188–196
journeys by horse or mule 17–25,
    211–21, 269–276
journeys by riverboat 280–286
journeys by train 150–156
jungle treks 248–255

Lawrence, DH 4, 145–156
Livingstone, David 5, 157–164
London, Jack 4, 165–177

Malawi 157
Malaysia 60
Mali 210–217
 Timbuktu 290
Mauritius 60
Morocco 5, 212, 287–294
 Fez 290, 291, 293; Marrakech 290,
 293; Meknes 293; Rabat 293
mountain travel 17–25, 188–196,
 238–244
Muir, John 4, 186–196

Nansen, Fridtjof 5, 197–208
New Zealand 6–14, 60
Norway 4, 199, 295, 296, 299–306
 Oslo 198

Pakistan 27
Palestine 294
Park, Mungo 209–217
Parry, William Edward 218–226
Polo, Marco 227–235
Portugal (Lisbon) 86–94, 113

Roosevelt, Theodore 4, 245–255
Russia (Siberia) 198

Saudi Arabia (Mecca) 290
scientific discovery 41–49, 52–60,
 61–70, 188–196, 200–208
Scotland 186, 209, 210
 Hebrides islands 5, 138–144
sea voyages 52–58, 61–70, 165–177,
 200–208, 220–226, 259–266,
 298–299
Serbia
 Belgrade 181; Nis 180
Shackleton, Ernest 5, 256–266
Solomon Islands 166
South Africa 157

Spain 289
 Cordoba 113, 122–123, 291, 293;

Gibraltar 113; Granada 4,
 113–124; Madrid 113; Seville
 122–123; Tenerife 59; Toledo 122;
 Zaragoza 113
Sri Lanka 146
Stevenson, Robert Louis 5, 267–276
Sweden 199, 296
 Strömstad 298
Switzerland (Geneva) 125
Syria 122, 294

Tahiti 50, 166
Tierra del Fuego 60
Tonga 51
Tunisia 291
Turkey 104, 180–185
 Istanbul 178–179
Twain, Mark 4, 277–286

Uruguay 60, 245
USA 146
 Arizona 187; Arkansas 278;
 California 165, 186–196, 267,
 279; Colorado 15–25; Hawaii 51,
 166–177; Illinois 95–103, 278;
 Indiana 186; Iowa 278; Kentucky
 278; Louisiana 278, 280, 286;
 Massachusetts 71, 95, 287;
 Michigan 186; Missouri 277, 278,
 280–286; Nevada 278; New York
 71, 73, 96, 186; Rhode Island 287;
 Tennessee 278; Washington 187;
 Washington, DC 72, 74–85;
 Wisconsin 186, 278; Wyoming 15

Wales (Cardiff) 38
Wharton, Edith 5, 287–294
wildlife 41–49, 52–58, 61–70, 97–103,
 107–112, 159–164, 188–196,
 248–255
Wollstonecraft, Mary 4, 295–306
Wortley Montagu,
 Lady Mary 178–185

Zambia 157